Python Programming

This Book Include

Python Crash Course, Python Machine Learning, Python for Data Analysis and Python Data Science

Steve Blair

DISCLAIMER

TABLE OF CONTENT

Python Crash Course

The Ultimate Guide for Beginners to Coding with Python Accompanied by Useful Tools

Steve Blair

Introduction

Congratulations on your decision to purchase this book, it is the bestdecision you have taken. You are a step away from becoming a professional Python programmer. If you are new to coding, it can be challenging. Perhaps you have considered programming languages such asJava, C++, or COBOL, and this has scared you. I am in no way trying tomake you scared, but this book contains symbols and letters that initially youmay not understand. Don't worry because that is not the case with Pythonprogramming because it is much easier than you can ever imagine. At the endof this book, you will program like a professional with over ten years of experience.

Learning Python: The Ultimate Guide for Beginners to Coding With Python Accompanied by ***Useful Tools*** doesn't include many assumptions regarding your knowledge of the Python language or any computer programming language. You don't require any prior experience to get thebest from this book. I will guide you by following a step-by-step approach. Furthermore, every new jargon, code, or concepts in this book are explained such that even a seven years old lad will understand. In the course of this book, you will encounter numerous programs and examples to improve your Python programming skills.

Let's Get Started!

Who Is This Book for?

This book is specifically for those to learn the basics of Python programming. Learning Python is ideal for both middle and high school educators whose desire is to guide their students into the programming world.

The purpose of this book is to equip you with the knowledge of Python programming and make you a more efficient programmer. You will also learn advanced Python techniques that will enable you to create whatever program and web application you envision.

Brief History of Python Language

Python programming language began in December 1989. Guido Van Rossum created the language, who started programming as a hobby. During thatperiod, he was busy with a project with the Dutch CWI research Institute. However, the project was later terminated, which enable him to start learning the fundamentals of the language.

The major advantage of the language is its ability to extend into more complex codes and supports multiple platforms. During the beginning days, these two features were important when personal computers became popular. In 2000, Python 2.0 was released to make it a community-oriented programming language. However, since the introduction of the Python 3 version, not many seems to use the previous version.

Why Python?

Interestingly, a beginner can choose from various programming languages. Despite this, Python is an important option to consider because it is easy for anyone to use. Additionally, it can be used on various platforms without any need to change things. The following are benefits that make people love using Python.

- **Readability:** The language is designed in such a way that it works with the English Language. This makes it easier for anyone to read without requiring any aid. Python also has strict rules as regards the punctuations.

- **Libraries:** The language has been in existence for over 30 years and contains codes that other programmers can use effectively.

- **Community:** The community for Python is significant because of its popularity. There are workshops where you can meet people to ask questions and learn more about the language. As a beginner, such a community can help you to learn faster and meet others who are experienced more than you are.

- **Different platform:** Python works on various operating systems such as Mac, UNIX, Windows, etc.

Features of Python Language

There are a lot of features that make Python Language one of the most sought languages to learn. These features include:

- It has a vast library, which works with other programming tasks.

- Platform compatibility – it can work on various platforms such as Mac OS X, Windows, Linux, and Unix.

- Expandable to other programming languages.

- Free to download.

- Contain advanced features such as list generators and comprehensions.

- Codes can be grouped into modules and packages.

- There are varieties of basics data types to choose from, such as strings, lists, dictionaries, and numbers.

How Python Runs Program

Every programming language has its way of working to execute the program. They all work differently, which is you must learn the process of organizing these words, and the various statements required by the programming language to avoid any issue or errors. In this section, I will briefly explore the way python executes its commands.

When you work with this language, you must understand that this is through an interpreter language. Therefore, you need a text interpreter to execute the programs line by line before converting into the language the computer can understand. Since python is a scripting language, you can directly write your code and execute it through the Python shell or decides to write the code and save it with its file extension.

What python does is to work on your source code and convert them into a byte code, which has the extension as .pyc; this makes it easier for your code to be executed, and within a few seconds, you see the output.

Each time you try to call a program you wrote, what python does is to check if it has a compiled version already with .pyc suffix. Python will check if a compiled version already exists with the .pyc suffix. If it does, it will load the code, but if it doesn't, a new code will be created before the program executes.

Python Implementations

Don't get confused about python implementation because it is the program or environment that provides the support needed for the execution of your plan. The CPython reference implementation represents this. What this does is to help you while executing the various statements and codes required for the program. We have various variants of CPython, with each making a big difference. The following are some features, which are available in these multiple variants. They include:

- Stackless Python – This has an importance on concurrency while using tasklets and channels. It is mostly used programs such as Nintendo DS

- CrossTwine Linker – This is a combinational feature between any add-on library you choose and CPython. It offers better performance, especially when the codes come with it.

- Wypthon – This involves the re-implementation of certain aspects of Python that doesn't allow the use of byte code.

Installation and Configuration on a Different Operating System

Since you know the benefits of learning Python, you are ready to get things started. However, before you begin to learn how to code, you must understand how to install and configure Python on the different operating systems. In this book, I will look at how you can install the language on various operating systems.

Installing Python on the Mac Operating System

Currently, the latest version of Python for the Mac operating system is Python 3.7.4. However, you can check the Python website (https//www.Python.org/downloads) if there is any latest update. On the website, click on "Download Python 3.7.4," then double-click on the file once the download is complete. This will give you access to the content of the disk image. After that, you have to run the installer by right-clicking on the file "Python.mpkg" and select open from the drop-down menu. If you get an error message indicating that, "Python.mpkg can't be opened because it is from an unidentified developer," then you have to click on the file, and select "Open with…" and then click on "Installer."

The diagrams below will help you install Python on Mac OS properly. Ensure to adhere to the instructions in the diagram below.

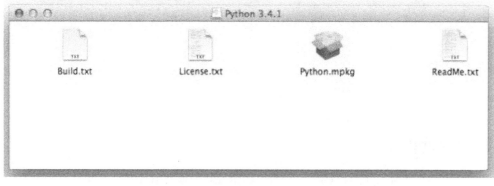

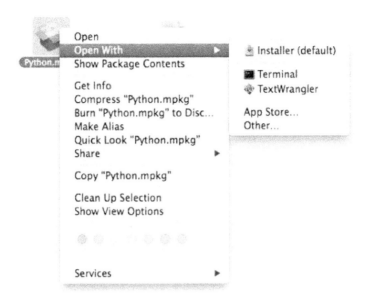

Installing Python

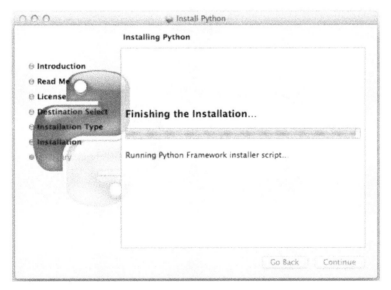

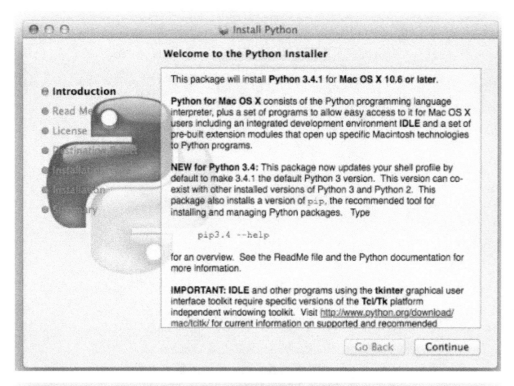

Window Installation

If you are using Windows 7, 8, or 10, adhere to the necessary steps to install the Python interpreter on your machine.

- Open your internet browser (Chrome, Firefox, Opera, or Internet

Explorer) and insert this link – https://www.Python.org/download

- Click on the Window links, and the installer will pop up. You can select the version you want.

- For the installer to work, your system must meet the essential requirement of having Microsoft Installer 2.0. Then save the file before running it.

- Then you can run the file you downloaded. Then run the downloaded file and follow the installation wizard, which is easy for anyone to follow. Additionally, accept all the default settings, and once the installation is complete, you are ready to begin your programming with Python. Linux and UNIX installation

Similar to the windows and Mac OS platforms, you can install Python on your Linux and UNIX OS. To do that, follow these steps below.

- Open your internet browser (Chrome, Firefox, Opera, or Internet Explorer) and insert this link – https://www.Python.org/download

- Click on the Unix/Linux link and down the zipped source code

- Once the file in question has finished downloading, you can extract the file using a file extracting software like WinZip.

- Edit the setup files to perform any form of personalization to suit your use.

- Run the./configure script to install.

With this, Python will be installed. The standard location and libraries are located at /usr/local/bin and /usr/local/lib/Python respectively

CHAPTER 1:

Basics in Python

O nce you have the software installed on your system, it is time to begin your programming adventure with Python. I will start with the fundamentals such as variables, strings, and keywords. In this chapter, you will learn and write your very first program in Python, the different data you can work with, how to use variables, and keywords. Let us begin with the basics to get your coding started right away.

Keywords

Some terms don't require much explanation. The word represents what they mean. The same applies to keywords. Keywords are reserved words that are explicitly used by the programming language. Each programming language has its unique keyword, which is meant for a particular purpose. Furthermore, avoid using these keywords elsewhere in your code. If you decide to neglect this instruction, you will end up with your program not working correctly or receive an error alert. The following are reserved keywords used in Python Programming Language:

async	assert	as	and
def	from	nonlocal	while
continue	for	lambda	try
elif	if	or	yield
else	import	pass	
global	not	with	del
in	raise	false	await
return	none	break	except
true	class	finally	Is

Let us begin with the fundamental "Hello" program that is the first step for any programmer.

```
print ("Hello, Welcome to Python Programming!")
```

When this program code is run, your output will be:

```
Hello, Welcome to Python Programming!
```

Python programs always end with the extension .py Let us save this program as Hello.py. **Please always remember to save each example using its name in order to recall them when necessary**. When you use your editor or IDE, the file is run via the interpreter, which then determines the words used in the program.

For instance, in the program below, the interpreter will see the word encircled in parenthesis and prints what is inside the parentheses.

In the course of writing Python codes, the editor may highlight certain parts of the program. For instance, it recognizes that print () is a function name and uses a particular color to differentiate it.

However, when it gets to the word "Hello, Welcome to Python Programming!" it recognizes that it is a Python program code. Therefore, it uses a different color to differentiate it from the other code. This unique feature is known as syntax highlighting and is useful for beginners.

Indentation and Lines

There is nothing like braces to indicate a block of code for function and class in Python. Normally, a block of code is represented by a line indentation that gets enforced in a strong manner. Importantly, the spaces in the indentation vary; however, every statement in the block must have the same amount of indentation. For instance,

```
if False:
    print "False"
else:
    print "True"
```

However, the block of the statement below will generate an error

```
if False:
print "Result"
print "False"
else:
print "Result"
print "True"
```

Consequently, all continuous lines you indent using the same number of spaces will for a block. Let us use another example to show various statement blocks. I will advise you not to try to understand the logic of the program. However, your aim is to understand the various blocks irrespective of their structure.

```
import sys

try:
    # open file stream
    file = open(fileName, "w")
except IOError:
    print "Error when writing to", fileName
    sys.exit()
print "Enter '", fileFinish,
print "' When finished"
while fileText != fileFinish:
    fileText = real_input("Enter text you want: ")
    if fileText == fileFinish:
        # close the file
        file.close
```

```
      break
    file.write(file_text)
    file.write("\n")
file.close()
fileText = real_input("Enter filename: ")
if len(fileName) == 0:
    print "Next time input something"
    sys.exit()
try:
    file = open(fileName, "r")
except IOError:
    print "Error reading file requested"
    sys.exit()
fileText = file.read()
file.close()
print fileText
```

Multiple Line Statements

These statements normally terminate with a new line. Though, it allows you to use a special character (\) to continue a statement. Check the code below:

```
Total_Number = number1 + \
        number2 + \
        number3
```

Notwithstanding, there is an exception to this situation if such statements contain brackets, such as (), {}, or []. For instance;

```
months = ['December,' 'November,' 'October,' 'September,' 'August,'
```

'July,' 'June,' 'May,' 'April,' 'March,' 'February,' 'January']

Variables

A variable is a storage location, which has a name assigned to it. In Python, we can assign a value to a variable and recall these variables. I believe an example will make things more transparent. Remember our first program (hello.py), let us add an additional two lines. Consider the program below:

```
outcome= "Hello, Welcome to Python Programming!"

print(outcome)
```

When you run the program, your output will be the same as the previous one, which was:

```
Hello, Welcome to Python Programming!
```

The only difference is that we added a variable called "outcome." Each variable always has a value assigned to it. In this situation, the value of "outcome" is "Hello, Welcome to Python Programming!"

Let us add two additional lines to the previous code. However, ensure to insert a blank line in the first code before adding the new codes.

```
outcome= "Hello, Welcome to Python Programming!"

print(outcome)


outcome = "Hello, Welcome to Learning Python!"
print(outcome)
```

After adding the two lines, save the file and rerun the program. Your output will be as follows:

```
Hello, Welcome to Python Programming!
Hello, Welcome to Learning Python!
```

Rules to Variable Naming

There are important rules to adhere to when naming variables in Python. If you break any of these rules, you will get an error message. Therefore, ensure to keep them in your mind when writing your programs.

- Variable names must have only numbers, underscores, and letters. You can begin your variable names with an underscore or a letter; however, it must not begin with a number. For example, your variable name can be outcome_1, but using 1_outcome is completely wrong.

- A variable name must not contain spaces between them. Notwithstanding, you can use underscores to separate two words. For instance, outcome_program will work; however, the outcome program will cause errors in your program.

- Avoid using function names and keywords as variable names

- Variable names must be short and descriptive when used. For instance, a score is preferable than using s, serial_name is better than sn.

Avoiding Variable Name Errors

As a beginner, you will make mistakes. Professionals aren't exempted from this situation, but they know how to tackle these errors efficiently. Let us look at a more likely mistake you will make as you beginning your Python-programming course. I will intentionally write an error code by misspelling the word "outcome."

```
outcome = "Hello, Welcome to Learning Python!"
#program will generate an error
print(outcom)
```

When such an error occurs, the Python interpreter figures the best way to solve the problem. It provides a traceback once the program cannot run successfully. Not many programming languages have this feature to traceback an error. Let us look at how the interpreter will respond to our program above.

Trackback (most recent call last):

1. File "hello.py," line 3, in <module>

2. Print(outcome)

3. NameError: name 'outcom' is not defined

Line 1 reports the presence of an error in **line 3** with filename "hello.py" however, the interpreter quickly identifies the error and informs us what particular type of error it is in **line 3**. In a situation like this, it will signify a name error. Additionally, it will report that our variable hasn't been adequately defined. Whenever you see a name error, it means there is a spelling error, or we didn't set a value to the variable. However, in this example, it was a wrong spelling where we didn't include the letter "e" from our variable name.

Note that the interpreter does not check the code for spelling; instead, it ensures the variable names are consistent when used. For instance, if we use the variable "outcom" in our previous program, it will print out the result successfully. Check the code below.

```
outcom= "Hello, Welcome to Python Programming!"

print(outcome)

outcom = "Hello, Welcome to Learning Python!"

print(outcome)
```

The program output will be:

Hello, Welcome to Python Programming!

Hello, Welcome to Learning Python!

You must understand that programming languages are strict; however, they disregard bad and good spellings. Because of this, you don't need to contemplate about grammatical and spelling procedures when creating a variable name.

Exercises to Try

Write a program that intends to perform the following things. Ensure to save the file and following the variable naming rules.

- Write a program that assigns a message to a variable name of your choice and print the message.

- In this second program, change the value and use a new message. Then print the message.

- Tick the wrong variable names from the list below:
  - 1_school
  - Fred Love
  - Fred_love
  - _exercises
  - Firsttwoletters

Data Types in Python

When writing codes, we need to store data into memory. These data cannot be stored in the same memory because a number will be different from a letter. For instance, a person's name is alphabetic; address can be alphanumeric characters, whereas age can be stored as a numeric value. Python has data types to define various operations and methods of storing these data types. There are five data types in Python; these are:

- String
- Numbers
- Tuple
- List
- Dictionary

Note, I will emphasize on the first two while the list, tuple, and the dictionary will be included in a single chapter.

String

It is a series of characters, which is enclosed in quotes. In Python, anything in quotes is regarded as a unique character. Both single and double quotes can be used to form a string in Python.

```
'Hello World'
"Hello World"
```

The two statements would produce the same output if we were to run it.

Using Quotes Inside Strings

In Python programming, when using strings, an opening string with a quote must match the ending quote. When you begin a string using a doublequotation mark, Python takes the next double quotation mark as the ending ofthe string. This applies to a single quotation mark.

If you decide to use double quotes inside a string, you have to place them in single quotes. The example below will show it better.

statement = 'Fred is "a boy that lives in New York"'

Let's assume you want to use both single and double quotes in a string. In this situation, you have to escape the single, and double quote misses up by using a backslash (\). The example below will demonstrate it.

```
statement_in_single = 'Fred "own\'s a wonderful car in his garage"'

statement_in_double = "Fred \ 'own's a wonderful car in his garage\""
```

Using Methods to Change Case in String

One simple task you can perform when using strings is to change the case of a particular word. What do you think the output will be for the code below?

```
full_name = "johnson boris"
print(full_name.title())
```

Once you write the code, save the file as name.py before running it. The output will be as follow:

```
Johnson Boris
```

If you observe, the variable full_name refers to the string in lowercase "johnson boris" after the variable name comes to the method title(). In Python, a method is an action upon which certain manipulation can be taken on a piece of data. Furthermore, the dot (.) that comes after the variable name informs the interpreter to allow the title() method to interact with our variable name. Parentheses always follow a method because they require additional information to perform their function. The function of the title() method is to change the first letter of each word to capital letter. Furthermore, Python allows us to change string to all lowercase or uppercase.

```
full_name = "Johnson Boris"
print(full_name.lower())
print (full_name.upper))
```

The output will be as follows:

```
johnson boris
JOHNSON BORIS
```

Using Variables in Strings

In certain scenarios, you may decide to use a variable, which contains a value in a string. For instance, you may want to use two variables to hold the first name and last name of a person, respectively. Additionally, these two variables must be combined to produce the individual's full name. Let us consider how that is possible in Python.

```
first_name = "johnson"
last_name = "boris"
    1. full_name    =    f    "{first_name} {last_name}"
```

```
print(full_name)
```

If you want to insert a variable value to a string, you have to add the letter "f" directly before the opening quotation mark

Consider the code below:

```
state = 'United Nation!'    #Assign the variable "state" to a string 'United Nation!'

print(state)        # Prints the complete string

print(state[0])     # Prints the first character of the string

print(state[0:3])    # Prints characters starting from 1st to 3th

print(state[3:])     # Prints string starting from 4th character

print(state * 3)     # Prints string three times

print(state + " United State") # Prints concatenated string
```

The output will be:

```
United Nation!
U
Uni
ted Nation!
United Nation! United Nation! United Nation!
United Nation!United State
```

Comments

If you observe in the program above, we use the symbol # to begin a statement after declaring a variable. Nevertheless, it shouldn't be used within a string literal. The Python interpreter ignores comments because they are notpart of the program, but provide an explanatory note for the programmer. Let us look at this example below:

```
#Learning about Comments in Python

print "Learning Python Language isn't complicated."

#Another comment to make things better
```

When you run this program, the output will be:

```
Learning Python Language isn't complicated.
```

How to Avoid Syntax Errors When Using Strings

A syntax error is a common error you will encounter when using Python. It normally occurs when the interpreter doesn't identify a particular section of the program. For instance, you wanted to use an apostrophe in a single quote; this will result in an error. Here is an example to show how you can easily use both single and double quotes properly.

```
statement = "One of American's problem is the lack of unity'"

print(statement)
```

In this situation, the apostrophe is inside the double quote. The interpreter won't see anything wrong with this program. However, consider the code below.

```
statement = 'One of American's problems is the lack of unity'

print(statement)
```

If you run it, the interpreter will indicate a syntax error. Ensure you avoid this kind of mistake.

Exercise to try

1. Use a variable name of your choice to represent your name and print the message "Python Language is the best!"

2. Declare a variable name and assign a name to it. Furthermore, print the name in title case, uppercase, and lowercase.

3. Write a simple program, which uses four variables. The variables must be address, phone_number, age, and sex. Then assign values

to each variable in the program.

Bonus Answer for Exercise 3

```
address = "23 London Street, New York"
phone_number = "0123456789"
age = "26"
sex = "Male"
print (address)
print (phone_number)
print (age)
print (sex)
```

Simple and short, your program is ready for execution. Remember to save it first before running. If you have done that, your output will be as follows:

```
23 London Street, New York
0123456789
26
Male
```

Operators in Python

Operators in a programming language are used to carry out various operations on variables and values. These operators allow programmers to manipulate variables and return results based on the operator used. In this section, you will learn various operators you need to manipulate operands.

Arithmetic Operators

These operators are by far the simplest you will find in any programming language. With these operators, you can perform arithmetic calculations such as addition, division, subtraction, multiplication, exponent, modulus, etc. Let us see how these operators can be used in a python program.

```
number1 = 6
number2 = 3
print(number1 + number2)
print(number1 – number2)
print(number1 * number2)
print(number1 / number2)
print(number1 % number2)
print (number1 **2)
```

The output will be as follow:

```
9
3
18
2
0
36
```

Arithmetic operators are elementary to use and straightforward for any beginner to understand.

Comparison Operators

From the name, you can easily understand what these operators are used for. They compare values on both sides of an operand and determine the relationship between them. At times, they are known as relational operators. These operators include <>, <=, >=, !=, == etc. They compare values and return the results in true or false. Let us rewrite our previous arithmetical operator example.

```
number1 = 6
number2 = 3
```

```
print(number1>number2)
print(number1<number2)
print(number1!=number2)
print(number1>=number2)
print(number1<=number2)
```

```
Output
True
False
True
True
False
```

Assignment Operators

The primary function of these operators is to assign a value to a variable. You assign what is on the left-hand side to the right. These operators include +=, *=, -=, /=, etc.

```
number1 = 6
number2 = 3
print(("The value of number1 is : ", number1))
print(("The value of number2 is : ", number2))
```

```
The value of number1 is: 6
The value of number2 is: 3
```

There are also compound assignment operators where you can subtract, add, multiply a right operand to the left before assigning it to the left. In the next program, we will add the value of number1 and number 2 before assigning the results to another variable and print out the output.

```
number1 = 6

number2 = 3

result = number1 + number2

print(("The result of number1 and number2 is:", result))
```

In the program above, we just perform a simple assignment. Our output will be 9.

Logical Operators

These operators are used to test if a particular conditional statement is true or false. They include, NOT, OR, and AND. However, some rules apply to these operators for them to either return true or false. These rules are:

- A NOT operator will return True only when the operand is false.

- An OR operator returns true if one of the operands is true.

- The AND operator returns true when both the operands are true.

Here is an example. We will use number1 and number2 to represent true and false respectively.

```
number 1 = 6

number2 = 3

print (not(number1<number2))

print (number1<number2 or number1>number2)

print (number1>number2 and number2>number1)
```

The output will be as follow:

```
True
True
```

False

Membership Operators

Although not commonly used, however, they are used in sequences like strings, lists, and tuples. In Python, we have two membership operators – "not in" and "in." The operators give you the result depending on the variable available in the string or sequence you specified. Let us see how you can use them in a program.

```python
number1 = 15
number2 =56
new_list = [11, 12, 13, 14, 15, 16, 17, 18, 19, 20 ]
if number1 in new_list:
    print("number1 is available in our given list.")
else:
    print("number1 is unavailable in our given list")
if number2 not in new_list:
    print("Number2 is not available in our given list.")
else:
    print("number2 is available in our given list")
```

Let see how the program runs line by line. In the first and second lines, we declare two variables and assign values for them. In the third line, we created a list "new_list" before using an if-else statement to test the membership operator on our list. We check if number1 is available on our list; depending on the number, it prints the expression based on the condition it fulfills. It does the same for number2 before printing out the desired result. In our program above, our output will be:

```
number1 is available in our given list.
```

number2 is not available in our given list.

Summary

Operators are important functions used in programming languages to perform various operations on operands. However, in Python, we use operations such as:

- Arithmetic operators perform operations on operands; these operators include addition, subtraction, multiplication, division, exponent, and modulus. Python also uses the call functions, declare variable $ calculate, and eval function.

- Comparison operators used to compare operands on both sides before determining the relationship between them.

- Assignment operators to assign values to variables; we also have a compound assignment operator, which allow you to assign theresult of an operand.

- Logical operators, which include "NOT, OR, and AND," as they return either true or false, depending on the condition set.

Sample Program to Illustrate Operators in Python

```
# Arithmetic Operators

number1 = 8
number2 = 4
print(number1 + number2)
print(number1 – number2)
print(number1 * number2)
print(number1 / number2)
print(number1 % number2)
print (number1 **2)
```

```python
#Comparison Operators
number3 = 13
number4 = 9
print("number3 > number4", number3 >number4)
print("number3 < number4", number3 <number4)
print("number3 != number4", number3 !=number4)
print("number3 >= number4", number3 >= number4)
print("number3 <= number4", number <= number4)

#Assignment Operators
number5 = 9
number6 = 6
print(("The value of number5 is : ", number5))
print(("The value of number6 is : ", number6))

#Logical Operators
number7 = 6
number8 = 3
print (not(number7<number8))
print (number7<number8 or number7>number8)
print (number7>number8 and number8>number7)

#Membership Operators
number9 = 5
number10 =63
new_list = [17, 5, 9, 7, 20, 63 ]
```

```
if number9 in new_list:

    print("number9 is available in our given list.")

else:

    print("number9 is unavailable in our given list")

if number10 not in new_list:

    print("Number10 is not available in our given list.")

else:

    print("number10 is available in our given list")
```

Numbers in Python

Numbers are used in programming to store information, represent data, and keep scores, etc., In Python, numbers are treated in several ways, depending on what they are used for. In this section, we will look at how Python supports various numerical types, such as integer, float, and complex numbers. Integers are easier to work with when writing programs.

Integers

You can perform operations such as addition, subtraction, multiplication, and division on integers. In the later chapter, we will explore more on these operators. I just want you to be familiar with them. For instance:

```
>>> 3+8
>>> 8 -7
>>>8*2
>>>8/4
```

If you want to use an exponent, then you have to use two multiplication symbols.

```
>>5**2
>> 12**5
```

Python follows the order of precedence when performing operations; with this, you can use several operations in a single expression. Additionally, if you want to modify an order of operation, you can use parentheses. Python evaluates the expression in the order you specify.

```
>>3+2*4
>>(3 + 2) * 4
```

In the first expression, the output will be 11. However, for the second, it will be 20. Note that spacing doesn't affect how expressions are evaluated in Python. Notwithstanding, it allows you to identify the operation with the highest priority when going through the code.

Summary of Number Data Types

int	long	float	complex
-786	0122L	-21.9	9.322e-36j
0x69	-4721885298529L	70.2-E12	4.53e-7
-0x260	-052318172735L	-32.54e100	3e+26J
10	51924361L	0.0	3.14j
100	-0x19323L	15.20	45.j
-0490	535633629843L	-90.	-.6545+0J
080	0xDEFABCECBDAECBFBAEl	32.3+e18	.876j

Floating-Point Numbers

A float is a number with a decimal point, and Python language has its way of managing decimal numbers. They can be written in scientific notation; the letter "e" represents the 10th power. Examples of floating numbers include 4.5e2, 0.25, 154.05588 etc. An important advantage of using floating-point values instead of integers is that they allow bigger storage space than integers. Additionally, they can also store numbers of smaller value. You can consider floating-point numbers as those with unlimited storage space. Interestingly, they can contain numbers as much as $2.4548899981236585 \times 10^{-452}$ and as little as $\pm 4.4879541268971562 \times 10^{-452}$

There are various ways of allocating values when using floating-point values. You can assign them directly or decide to use scientific notation. Don't forget that negative exponents will result in fraction equivalents.

Complex Numbers

Another type of number data types we have in Python is complex numbers, which include both real and imaginary numbers. They are usually in this form – a + cJ where "a" represents a float and a real part of the complex number. Alternatively, the "cJ" comprises of the float "c" whereas "J" is the square root of an imaginary number. In this situation, this makes c to be the imaginary part of the number.

This may look complex, but let us use an example to make it simple

```
x = 5 + 9j
y= 9 – 5j
z = x + y
print(z)
```

The output will be as follow:

(14 + 4j)

Chapter Review

- A variable is a storage location, which has a name assigned to it.

- Variables must begin with a letter. However, they can have underscores and numbers.

- Variable declaration: variable_name = value.

- Strings are a series of characters enclosed in quotation marks.

- Python data types include numbers, tuple, dictionary, list, and string.

- Python number data types comprise of integer, floating numbers, and complex numbers.

#### CHAPTER 2

List & Tuples in Python

In this chapter, you will learn everything you need to learn about a list in Python programming. Lists allow you to store a particular set of information on the number of items in such a list. They are essential features in Python that are accessible to programmers.

Definition of List

A list refers to a data type that contains a collection of items in an orderly manner. For instance, a list can comprise the alphabets, digits, or the names of the street in a country. Below is the syntax structure for a list:

list = [item1, item2, item3, itemN]

Consider the list of items in a kitchen in this code.

```
kitchen_item = ["pot", "kettle", "fridge", "dishwasher", "microwave",
"knife", "bowls"]

print(kitchen_item)
```

If you decide to print this code, the output will be as follows:

```
["pot", "kettle", "fridge", "dishwasher", "microwave", "knife", "bowls"]
```

Accessing a List Item

Perhaps, you don't want the users to see certain items in a list; you can decide to access only the items you want. To have access to a particular element in a list, you have to write the list name then followed by the index of the item, which is enclosed in squared brackets. For instance, we can pull the third item in our list of items in the kitchen.

```
kitchen_item = ["pot", "kettle", "fridge", "dishwasher", "microwave",
"knife", "bowls"]
```

```
print(kitchen_item [3])
```

The output will be as follow:

```
dishwasher
```

Index Positions

The first index position in Python is not 1 but 0. If you observe in the example above, you will see that when indexed the third item, we started counting from 0. You can see that pot (0), kettle (1), fridge (2), while dishwasher (3). Peradventure, you run a Python program and get a different result; you have to check if you are making a number error.

Always remember that the second element in any list starts with an index of 1. A simple way of knowing what the particular index number will be is to substrate one from the item you want to index. Does that sound simple?

```
kitchen_item = ["pot", "kettle", "fridge", "dishwasher", "microwave",
"knife", "bowls"]

print(kitchen_item)
```

For instance, we want to access only the item "microwave. To do that, you have to count the number of items to get to "microwave" and subtract one. From the code, if you count first, you will discover that "microwave" is the 5th element. However, to index it to print only "microwave," you have to substrate one from the element. Your code will be like this:

```
kitchen_item = ["pot", "kettle", "fridge", "dishwasher", "microwave",
"knife", "bowls"]

print(kitchen_item [4])
```

Let us use another example to index the third and sixth items.

```
kitchen_item = ["pot", "kettle", "fridge", "dishwasher", "microwave",
"knife", "bowls"]

print(kitchen_item [3])
```

```
print(kitchen_item [6])
```

The output will be as follows:

```
dishwasher
bowls
```

Assuming you only want to access the last element, Python has a unique way of doing that. You can do this by using an index of -1. With this, Python returns the last item.

```
kitchen_item = ["pot", "kettle", "fridge", "dishwasher", "microwave",
"knife", "bowls"]

print(kitchen_item [-1])
```

In this example, the code will return "bowls." It is easy to remember this syntax. You do not have to know the particular length of the list. This also applies to other negative index values. It is like going backward. You can use the negative index to access the second or third items in a list. For instance,

```
kitchen_item = ["pot", "kettle", "fridge", "dishwasher", "microwave",
"knife", "bowls"]

print(kitchen_item [-2])

print(kitchen_item [-3])
```

The output will be as follows

```
knife
microwave
```

Exercise to Try

- Write a Python program, which contains a list of all your special friends. Then print their names by accessing each element in your list.

- From the list you created above, print a greeting message to each name you access in the list.

- Think of any means of transportation you can remember and write a list of items used within them. Then make a statement on some of these elements in the list and print it.

Adding, Changing, and Removing Elements in a List

The lists you will mostly create in Python are dynamic in nature. This means you have to build the list, add elements to it, and remove it in the course of running your program. For instance, you may decide to create a game where the player must shoot birds flying. You may record the first set of birds in a particular list before removing each bird that is shot down. Once a new bird appears, it is added to the screen. Your bird lists will increase, whereas the length will decrease throughout the game.

Modifying Elements

You can modify elements in an element similar to how you can access it. Furthermore, the same syntax applies to when you want to access an element. To modify an element, you will use the list name, followed by the index element that you want to modify, and then provide the new value to want to change. Well, this may sound foreign; however, let me use a simple example to illustrate how you can do this. For instance, we want to change dishwasher to spoon in the example below, how can you do that.

```
kitchen_item = ["pot", "kettle", "fridge", "dishwasher", "microwave", "knife", "bowls"]

print(kitchen_item)


kitchen_item[3] = "spoon"

print(kitchen_item)
```

The first two lines of code define our original list, which contains the word "dishwasher." The third line changes the element from dishwasher to spoon. If you do it correctly, you will get the output as:

["pot", "kettle", "fridge", "dishwasher", "microwave", "knife", "bowls"]

["pot", "kettle", "fridge", "spoon", "microwave", "knife", "bowls"]

You can change any element irrespective of where it is positioned.

Adding Elements

At times, you may want to add an element in a list to expand your program. Remember the bird scenario, where you have additional new birds each time you shoot. It doesn't apply to that alone; you may want to expand your database to include new users or add new items to a list. Python provides various means of adding elements in a list. In this section, we will focus on two ways you can do this as a beginner.

Append an Element to the List End

This method is the simplest to use when adding an element to a list. By appending the element, you add the item to the list end. Remember, we use the word "append" to add new items. However, for consistency purposes, I will use our previous kitchen_item example to explain. In this example, we will add cooking gas to the list.

```
kitchen_item = ["pot", "kettle", "fridge", "dishwasher", "microwave", "knife", "bowls"]

print(kitchen_item)


kitchen_item.append("spoon")

print(kitchen_item)
```

The append()method allows us to add an element at the end of the list. The output will be:

["pot", "kettle", "fridge", "dishwasher", "microwave", "knife", "bowls", "spoon"]

If you have an empty list, you can utilize the append() method to add a new list. Assuming we want to add a new list element, such as pot, kettle, and microwave, we can do that as follows:

```
kitchen_item []

kitchen_item.append("pot")

kitchen_item.append("kettle")

kitchen_item.append(microwave")


print(kitchen_item)
```

This code will produce:

```
["pot", "kettle", "microwave"]
```

It is very common to build the list this way because you may not know the particular data type the users want to keep track of in the program. However, to give the users full control, first define an empty list, which will hold the values of the users. With this, you can use the append method to add new elements to the list created.

Inserting Elements

The second way of adding an element in a list is by inserting the element to the position you want through the insert() method. You have to specify the index of both the new element and the value, respectively. For instance, we want to insert a "spoon" after the microwave item on the list.

```
kitchen_item = ["pot", "kettle", "fridge", "dishwasher", "microwave", "knife", "bowls"]

print(kitchen_item)


kitchen_item.insert(3, "spoon")

print(kitchen_item)
```

Your output will be:

```
["pot", "kettle", "fridge", "spoon", "dishwasher", "microwave", "knife",
"bowls"]
```

What happened in the example above is that I inserted the value "spoon" at the third index. The insert method enables us to create a space between the "dishwasher" and the "microwave" while storing the value "spoon" to the location created.

Removing Elements

Some situations may warrant you to remove an item in a list. For instance, a player may decide to remove a bird; he shoots down from the sky from the active list. Perhaps, you want to delete a customer's account or cancel their account. You can remove such detail from the list. You can use the following two ways to remove elements in a list.

Remove Items Using del Statement

Python provides a unique way of removing or deleting an item if you know the position of such an item from the list. Look at the code below:

```
kitchen_item = ["pot", "kettle", "fridge", "dishwasher", "microwave",
"knife", "bowls"]

print(kitchen_item)


del kitchen_item [4]

print(kitchen_item)
```

What did you think will be deleted from the snippet above? If your answer is a dishwasher, then you are wrong. Remember that Python index begins at 0. This means we start counting 0 from the first element. Therefore, the final output will be:

```
["pot", "kettle", "fridge", "dishwasher", "knife", "bowls"]
```

You can remove any item from the position of your choice.

Using the pop() Method to Remove an Item

There are situations where you want to use an item value after removing it from the list. For instance, you want to know the coordinates of the bird you shot, to enable you to draw an explosion in such a position. The function of the pop()method is to remove the last item in the list. For clarity, let us popan example.

```
kitchen_item = ["pot", "kettle", "fridge", "dishwasher", "microwave", "knife", "bowls"]

print(kitchen_item)


poppedkitchen_item = kitchen_item.pop()

print(kitchen_item)

print(poppedkitchen_item)
```

I won't explain the first two lines since you are already conversant with it. However, if you forget, I will refresh your memory. The first line begins by declaring "kitchen_item" as a variable with values including pop, kettle, fridge, dishwasher, microwave, knife, and bowls—the second line prints out the items in the kitchen_item list.

In the third line, we popped a value from our list and stored the value to the new variable "popped.kitchen_item" additionally, we print out the remaining items in the kitchen_item list. From the code above, our output will be:

```
"pot", "kettle", "fridge", "dishwasher", "microwave", "knife", "bowls"]


"pot", "kettle", "fridge", "dishwasher", "microwave", "knife"]
bowls
```

The first line shows the complete kitchen_items, whereas the second shows the remaining items after the popped method was used. Finally, line three shows the item removed from our list.

How to Remove an Item Using Value

It is not in every situation that you will know the exact position of a value you want to remove from your list. Remember, if you identify the value, then you can use the remove()method because it serves the best option in this situation. Do you remember our previous example where we use the del function? However, this is different. Let's remove an item from the list of our kitchen_item.

```
kitchen_item = "pot", "kettle", "fridge", "dishwasher", "microwave", "knife", "bowls"]

print(kitchen_item)


kitchen_item.remove("kettle")

print(kitchen_item)
```

In the example above, we aimed to remove the kettle from the list of kitchen items. The output will be as follow:

```
["pot", "kettle", "fridge", "dishwasher", "microwave", "knife", "bowls"]


["pot", "fridge", "dishwasher", "microwave", "knife", "bowls"]
```

Exercise to Try

The following exercises to try may seem complex; however, the offer you a huge opportunity to include all the lists we have described in this section.

- **First list** – If you are allowed to invite ten persons (dead or alive) for a love feast, who will you invite? Then print a message for each individual, inviting him or her to your love feast.

- **Alter the first list** – Due to unforeseen circumstances, two of your invitees fell ill and won't make it. It means you have to send a new invite to replace the absentees. Using a print call, list the invitees that won't make it. Furthermore, replace the list with new invitees and print out the full list.

- **Special list** – Now create a new list by using the insert() method to add your best five invitees to the love feast.

Organizing a List in Python

Most times, you may create your list in an unorderly manner because you link the ability to control what the user is providing. However, you can avoid such a situation and organize the list properly. You can preserve the order in the list, or change it from its original order. There are ways of doing this, depending on your particular situation.

Using the sort() Method

An easier means of organizing a list in Python is by using the sort method. Consider our kitchen items in previous examples, and you want to sort them alphabetically. To make it easier, we assume all the items are in lowercase.

```
kitchen_item = ["pot", "kettle", "fridge", "dishwasher", "microwave", "knife", "bowls"]

kitchen_item.sort()

print(kitchen_item)
```

The output will be as follows when the sort method operates on the list items. Remember, it sorts the item in alphabetical order.

```
["bowls", "dishwasher", "fridge", "kettle", "knife", "microwave", "pot"]
```

Look at the code below:

```
kitchen_item = ["pot", "kettle", "fridge", "dishwasher"]

kitchen_item.sort(reverse=true)

print(kitchen_item)
```

What do you think will happen to our list? Well, the kitchen items will be reversed, and your output will be:

```
[ "dishwasher", "fridge", "kettle", "pot"]
```

List Length

Another important thing you can do with a list is to determine the length. To do this, you have to use the len() function. Using our kitchen item list, we can demonstrate this.

---

kitchen_item = "pot", "kettle", "fridge", "dishwasher", "microwave", "knife", "bowls"]

length = len(kitchen_item)

print(lenght)

The output will be

7

This function comes handy, especially when you want to determine the number of birds that remain to be shot.

Summary

I am convinced that you know what lists are, how to work with them, including adding and removing elements in a list. Furthermore, you know how to determine the length of a list; however, I want to go a step higher by introducing how you can work with items in a given list effectively. We will loop through these items with a few line codes. With looping, you can work with any list, irrespective of how many items contained in it.

Looping Through a Complete List

At times, you may want to go through all elements in a list to perform the same activity on each item. For instance, you might want to perform certain statistical operatives on all elements in a list or display every headline contained in a list on your website. Well, you can do this and more activities on items in a list by using a loop.

For instance, the list below comprises of famous magician's name, and we aim to print their names from the list. There are several ways of doing this; it could be by retrieving each name individually or allow Python to perform the magic. Nevertheless, the problem with the first option is that it can create numerous issues for us because it can be repetitive to do this if the list is long.

Furthermore, there is a need to change the code whenever the length of the list changes. You see how tedious it could be if we decide to take the first approach. To save you the stress, let me show you the easiest way of printing out the list individually.

```
magicians_name = ["Greg", "Perpetual", "Amos"]
magician in magicians_name:
print(magician)
```

In the first line, we began by assigning elements to the variable name "magicians_name." You should be familiar with this by now if you have been following. The second line tells the interpreter to bring a name from our magicians_name list and assign the element to the variable magician. Then the third line prints the name assigned to the variable magician. The interpreter repeats the process for the remaining items in the list and produces the output. If you type the code properly, your output will be as follow:

```
Greg
Perpetual
Amos
```

Note: Always remember to save your programs.

Looping in Python

The theory of looping is significant in any programming language, including Python, because it provides a more natural way for a computer to perform automatic repetitive tasks. For instance, in our previous magician program, in the second line, the interpreter reads the line (magician in magicians_name). The line informs the interpreter to retrieve the first value of the magicians_name list. It further assigns it to the variable magician. The first value is "Greg," and the interpreter goes to read the next line – **print(magician)**.

The interpreter goes back to the second line and retrieves the second name "Perpetual" before assigning it to the variable magician. Then the last line is executed, which prints the name "Perpetual." Once this is completed, the interpreter repeats the loop to evaluate the previous value and print "Amos." Since that is the last loop, there is no more instruction to execute, the program halts. In the course of using a loop in Python, remember that the steps are repeated once for each element in the list, irrespective of the number of elements in the list you created. Additionally, you have the liberty to select the name you desire to store your values in the program. However, it is essential to use a meaningful name. For instance, let us use a list of lions, horses, and cars.

```
for lion in lions

for horse in horses

for car in cars
```

This kind of naming convention will enable you to follow the actions performed on each item in the loop. You can also identify the section of the code with errors when you use singular and plural names.

More actions on a "for Loop"

You can perform whatever thing you want on each item when using a for loop. Instead of using a new example, I will use our magician example. In this example, I will print a message indicating that each magician did perfectly well.

```
magicians_names =["Greg," "Perpetual," "Amos"]

for magician in magicians_names:

print(f"{magician.title()}, you did an excellent trick today!")
```

The first two lines do not require any explanation. However, the only alteration in the code is the third line, where we created a piece of unique information to every single magician, beginning with his or her name. During the loop, it goes through the first value, which is "Greg" and prints the message after the name. It does the same thing for the value "Perpetual" before running through the loop for the third time to print the value "Amos" with the message. The output will show a customized message as follows:

```
Greg, you did an excellent trick today!
```

Perpetual, you did an excellent trick today!

Amos, you did an excellent trick today!

You can write many codes as possible inside a for loop. Each indented line that follows the line "for magician in magicians_name" is regarded to be within the loop with each indented line performed once for every single item.For instance, let us add another line to our previous example, telling the magicians to keep the good work going every day.

```
magicians_names =["Greg," "Perpetual," "Amos"]
for magician in magicians_names:
print(f "{magician.title()}, you did an excellent trick today!")
print(f "Keep the good work going every day, (magician.title()}. \n")
```

If you observe clearly, each print() method is indented correctly; therefore, each line will be executed once for the element in the list. However, (\n) in the second print line is a newline, which requests for a blank line inserted after the last statement before going through the loop. With this newline, the message becomes neatly grouped for the magician list. Let us see how the output of the program will be.

Greg, you did an excellent trick today!

Keep the good work going every day

Perpetual, you did an excellent trick today!

Keep the good work going every day

Amos, you did an excellent trick today!

Keep the good work going every day

You see how neatly the output is; this makes your program understandable. You can add as many lines of codes you want in a "for loop." Ensure to include some lines of codes in this program to understand the concept behind looping in Python.

Performing Actions After a for Loop

What will happen when a "for loop" finishes execution? Normally, you may want to summarize an output or continue with other work that your code must complete. Well, in our previous example, the code is well indented; however, if the code is after the loop, then it will be executed once since it wasn't indented. Let us include an appreciation message to the magicians for their wonderful work. This message will be a group message instead of the personalized messages we have written before. To do that, we have to place our message after the for loop. Additionally, we won't indent this line of code. An example will clarify these properly.

```
magicians_names =["Greg," "Perpetual," "Amos"]

for magician in magicians_names:

print(f "{magician.title()}, you did an excellent trick today!")

print(f "Keep the good work going every day, (magician.title()}. \n")

print("We appreciate your wonderful work. It was a masterpiece performance!")
```

The only inclusion of this line of codes is the last statement. If you look closely, the first two print() methods were adequately indented. However, thethird one is different; hence, it will be printed once. The output will be as follows.

```
Greg, you did an excellent trick today!

Keep the good work going every day


Perpetual, you did an excellent trick today!

Keep the good work going every day


Amos, you did an excellent trick today!

Keep the good work going every day
```

> We appreciate your wonderful work. It was a masterpiece performance!

Dealing with Indentation Errors

The importance of indentation in Python is that it helps to determine the relationship(s) between a line or group of lines from the rest of the program. Furthermore, it makes the program easier to read for anyone. However, Python introduces whitespace to format your code neatly in order to have a clear visual structure of your codes. As you continue writing Python programs, you will observe the line of codes is indented at different levels. Through this, one can have a general structure of the program. Well, while Python helps with indentation, it is important to watch out for commonerrors. For instance, some beginners indent a line of codes that don't require indentation or may also forget to indent them. I will write some indentation errors and provide ways of dealing with such a situation in the future. The following are common indentation errors that most beginners commit when starting their Python programming course.

Forgetting to Indent

A for loop always requires indentation; however, if you forget it, Python will remind you. save this program with magic.py Let us look at the example below.

```
magicians_name =["Greg," "Perpetual," "Amos"]

magician in magicians_name:

print(magician)
```

In this code, the third line should be indented but wasn't. Once the Python interpreter encounters such statement that should have an indented block but didn't find any, it indicates an error with the code as follows:

```
File "magic.py," line 3
```

```
   print(magician)
        ^
IndentationError: expected an indented block
```

To solve this error, you have to indent the line of code properly. As simple as this mistake may be, it can keep you from getting an error each time you run a program.

Besides forgetting to indent, you may forget to indent statements in a loop. Your loop may run successfully without any errors, but your output will be different from what you expected. When this happens, it signifies you are doing several tasks inside your loop and don't indent some of the lines of codes. For instance, you didn't indent the second line in the magician code that says, "***keep the good work going every day, (magician.title()}. \n")***

```
magicians_names =["Greg," "Perpetual," "Amos"]

for magician in magicians_names:

print(f "{magician.title()}, you did an excellent trick today!")

print(f "Keep the good work going every day, (magician.title()}. \n")
```

The line in bold and italicize should have been indented, but the interpreter finds at least a statement indented after the "for magician in magicians_name" a statement. However, it doesn't indicate any error; when the first print() method takes action for each name contained in our magician list, it prints the same message to the names. However, for the second print() method, because it is not indented, it executes the loop once before haltingthe program. Among the three magicians (Greg, Perpetual, and Amos), only Amos will receive the message, "Keep the good work going every day." The output of this program will be as follow:

```
Greg, you did an excellent trick today!

Perpetual, you did an excellent trick today!

Amos, you did an excellent trick today!
```

This error is also known as a logical error because the syntax is an acceptable Python code. However, it doesn't produce the result we expected because of the logic error in the code. Therefore, if your goal is to repeat a certain code once for every item in a list, then you can do that with indentation.

Exercise to Try

- **Fruits** – Consider at least four of your much-loved fruits. Store these preferred fruit names in the list of your choice and use a "for loop" to generate each fruit's name. Then modify the "for loop" to produce a statement using the fruit name rather than printing the name of your favorite fruit only. Additionally, for every fruit in the list, you should generate an output that says, I like apple fruit.

- **Animals** – Think of four animals with common features in life. Store their names in a list of your choice. Furthermore, implement a conditional test using "for loop" to display every animal you on your list.

  - Modify your line of code to produce a sentence about each animal. For instance, you can say, A lion is the bravest animal I have ever known.

  - Add another line to your program, indicating the unique features of these animals. For instance, you can print a general statement like; these animals are dangerous to human beings.

Note: These programs are elementary to write if you have followed our previous examples above. Study them properly and write your own code. Practice more, and you will be perfect when it comes to writing Python programs.

Numerical Lists

So far, we have been dealing with string as it relates to the list. However, in this section, you will learn how to perform certain operations on numerical values. In Python, many reasons may warrant us to store a number. For storing numbers, lists are very important, and Python provides various tools to perform such action effectively. If you can understand these tools effectively, you can work perfectly well even if the list contains thousands of items in it. Let us look at certain operations you can perform on a number as it relates to the list.

Range() Function

This function is a unique function that allows a programmer to generate a sequence of numbers quickly. In the example below, we can print a range of numbers from 6 to 15.

```
for scores in range(6, 15):
print(scores)
```

In as much as the code seems like printing the numbers from 6 to 15, however, it doesn't print the number 15. Our output will be as follow:

```
6
7
8
9
10
11
12
13
14
```

In our example below, the range() function prints only the numbers from 6 to 15. Well, this is the product of the off-by-one behavior, which exists in most programming languages. The function makes the interpreted to start the counting process at the initial number, but stops at the second number before reaching the number indicated. However, if you wanted to print out the number 15, that means you have to extend the stopping point by one. In this case, it is 16. Therefore, your code will be as follows:

```
for scores in range(6, 16):
print(scores)
```

Moreover, your output will be:

```
6
7
8
9
10
11
12
13
14
15
```

If your output doesn't match what you wanted when using the range() function, then you have to adjust the ending value by 1.

Making a List Using range() Function

You can exchange a number list by using the list() function. Nevertheless, you need to wrap the list() within the range() function. With this, your final outcome will be similar to a number list. We will use our previous example of a number range to illustrate this example. You will see the difference between the previous program code and this new one.

```
num = list(range(1, 16))
print(num)
```

Our output will be as follows:

```
1, 2, 3, 4, 5, 6, 7, 8, 9, 10, 11, 12, 13, 14, 15
```

It is also possible to skip some numbers in the list by using range() function. If we add a third argument to the range(), the interpreter uses that value to perform a step size. For instance, we want to print even numbers from 1 to 16. What the program does is, to begin with, the value 2 and increases that value by 2. In order words, it starts at 2 and repeatedly adds 2 to the initial number and continue until it reaches the last number.

```
Even_num = list(range(2, 16, 2))
print(even_num)
```

The output will be as follows:

```
2, 4, 6, 8, 10, 12, 14
```

Let us try another example.

```
odd_num = list(range(1, 16, 2))
print(even_num)
```

The output will be as follows:

```
1, 3, 5, 7, 9, 11, 13, 15
```

```
number_squares=[]
for numb in range(1, 15)
numbers = numb**2
number_squares.append(numbers)
print(number_squares)
```

Besides getting even and odd numbers, you can generate any set of numbers or operations you can envision. Programming is about thinking outside the box. For instance, you can find the square of any number of your choice. In this example below, we will make a list comprising of the first 15 square numbers. When you want to represent exponents in Python, we use double asterisks (**). This is the program to illustrate the first 15 square numbers.

Initially, the program will look confusing; however, I will explain it line by line. We began by creating an empty list and called it "number_squares." In line two, we created a loop and request each "numb," ranging from 1 to 15, by using the range() function. Then, in line three, we raised the current "numb" to its second power before assigning it to the variable "numbers"; in line four, every new "numb" of numbers is joined to our list number_squares.Lastly, the list of number_squares is printed when the loop is finished. Then, the outcome of the program will be:

```
1, 4, 9, 16, 25, 36, 49, 64, 81, 100, 121, 144, 169, 196, 225
```

We can rewrite this code concisely by omitting the variable "numbers" while appending each new "numb" directly to our list. Let us see how that is possible.

```
number_squares=[]
for numb in range(1, 15)
number_squares.append(numb**2)
print(number_squares)
```

As you can see, the two different approaches create a complex list. Remember, we omitted the temporary variable "numbers" in the last approach. With this method, you make your program more comfortable to read. However, the goal is to focus on the one you understand and not to rushthings. Review the two approaches and look for the more efficient one.

Performing Statistics on Number List

Python has certain functions that allow you to perform statistical operations on a number list. For instance, you can execute operations such as finding thesum, minimum, and maximum numbers in a particular list.

```
>>>numbers= [11, 12, 13, 14, 15, 16, 17, 18, 19, 20]
>>>min(numbers)
11
>>>max(numbers)
```

```
20
>>>sum(numbers)
155
```

This example is just to show you how possible you can manipulate numbers in a list. You can do the same even if the list contains a million numbers.

List Comprehensions

Previously, I explained how you could create a list of squares using four lines of code. However, there is a simpler approach, which allows you to use a single line. A list comprehension comprises of a "for loop" with the creation of new elements in the list, and repeatedly append each new element. Although beginners should use the list comprehension, however, I included them for you to be aware of them. Let us use an example to show you how you can rewrite this program on a line to create a square of the first 15 numbers.

```
number_squares = [numbers**2 for numb in range(1, 15)]
print(number_squares)
```

We started by creating a descriptive name (number_squares) for our list. We then open a set of square brackets, which allows us to define the expression "[numbers**2 for numb in range(1, 15)]" for the numbers we want to keep track of in our new list. Furthermore, a loop is created to repeat the expression pending when the condition is completed. The loop goes through the range()function, with values from 1 to 15. If you observe carefully, we didn't include a colon at the end of the loop. When we run the program after saving it, our output will be as what we got in our previous example.

```
1, 4, 9, 16, 25, 36, 49, 64, 81, 100, 121, 144, 169, 196, 225
```

Because the list comprehension isn't advisable for beginners, it doesn't mean you can't give it a try. It takes consistent practice to understand the list comprehension before it will be worthwhile to create lists comfortably.

Exercise to Try

- **Counting to forty** – Write a program using a "for loop" to create and output numbers ranging from 10 to 60 with 60 inclusive.

- **One hundred** – Create a list of numbers ranging from 1 to 100. Furthermore, use the conditional test "for loop" to display the numbers on the screen.

- **Summing one hundred numbers** – After creating your 100 numbers, save using another name, and perform the followingtasks on it. Find the minimum, maximum, and sum of the 100 numbers with 100 excluded.

- **Four** – Compile a list of multiples of 4 from 4 to 40. Ensure to use a for loop for this program and print the output.

- **Cube** – Calculate the cube of the first 10 numbers. A cube is the third power of a number. Use a "for loop" to generate the number and print the value of the cube.

Working with List Part

In the course of learning this tutorial, you have understood how to easily access single elements in a list, perform manipulations on numbers, and strings. However, I want to go a step ahead into ways how you can work withspecific elements in a list. In Python, we call them a slice. Consider a full loafof bread, which is in slices. Depending on the same, you may not finish a full loaf; therefore, when you take four slices and wrap up the other, you have taken a specific number of slice instead of all the slices in the full loaf.

Slicing a List in Python

If you want to perform a slice in Python, you have to stipulate the first and last index of the elements in the list. Similar to the range() function we use previously, Python halts at one item before the second index you stipulate. To display the first five elements, you have to request indices from 0 to 5. In this situation, this would return the following elements 0, 1, 2, 3, 4, and 5.

The following are team members in Manchester United Football club

```
united_players =[ "Rashford," "Young," "Pogba," "James," "De Gea"]
print(united_players [1:4]
```

The second line prints a slice of the element in the list, which comprises of the following players.

> "Young," "Pogba," "James," "De Gea"

If you mistakenly forget the first index when slicing a list, Python spontaneously begins your slice at the start of your list. For instance,

> united_players =["Rashford," "Young," "Pogba," "James," "De Gea"]
>
> print(united_players [:4]

Since there is no starting index, the output will be:

> "Young," "Pogba," "James," "De Gea"

The same thing applies if you omit the last index of the list. For instance, you want to start your index at two while omitting the second index.

> united_players =["Rashford," "Young," "Pogba," "James," "De Gea"]
>
> print(united_players [2:]

Python will return the following value:

> "Pogba," "James," "De Gea"

With this, you can print out all elements in a list irrespective of the length and its position. You can use a negative index, but it recalls a number from thelist end. For instance, our goal to display the last four United players in our list

> united_players =["Rashford," "Young," "Pogba," "James," "De Gea"]
>
> print(united_players [-4:]

This will print the last four players

> "Young," "Pogba," "James," "De Gea"

Using Loop in a Slice

Python allows the use of for loop in a slice to go through a subset of elements in the list. We can create a loop to pass through the first four players on our list and display their names. Let us see how that works.

```
united_players =[ "Rashford," "Young," "Pogba," "James," "De Gea"]

print ("My favorite Manchester United Players are:")
for players in united_players [ :4]:
print(players.title())
```

Rather than the interpreter looping through the full list of players in line 3, it loops only through the first four players in the team. Then our output will be:

```
My favorite Manchester United Players are:
Rashford
Young
Pogba
James
```

Slice comes handy in various situations, such as when you want to add the final score of a player in a game when working with data or building a website application.

Tuples

If you want to store items, which can change during the course of the program, then the list works perfectly for this situation. Modifying data or a list is very important when working with various applications or creating web applications. Notwithstanding, at times, you may want a list of items whose value doesn't change throughout the program. In such a situation, you can use a tuple to replace using a list. In Python, we call values, which cannot change throughout the life of the program as immutable. Therefore, an immutable list can also be known as a tuple.

What is a Tuple?

A tuple is similar to the list I explained earlier. However, we use parentheses for tuple as an alternative to square brackets used in a list. You can access each element after defining a tuple by using each index. It is similar to what you would do if you want to access a list.

For instance, let us take the length and width of a room to be 200 by 100, which will always remain the same size unless the building is destroyed. Therefore, putting the length and width into a tuple, we have ensured that its size won't change.

```
size = (200, 100)
print(size[0])
print(size[1])
```

What we have done in the first line is to define the tuple size by using parentheses rather than square brackets. Then in the second and third lines, we print the elements individually. Then save and run the program, your output will be:

```
200
100
```

Let me modify the program to show you when Python recognizes an error when you try to alter the tuple value.

```
size = (200, 100)
size[0] = 220
```

In the second line, I try to change the value from 200 to 220. However, Python will return an error. We try to change a tuple, which isn't possible with such an object.

Using loop in a Tuple

Similar to what we did in a list using the "for loop," tuple allows us to loop through the elements in it. For instance,

```
sizes =(200, 100)
for size in sizes:
print(size)
```

The output will be:

```
200
100
```

Writing Through a Tuple

As already stated, you cannot modify or alter a tuple; however, you can allocate new values to the variable representing the tuple. Assuming something happens and you decide to change the size of the room, you can redefine the entire tuple.

```
sizes =(200, 100)
print("This is our original room size:"
for size in sizes:
print(size)

sizes = (300, 150)
print("Our new room size:")
for size in sizes
print(size)
```

The output will be as follows:

```
This is our original room size:
200
100
```

```
Our new room size:
300
150
```

Summary

So far, in this chapter, you have learned everything you need to know as it concerns lists and tuple. I am convinced that you can efficiently work with elements in a list. We also went through how to use a "for loop" in a list, the structure of indenting a Python program, and popular indentation errors to avoid. You learned how to make numerical lists and perform certain operations such as finding the maximum, minimum, and sum in a list. Additionally, we learned more about slicing a list and getting only the details you want in a list.

Finally, you learned about tuples. You also know what makes it different from a list. The values of a tuple cannot change, whereas that of a list can be changed in the course of the program. In the next chapter, you will learn about using various conditional statements in Python. Endeavor to practice the exercise provided in this chapter, as it will enhance your programming skills in Python. If peradventure you encounter an error, take your time to go through the line indicated. Congratulations on your promotion to the next chapter of this course.

CHAPTER 3:

Dictionary

The Dictionary offers programmers a whole lot of options, especially in storing a limitless volume of information. In this chapter, you will understand what dictionaries are, how you can use them in a loop, build lists inside them, and create a dictionary insider another dictionary. If you can understand the concept of dictionaries in Python, it will equip you in various ways and allow you to model different live situation situations. You can create a simple dictionary, which represents an individual. With this, you can store various information, including the person's name, location, age, phone details, security number, anything you can think of as it concerns the person. You can do so much a dictionary in Python, such as storing people's names with their best food, words with their meaning, countries and their presidents, etc.

Let us look at a game with teams having different scores and colors. This code stores information as it relates to a particular team.

```
team1 ={'color': 'red', 'scores' : 3}

print(team1 ['color'])
print(team1 ['scores'])
```

The dictionary team1 stores the color and scores, whereas the last two lines access the dictionary before displaying the information as seen below

```
red
3
```

New programming concepts require consistent practice to perfect it. Since you are learning a new language, it is crucial to understand this concept painstakingly. If you understand it, you can apply it in all real-world situations.

What is a Dictionary?

From the program above, you can have an idea of what dictionaries are. A dictionary is a group of key-value pairs. Every single key in the dictionary has its corresponding value; the key enables you to have access to the value, and it can be a list, string, number, or dictionary. Dictionaries are usually enclosed in braces with the keys and values placed inside the braces. For instance:

```
team1 ={'color': 'red', 'scores' : 3}
```

A key to value pair always has values corresponding to each other. Once you provide the key in a dictionary, Python returns the value corresponding with such key. Each key is linked to a value by a colon, whereas individual key-value pairs are disconnected by a comma.

```
team1 ={'color': 'red', 'scores' : 3}
```

The program above has only one pair, with each matching its value, respectively. The color matches red, whereas scores match the value 0.

How to Access Values

If you want to access the value of a key, you have to include the dictionary name before placing the key in square brackets.

```
team1 ={'color': 'red', 'scores' : 3}
print(team1['color'])
```

The output for this code will return the corresponding key value from the dictionary "team1," which in this situation is red.

Python allows us to have an unlimited number of key-value pairs. We can add more codes to illustrate this. Additionally, we can decide the particular key-pair to print or display on the screen. In this code, it will display 'London.'

```
team1 ={'color': 'red', 'scores' : 3, 'S/N' : 1, 'place' : 'London'}
print(team1['place'])
```

```
London
```

Adding Key-Value Pairs

Since dictionaries are structurally dynamic, we can add new pairs to them whenever we want. For instance, we can add additional information to our original program to include positions, which will display the position score is taken. Let the home team be on the left position while the away team is on the right.

```
team1 ={'color': 'red', 'scores' : 3}
print(team1)

team1['home_team'] = left
team1['away_team'] = right
print(team1)
```

We began by defining a dictionary "team1" and included its key and values, respectively, before printing the dictionary. In the second phase of the code, we assign the home team to be on the left position while the away team is on the right. If we print the program, our output will be:

```
{'color': 'red,' 'scores' : 3}
{'color': 'red', 'scores' : 3, 'home_team': left, 'away_team' : right}
```

In our final program, we have four key-value pairs, where we added two positions, whereas the original two specifies only the color and score.

At times, most programmers find it convenient to begin with an empty dictionary, unlike what we did by adding elements first. To fill an empty dictionary, you have to define the dictionary without adding any key-value pairs. The dictionary will be empty with a set of braces. For instance, if we are to define the color and scores dictionary, that will be as follows:

```
team1 = {}
team1['color'] = 'red'
team1['score'] = 3

print(team1)
```

What we did here is to define an empty team1 dictionary before adding color and score values, respectively. We will get the same results as what we got in our previous examples.

```
{'color': 'red,' 'scores' : 3}
```

How to Modify Values

Besides adding and creating an empty dictionary list, you can also modify a value in your dictionary. To do this, you have to specify the dictionary name before adding the new value. Let us change the color from red to blue.

```
team1 ={'color': 'red'}
print(f "The color of the team is {team1['color']}.")

team1 = ['color'] = 'blue'
print(f "The team's new color is {team1['color']}.")
```

What we did is first to define the team1 dictionary, which contains only the team's color. We then print the team's color before changing the value of the corresponding key from red to blue. The output shows that we have changed the team color from red to blue.

```
The color of the team is red.
The team's new color is blue.
```

To make the program more interesting, I will track the position of the team based on their speed in the opponent's direction. With the ball speed, we can determine if the team is on the left or right.

```
team1 = {'home_team' : 'left', 'away_team': 'right', 'ball': ' neutral'
print(f "Original direction: {team1('home_team')}")
#The team is on the left position
#Current speed of the team
if team1['ball'] == 'slow':
     home_incre = 1
elif team1['ball'] == 'medium':
     home_incre = 2
else:
     #in opposition half
     home_incre = 3

team1['home_team'] = team['home_team'] + home_incre

print(f "Position of team: {team1['home_team']}")
```

If you observe, I intentionally avoided the color and its point value in order to make the program simple. We began by defining a team with the left and right position; a ball speed set medium.

In the line "if team1['ball'] == 'home':" we use an if-elif-else conditional statement to test the position of the ball. If the ball is slow, then it is on the home team, if it is medium, then it is positioned in the middle. Run the program and notice what the output will be. Towards the end of this chapter, I will unveil the outcome of this program.

How to Remove key-value Pairs

So far, you have learned how to add, modify, and create an empty dictionary list. What if you decide to remove a piece of information in your dictionary? You can take advantage of the "del" statement to remove your information. Let us use our original program to illustrate how you can easily remove a key-value pair in Python.

```
team1 = {'color': 'red', 'scores' : 3}
print(team1)

del team1['color']
print(team1)
```

The only difference to our original program is the last two lines we added. We use the del statement to delete the "color" key from our team1 dictionary. This will eventually remove the corresponding value of the key. Our initial output will display the keys and its corresponding value, but after the "del" statement, it will print only the scores. Let's see how that will be:

```
{'color': 'red,' 'scores' : 3}
{'scores' : 3}
```

Dictionary with Similar Objects

Throughout this chapter, we have only stored different information as it relates to a single object, which in this case, is our team1. However, you are not limited to a particular team as you can store information on different objects. For instance, we want to conduct an election for a community. We can use a dictionary to store the list of candidates, along with their parties.

```
election_list = {
    'John Campbell' : 'Freedom Party,'
    'Eric Longman': 'Sovereign Nation Party,'
    'Amanda   Drill':   '   Women   Liberation
```

```
    Movement,'
'Condolence Rice': 'Democratic Party,'
'Donald Trump': 'Republican Party,'

}
```

If you observe, there is a difference from our previous list as we broke this list into several lines, unlike the team1 dictionary, where everything is written on a single line. Each candidate corresponds to his or her party; additionally, there is always an opening and closing brace. Don't forget to add a comma to signify the end of a pair. With this, you can add another key-value pair. Let us pick a candidate of our choice

```
list = election_list['Donald Trump'].title()
print("Our Vote will be for {list}.")
```

In this portion, we see that the user picked Donald Trump as their favorite candidate.

```
Our Vote will be for Donald Trump.
```

Exercise to Try

- Create a new dictionary to keep information about people you know about living in your country. Then store the last name, first name, city, and age of each individual. Ensure you use a uniquekey for this information and print each information in the dictionary.

- Store the favorite food of 8 people in a dictionary, you know. Print their names and corresponding food.

Looping Through Dictionaries

A dictionary can have a single key-value pair and even up to millions of pairs due to its capability of accommodating large amounts of data. With this, you can loop through a dictionary. Since we have different ways of storing information when using dictionaries, it makes it possible to loop through the dictionary in various ways. In this section, we will explore ways of looping through dictionaries.

However, before we begin to explore the various ways of approaching looping through dictionaries, let us look at a dictionary that saves the information about users visiting a website. The dictionary stores the last name, first name, and username of the person.

```
user = {
  'last_name':
  'Trump,'
  'first_name':
  'Donald,'
  'username':
  'dotrum,'
  }
```

If you remembered what you have learned, you could easily access every information in our user dictionary. However, what will you do if you want to see all the information stored in our dictionary? Well, to do that, you have to use a "for loop" to go through the dictionary. Let see how you can put that into action.

```
user = {
  'last_name':
  'Trump,'
  'first_name':
  'Donald,'
  'username':
  'dotrum,'
  }
for k, v in user.item():
  print(f "\nK: {k}")
  print(f "V: {v}")
```

As you can see, for you to loop through a dictionary, you have to create names for our two variables, which will hold last and first names in our key- value pair. You can use any variable name of your choice. In this case, weuse k and v to represent key and value, respectively. Our output will be:

```
K: last_name
V: Trump

K: first_name
V: Donald

K: username
```

Looping through a dictionary works perfectly for a program like the list of candidates in an election we wrote previously. Remember, it stores the name and party of candidates approved to participate in the election. If we were to loop through the list, we will get the names of every candidate and generate their respective parties. Since the keys represent the person's name, whereas the value is the party, we can use variable names such as name and party in our loop rather than using key and value. This will make it easier for you to understand fully.

```
election_list = {
    'John Campbell' : 'Freedom Party',
    'Eric Longman': 'Sovereign Nation Party',
    'Amanda    Drill':    '    Women    Liberation
    Movement',
    'Condolence Rice': 'Democratic Party',
    'Donald Trump': 'Republican Party',
    }
for name, party in election_list.item():
    print(f    "{name.title()}'s    party    is    the
    {party.title()}.")
```

The program loops through every key-value pair in our election_list, and it goes through every pair of the key assigned to the name variable while the value is assigned the party variable. With only the last two lines, we can generate a full list of all candidates in the election.

```
John Campbell's party is the Freedom Party.
Eric Longman's party is the Sovereign Nation Party.
Amanda Drill's party is the Women Liberation Movement.
Condolence Rice's party is the Democratic Party.
Donald Trump's party is the Republican Party.
```

With this, you can display from a single name to millions of names in a list to the screen.

Looping Through Keys Only

We can use the keys() method to display only the key values while omitting the values contained in the dictionary. Let us use our election_list to demonstrate this feat.

```
election_list = {
    'John Campbell' : 'Freedom Party,'
    'Eric Longman': 'Sovereign Nation Party,'
    'Amanda  Drill':  '  Women  Liberation
    Movement,'
    'Condolence Rice': 'Democratic Party,'
    'Donald Trump': 'Republican Party,'
    }
for name in election_list.keys():
    print(name.title())
```

The line after the closing brace is the beginning of the "for loop," which tells the interpreter to pull only the keys from our election_list. Remember, we assign names as the key. The output will be as follows:

```
John Campbell
Eric Longman
Amanda Drill
Condolence Rice
Donald Trump
```

Looping Through Values Only

In the same manner that we can easily loop through the keys in a given dictionary, we can also loop through the value and display the value list. We can use the values() method to achieve this feat. Remember, in the previous example, we use the keys() method.

```
election_list = {
    'John Campbell' : 'Freedom Party,'
    'Eric Longman': 'Sovereign Nation Party,'
    'Amanda Drill': ' Women Liberation Movement,'
    'Condolence Rice': 'Democratic Party,'
    'Donald Trump': 'Republican Party,'
    }
print("This is the list of Political Party for the election:")
for party in election_list.values():
    print(party.title())
```

The "for" statement pulls all the value in our dictionary list and assigns it to the party. The print statement, then prints all the values in the election_list.

```
This is the list of Political Party for the election:
```

```
Freedom Party
Sovereign Nation Party
Women Liberation Movement
Democratic Party
Republican Party
```

This approach prints all the value available in the dictionary without verifying any repetition. Although this may work perfectly in a small list, however, when you have to pull a significant name or item, there may be room for repetition. To avoid such repetition, it is a way out. We can use aset, which is a group where every item is unique.

```
election_list = {
    'John Campbell' : 'Freedom Party,'
    'Eric Longman': 'Sovereign Nation Party,'
    'Amanda Drill': ' Women Liberation Movement,'
    'Condolence Rice': 'Democratic Party,'
    'Donald Trump': 'Republican Party,'
    'Nicolas Fred': ' Sovereign Nation Party,'
    }
print("The following Political Parties have been mentioned already:")
for party in set(election_list.values()):
    print(party.title())
```

We added another name and party to the list – Nicolas Fred. Assuming we are printing only the value list and don't want a repetition of the party. Once you use the set() around the list, you don't wish to duplicate; python identifies this as a unique item in the list. In the end, there won't be any repeated detail.

```
The following Political Parties have been mentioned already.
Freedom Party
Sovereign Nation Party
Women Liberation Movement
Democratic Party
Republican Party
```

Nesting Dictionary

Some situations may warrant you to store several dictionaries on a particular list. This is referred to like nesting in Python because you can include a dictionary in another dictionary. Nesting is very powerful if you understand them properly, and we will use an example to explain it better.

The team1 dictionary list comprises of a single team, but doesn't have the space to store additional information concerning a second team. How can you control a group of teams? You can do this by making a list, which has each team in a dictionary. Consider the program below:

```
team1 = {'color': 'red', 'scores' : 3}
team2 = {'color': 'black', 'scores' : 5}
team3 = {'color': 'blue', 'scores' : 0}
team4 = {'color': 'brown', 'scores' : 9}

teams = [team1, team2, team3]

for team in teams:
    print(team)
```

First, we create four dictionaries with each representing a different team. In the fourth line, we stored each of the dictionaries in a particular list called teams. Then, we loop through our list before printing each team.

```
{'color': 'red,' 'scores' : 3}
{'color': 'black,' 'scores' : 5}
{'color': 'blue', 'scores' : 0}
{'color': 'brown,' 'scores' : 9}
```

This example looks simple and very straightforward. Let us look at a realistic one that will involve over four teams with code, which automatically creates each team. In the example below, we use range() to generate 40 teams.

```
#Create an empty list to store the teams.
teams =[]

#create 40 teams.
for team_num in range(40):
    new_team = {'color': 'red', 'scores': 3, 'position':
    'middle'}
    teams.append(new_team)

#display the first 6 teams.
for team in teams[:6]:
    print[team]
print["…"]
#display the number of teams we have in our dictionary
```

```
print(f "Total teams available in our list: {len(teams)}")
```

In this example, we began by creating an empty list comprising of all teams to be created in our dictionary. We use the range() method to determine the number of times the loop will repeat. Whenever the loop goes through the range() method, it creates a new team and appends the new team to our list "teams." In the line "for team in teams [:6]:", we use a slice to print our first six teams. Finally, the last statement prints the length of the teams, which in this case is 40 teams.

```
{'color': 'red,' 'scores': 3, 'position': 'middle'}
{'color': 'red,' 'scores': 3, 'position': 'middle'}
{'color': 'red,' 'scores': 3, 'position': 'middle'}
{'color': 'red,' 'scores': 3, 'position': 'middle'}
{'color': 'red,' 'scores': 3, 'position': 'middle'}
{'color': 'red,' 'scores': 3, 'position': 'middle'}
...

Total teams available in our list:40
```

If you observe, the teams all have the same features – color, scores, and positions. However, it doesn't mean that Python sees them as one iteminstead of a separate object. With this, we can modify any team of our choice without affecting the other.

How possible is it to work with a collection of teams like we have? Assuming a particular team decides to change their color and scores, how can you do this? If you decide to change the color of a team, you can use the "for loop" conditional test with an if statement. For instance, let us change the first four teams' colors to black, scores to 5, and position to center.

```
#Create an empty list to store the teams.
teams =[]

#create 40 teams.
for team_num in range(40):
    new_team = {'color': 'red', 'scores': 3, 'position':
    'middle'}
    teams.append(new_team)

for team in teams[:4]:
    if team['color'] == 'red'"
      team['color'] = 'black'
```

```
        team ['scores'] = 5
        team ['middle] = 'center'

#display the first 6 teams.
for team in teams[:6]:
    print[team]
print["…"]
#display the number of teams we have in our dictionary
print(f "Total teams available in our list: {len(teams)}")
```

When you run the program, your output should be:

```
{'color': 'black,' 'scores': 5, 'position': 'center}
{'color': 'black,' 'scores': 5, 'position': 'center'}
{'color': 'black,' 'scores': 5, 'position': 'center'}
{'color': 'black,' 'scores': 5, 'position': 'center'}
{'color': 'red,' 'scores': 3, 'position': 'center'}
{'color': 'red,' 'scores': 3, 'position': 'center'}
…

Total teams available in our list:40
```

How to Use a List Inside a Dictionary

In our previous examples, our dictionary is inside a list; however, we can also use a list inside our dictionary depending on what you want. For instance, you may decide to react to a particular way to describe when ordering a meal. If you use a list, all you need is to store the meals. In the program below, we only stored two-piece of information for each meal

```
meal = {
    'food' : ' beans,'
    'drink': ['Fanta,' 'Water'],
    }
#summary of the order
print(f "You ordered {meal ['food']} with the following drink:"]

for drink in meal['drink']:
    print("\t" + drink)
```

We begin by creating a dictionary "meal" to hold information about the food you ordered. Remember, every list has a key-value pair, respectively. In this case, the key for food is beans, whereas that of the drink includes Fanta and Water. Then we summarize our order before creating the meal. To access our drink list, we use the "for loop" to print the drink list. Let us see how the output for this program will be:

```
You ordered beans with the following drinks:
    Fanta
    Water
```

Easily done in such a way that you can understand each line. Besides this, you can also nest your list in a dictionary when you want a key to have more than one value. Let us look at our previous election_list program, where candidates can choose two political parties. Assuming we have to store their responses in a list, a particular person can belong to more than one political party.

```
election_list = {
        'John Campbell' : ['Freedom Party'],
        'Eric Longman': ['Sovereign Nation Party'],
        'Amanda Drill': ['Freedom Party,' ' Women Liberation
        Movement'],
        'Condolence Rice': ['Democratic Party,' ' Sovereign Nation
        Party'],
        'Donald Trump': ['Republican Party,' 'Democratic Party'],
        'Nicolas Fred': ['Sovereign Nation Party'],
        }
for name, party in election_list.items():
    print(f "\n{name.title()}'s party are: ")
        for party in parties:
    print (f "\t{party.title()}")
```

In the first bolded line, we create a list. If you observe, some names have one political party, while others have two. We then loop through the dictionary to run through the political party of each candidate.

```
John Campbell's party are:
    Freedom Party

Eric Longman's party are:
    Sovereign Nation Party
```

```
Amanda Drill's party are:
    Freedom Party
    Women          Liberation
    Movement

Condolence Rice's party are:
    Democratic Party
    Sovereign Nation Party

Donald Trump's party are:
    Republican Party
    Democratic Party

Nicolas Fred's party are:
    Sovereign Nation Party
```

Exercise to Try

- Write a program that creates three dictionaries, which represent three different meals with each person choosing at least a meal of their choice. Use "for loop" to scan through the list and prints the choice of each individual.

- Make a dictionary list comprising of your favorite pets. The dictionary must contain the type of pet, owner's name, best food, and unique sound. Next, loop through your pest list and display two of this information in the list.

- Create a list of your favorite cities in the world. Create a key-value dictionary system that includes the name of the city, population, currency, and contact details of the mayor. Furthermore, print each city with at least three of the information you want people to know.

Summary

In this section, you have learned what dictionaries are, how to work with them and store information in it. Undoubtedly, you can write a program that can access and modify each item in a dictionary. Additionally, you can loop through the information contained in your dictionary. You can also loop through a dictionary key, value, and key-value pairs. Furthermore, you can nest multiple dictionaries in a list, nest dictionary in a dictionary, and nest listin your dictionary.

CHAPTER 4:

Conditional or Decision Statements

Introduction

I n programming, we usually set certain conditions and decide which particular action to perform depending on the conditions. To do this, Python uses the "if statement" to check the current program state before responding suitably to that state. However, in this chapter, you will be exposed to various ways to write conditional statements. Furthermore, you will learn basic "if statements," create complex if statements, and write loops to handle items in a list. There is so much more loaded in this chapter for you to learn. Without further ado, let us begin with a simple example.

The program below shows how you can use "if statement" to respond to a particular situation correctly. For instance, we have a list of colors and want to generate an output of different colors. Furthermore, the first letter should be in the title case of the lower case.

```
colors =["green," "blue," "red," "yellow"]
for color in colors:
print(color.title())
```

The output will be as follows:

```
Green
Blue
Red
Yellow
```

Consider another example where we want to print a list of cars. We have to print them in the title case since it is a proper name. Additionally, the value "kia" must be in uppercase.

```
cars = ["toyota," "kia," "audi," "infinity"]

for car1 in cars:

if car1 == "kia":

print(car1.upper())

else:

print(car1.title())
```

The loop first verifies if whether the current value of the car is "kia." If that is true, it then prints the value in uppercase. However, if it is not kia, it prints it in title case. The output will look like this:

```
Toyota
KIA
Audi
Infinity
```

The example above combines different concepts, which at the end of this chapter, you will learn. However, let us begin with the various conditional tests.

Conditional Tests in Python

The center of any if statement lies an expression, which must be evaluated to be either true or false. This is what is normally known as a conditional test because Python uses both values to determine if a particular code should be executed. If the particular statement is true, Python executes the code that follows it. However, if it is false, it ignores the code after it.

Checking Equality

At times, we may test for the equality of a particular condition. In this situation, we test if the value of the variable is equal to the other variable we decide. For instance:

```
>>>color = "green"
>>> color == "green"
True
```

In this example, we first assign the variable color with the value "green by using the single equal sign. This is not something new, as we have been using it throughout this book. However, the second line checks if the value of color is green, which has a double equal sign. It will return true if the value on the left side and that on the right side are both true. If it doesn't match, then the result will be false. When the value of the color is anything besides green, then this condition equates to false. The example below will clarify that.

```
>>>color = "green"
>>> color == "blue"
False
```

Note: When you test for equality, you should know that it is case sensitive. For instance, two values that have different capitalizations won't be regarded as equal. For instance,

```
>>>color = "Green"
>>> color == "green"
False
```

If the case is important, then this is advantageous. However, if the case of the variable isn't important, and you want to check the values, then you can convert the value of the variable to lowercase before checking for equality.

```
>>>color = "Green"
>>> color.lower() == "green"
True
```

This code will return True irrespective of how to format the value "Green" is because the conditional tests aren't case sensitive. Please note that the lower()

function we used in the program does not change the value originally stored in color.

In the same way, we can check for equality; we can also check for inequality in a program code. In checking for inequality, we verify if two values are not equal and then return it as true. To check for inequality, Python has its own unique symbol, which is a combination of the exclamation sign with an equal sign (!=). Most programming language uses these signs to represent inequality. The example below shows the use of if statement to test for inequality

```
color = "green"

if color != "blue"

print("The color doesn't match")
```

In the second line, the interpreter matches the value of color to that of "blue." If the values match, then Python return false; however, if it is true, Python returns true before executing the statement following it "The color doesn't match"

```
The color doesn't match
```

Numerical Comparison in Python

We can also test numerical values in Python, but it is very straightforward. For instance, the code below determines if a person's age is 25 years old:

```
>>>myage = 25
>>>myage == 25
True
```

Additionally, we can also test if two numbers are unequal. Consider the code below.

```
number = 34
```

```
if number != 54:

print("The number does not match. Please retry!")
```

The first line declares number as a variable and stores the number "34" in it. The conditional statement begins in line two and passes through the line because the number 34 is not equal to 54. Since the code is indented, the code is then executed to produce

```
The number does not match. Please retry!
```

Besides this, you can perform various mathematical comparison inside your conditional expressions including greater than, greater than or equal to , less than, and less than or equal to.

```
>>> number = 22
>>> number <25
True
>>> number <= 25
True
>>> number > 25
False
>>> number >= 25
False
```

Every mathematical comparison you want can be included as part of an "if statement" that allows you to detect the particular condition in question.

Creating Multiple Conditions

When writing code, some situations may warrant you to verify multiple conditions simultaneously. For instance, you require conditions to be false in order to take action. At times, you may want only one condition to besatisfied. In this situation, you can use the keyword "or" and "and." Let first use the "and" keyword to check multiple conditions in Python programming.

Using "AND"

If you want to verify that two expressions are both true at the same time, the keyword "and" serves that purpose. The expression is evaluated to be true when both conditions test to return true. However, if one of the condition falls, then the expression returns false. For instance, you want to ascertain if two students in a class have over 45 score marks.

```
>>> score_1 = 46
>>> score_2 = 30
>>> score_1 >=45 and score_2 >= 45
False
>>> score_2 = 47
>>> score_1 >= 45 and score_2 >= 45
True
```

The program looks complicated but lets me explain it step-by-step. In the first two lines, we define two scores, score_1, and score_2. However, in line 3, we perform a check to ascertain if both scores are equal to or above 45. The condition on the right-hand side is false, but that of the left-hand side is true. Then in the line after the false statement, I changed the value of score_2 from 30 to 47. In this instant, the value of score_2 is now greater than 46; therefore, both conditions will evaluate to true.

In order to make the code more readable, we can use parentheses in each test. However, it is not compulsory to do such but makes it simpler. Let us use parentheses to demonstrate the difference between the previous code and the one below.

```
(score_1 >= 45) and (score_2 >=45)
```

Using "OR"

The "OR" keyword allows you to check multiple conditions as the "AND" keyword. However, the difference here is that the "OR" keyword is used when you want to ascertain that one expression is true for multiple conditions. In this situation, if one of the expression is false, the condition returns true. It returns false when both conditions are false.

Let us consider our previous example using the "OR" keyword. For instance, you want to ascertain if two students in a class have over 45 score mark.

```
>>> score_1 = 46
>>> score_2 = 30
>>> score_1 >=45 or score_2 >= 45
True
>>> score_1 = 30
>>> score_1 >= 45 or score_2 >= 45
False
```

We began by declaring two variables score_1 and score_2 and assign values to them. In the third line, we test the OR condition using the two variables. The test in that line satisfies the condition because one of the expressions is true. Then, it changed the value of the variable score to 30; however, it fails both conditions and therefore evaluates false.

Besides using the "And" and "OR" conditional statements to check multiple conditions, we can also test the availability of a value in a particular list. For instance, you want to verify if a username requested is already in existence from a list of usernames before the completion of online registration on a website.

To do this, we can use the "in" keyword in such a situation. For instance, let us use a list of animals in the zoo and check if it already on the list.

```
>>>animals = ["zebra", "lion", "crocodile", "monkey"]
>>> "monkey" in animals
True
>>> "rat" in animals
```

```
False
```

In the second and fourth lines, we use the "in" keyword to test if the request word in a double quote exists in our list of animals. The first test ascertains that "monkey" exists in our list, whereas the second test returns false because the rat is not in the animal's list. This method is significant because we can generate lists of important values and check the existence of the values in the list.

There are situations where you want to check if a value isn't in a list. In such a case, instead of using the "in" keyword to return false, we can use the "not" keyword. For instance, let us consider a list of Manchester United players before allowing them to be part of their next match. In order words, we want to scan the real players and ensure that the club does not field an illegible player.

```
united_player = ["Rashford," "Young," "Pogba," "Mata," "De Gea"]

player = "Messi"


if player not in united_player:

print(f "{player.title()}, you are not qualified to play for Manchester United.")
```

The line "if player, not in united_player:" reads quite clearly. Peradventure, the value of the player isn't in the list united_player, Python returns the expression to be True and then executed the line indented under it. The player "Messi" isn't part of the list united_player; therefore, he will receive a message about his qualification status. The output will be as follow:

```
Messi, you are not qualified to play for Manchester United.
```

Boolean Expressions in Python

If you have learned any programming language, you might have come across the term "Boolean Expression" because they are significant. A Boolean expression is another term to describe the conditional test. When evaluated, the outcome can only be either True or False. However, they are essential if your goal is to keep track of specific conditions like if a user can change content or light is switched on or not. For instance,

```
change_content = False
light_on = False
light_off = True
```

Boolean values provide the best means of tracking the particular condition of a program.

Exercises to Try

- **Conditional Testing** – Write various conditional expressions. Furthermore, print a statement to describe each condition and what the expected output of each test will be. for instance, your code can be like this:

```
car = "Toyota"
print("Is car == 'Toyota'? My prediction is True."(
print (car == "Toyota")


print("\nIs car == 'KIA'? My prediction is False.")
print(car== "KIA")
```

- Test the following condition to evaluate either True or false using any things of your choice to form a list.
    1. Test for both inequality and equality using strings and numbers
    2. Test for the condition using the "or" and "and" keywords
    3. Test if an item exists in the above list
    4. Test if an item doesn't exist in the list.

If Statements

Since you now know conditional tests, it will be easier for you to under if statements. There are various types of if statements to use in Python, depending on your choice. In this section, you will learn the different if statements possible and the best situation to apply them, respectively.

Simple if Statements

In any programming language, the "if statement" is the simplest to come across. It only requires a test or condition with a single action following it, respectively. The syntax for this statement is as follows:

```
if condition:
perform action
```

The first line can contain any conditional statement with the second following the action to take. Ensure to indent the second line for clarity purposes. If the conditional statement is true, then the code under the condition is executed. However, if it is false, the code is ignored.

For instance, we have set a standard that the minimum score for a person to qualify for a football match is 20. We want to test if such a person is qualified to participate.

```
person =21
if person >= 20
print("You are qualified for the football match against Valencia.")
```

In the first line, we define the person's age to 21 in order to qualify. Then the second line evaluates if the person is greater than or equal to 20. Python then executes the statement below because it fulfills the condition that the person is above 20.

```
You are qualified for the football match against Valencia.
```

Indentation is very significant when using the "if statement" like we did in the "for loop" situations. All indented lines are executed once the condition is satisfied after the if statement. However, if the statement returns false, then the whole code under it is ignored, and the program halted.

We can also include more code inside the if statements to display what we want. Let us add another line to display that the match is between Chelsea and Valencia at the Standford Bridge.

```
person =21
if person >= 20
print("You are qualified for the football match against Valencia.")
print("The match is between Arsenal and Valencia.")
Print("The Venue is at the Emirate Stadium in England.")
```

The conditional statement passes through the condition and prints the indented actions once the condition is satisfied. The output will be as follow:

```
You are qualified for the football match against Valencia.
The match is between Arsenal and Valencia.
The Venue is at the Emirate Stadium in England.
```

Assuming the age is less than 20, and then there won't be any output for this program. Let us try another example before going into another conditional statement.

```
name = "Abraham  Lincoln"
if name = "Abraham Lincoln"
print("Abraham Lincoln was a great United State President.")
print("He is an icon that many presidents try to emulate in the world.")
```

The output will be:

```
Abraham Lincoln was a great United State President.
He is an icon that many presidents try to emulate in the world.
```

If-else Statements

At times, you may want to take certain actions if a particular condition isn't met. For example, you may decide what will happen if a person isn't qualified to play a match. Python provides the if-else statements to make this possible. The syntax is as follows:

```
if conditional test
perform statement_1
else
perform statement_2
```

Let us use our football match qualification to illustrate how to use the if-else statement.

```
person =18
if person >= 20:
print("You are qualified for the football match against Valencia.")
print("The match is between Arsenal and Valencia.")
Print("The Venue is at the Emirate Stadium in England.")
else:
print("Unfortunately, you are not qualified to participate in the match.")
print("Sorry, you have to wait until you are qualified.")
```

The conditional test (if person>=20) is first evaluated to ascertain that the person is above 20 before it passes to the first indented line of code. If it is true, then it prints the statements beneath the condition. However, in our example, the conditional test will evaluate to false then passes control to the else section. Finally, it prints the statement below it since it fulfills that part of the condition.

```
Unfortunately, you are not qualified to participate in the match.
("Sorry, you have to wait until you are qualified.
```

This program works because of the two possible scenarios to evaluate – a person must be qualified to play or not play. In this situation, the if-else statement works perfectly when you want Python to execute one action in two possible situations.

Let us try another.

```
station_numbers = 10

if station_numbers >=12:

print("We need additional 3 stations in this company.")

else:

print("We need additional 5 stations to meet the demands of our audience.")
```

The output will be:

```
We need an additional 5 stations to meet the demands of our audience.
```

The if-elif-else Chain

At times, you may want to test three different conditions based on certain criteria. In such a situation, Python allows us to use the if-elif-else conditional statement to execute such a task. We have many real-life situations that require more than two possibilities. For instance, think of a cinema hall with different charge rates for different sets of people.

- Children under 5 years are free

- Children between 5 years and 17 years are $30

- People older than 18 years is $50

As you can see, there are three possible situations because the following set of people can attend the cinema to watch the movie of their choice. In this situation, how can you ascertain a person's rate? Well, the following code will illustrate that point and print out specific price rates for each category of people.

```
person_age = 13
```

```
if person_age < 5:
print("Your ticket cost is $0.")
elif person_age < 17:
print("Your ticket cost is $30.")
else:
print("Your ticket cost is $50)
```

The first line declares a variable "person_age" with value 13. Then we perform the first conditional statement to test if the person is under the age of 5. If it fulfills the condition, it prints the appropriate message, and the program halts. However, if it returns false, it passes to the elif line, whichtests if the person_age is less than 17. In this post, the person's minimum age must be 5 years and not above 17. If the person is above 17, then Pythonskips the instruction and goes to the next condition.

In the example, we fix the person_age to 13. Therefore, the first test will evaluate false and won't execute the block of line. It then tests the elif condition, which in this case is true, and will print the message. The output will be:

```
Your ticket cost is $30.")
```

Nevertheless, if the age is above 17, then it will pass through the first two tests because it will evaluate to false. Then the next command will be the else condition, which will print the statement below.

We can rewrite this program in such a way that we won't have to include the message "Your ticket cost is…" All we need is to put the prince inside the if-elif-else chain with a simple print() method to execute after the evaluation of the chain. Look at the line of code below:

```
person_age = 13
if person_age < 5:
cost = 0
```

```
elif person_age < 17:

cost =30

else:

cost = 50

print(f "Your ticket cost is ${cost}.")
```

In the third, fifth, and seventh lines, we defined the cost based on the person's age. The cost price is already set within the if-elif-else statement. However, the last line uses the cost of each age to form the final cost of the ticket.

This new code will produce the same result as the previous example. However, the latter is more concise and straightforward. Instead of usingthree different print statement, our reverse code only uses a single printstatement to print the cost of the ticket.

Multiple Elif Blocks

You can also have more than one elif block in your program. For instance, if the manager of the cinema decides to implement special discounts for workers, this will require additional, conditional tests to the program toascertain whether the person in question is qualified for such a discount. Assuming those above 55 years will pay 70% of the initial cost of each ticket.Then the program code will be as follows:

```
person_age = 13

if person_age < 5:

cost = 0

elif person_age < 17:

cost =30

elif person_age < 55

cost = 50

else:
```

```
cost = 35
print(f "Your ticket cost is ${cost}.")
```

The cost is identical to our previous example; however, the only including is the "elif person_age < 55" and is respective else condition. This second elif block checks if the person's age is less than 55 before assigning them the cost of the ticket for $50. However, the statement after the else needs to be changed. In this situation, it is applicable if the person's age is above 55 years, which is this situation fulfills the condition we want.

The "else" statement isn't compulsory because you can omit it and use the elif statement instead. At times, it is better to use additional elif statements to capture specific interests. Let us see how to implement it without using the else statement.

```
person_age = 13

if person_age < 5:
cost = 0
elif person_age < 17:
cost =30
elif person_age < 55:
cost = 50
elif person_age >= 55:
cost = 35
print(f "Your ticket cost is ${cost}.")
```

The additional elif statement helps to assign the ticket cost of "$30" to those above 30 years. This format is a bit clearer when compared with the else block.

Performing Multiple Conditions

Using the if-elif-else statement comes handy when especially when you want to pass only one test. Once the interpreter discovers that this test is passed, it skips other tests and halts the program. With this feature, you test a specific condition in a line of code.

Nevertheless, some situations may warrant you to check all the conditions available. In such a scenario, you can use multiple if statements without adding the elif or else blocks. This method becomes relevant when more thanone of the conditions returns true. For instance, let us consider the previous example of players in Manchester United to illustrate this. In this, we want to include the players in an upcoming match against their rivals Manchester City.

```
united_players = ["Rashford," "Young," "Pogba," "Mata," "De Gea"]

if "Young" in united_players:

print("Adding Young to the team list.")

if "De Gea" in united_players:

print("Adding Dea Gea to the team list.")

if "Messi" in united_players:

print("Adding Messi to the team list.")


print( "\ Team list completed for the match against Manchester City!")
```

In the first line, we defined united_players as a variable with values Rashford, Young, Pogba, Mata, and De Gea. The second line uses the "if statement" to check if the person requested for Young. The same applies to the lines with the "if statement" and the condition is run regardless of the outcome of the previous tests. For this program above, the output will be:

```
Adding Young to the team list.

Adding Dea Gea to the team list.


Team list completed for the match against Manchester City!
```

If we decide to use the if-elif-else block, the code won't function properly because once a particular test returns true, the program will stop. Let us try it and see.

```
united_players = ["Rashford," "Young," "Pogba," "Mata," "De Gea"]

if "Young" in united_players:
print("Adding Young to the team list.")
elif "De Gea" in united_players:
print("Adding Dea Gea to the team list.")
elif "Messi" in united_players:
print("Adding Messi to the team list.")

print( "\ Team list completed for the match against Manchester City!")
```

In this code, Python will evaluate the first condition, and once it is true, the program stops. The output for this program will be:

```
Adding Young to the team list.

Team list completed for the match against Manchester City!
```

Exercise to Try

- Consider the list of colors we have in the world. Create a variable name color and assign the following colors to it – blue, red, black, orange, white, yellow, indigo, green.

- Use an "if statement" to check if the color is blue. If the color is blue, then print a message indicating a score of 5 points.

- Write a problem using the if-else chain to print if a particular selected is green.

- Write another program using the if-elif-else chain to determine the scores of students in a class. Set a variable "score" to store the student's score.

- If the student's score is below 40, indicate an output a message that such student has failed.

- If the student's score is above 41 but less than 55, print a message that the student has passed.

- If the student's score is above 56 but less than 75, print a message that the student did well.

- If the student scores above 76, print a message that the student did excellently.

CHAPTER 5:

User's Input and Loop

T he primary purpose why most programs are written is to solve a particular problem. In order to solve these problems, users must input certain information while interacting with the program. For instance, a player that determines if someone is eligible to vote or not will require input from the user. Such a program will request the user to input their age, which will enable the program to compare their value with the laid down condition of the program before displaying the outcome.

In this chapter, you will learn the different ways of accepting input from the users and how it works. Additionally, you will learn how to prompt users to provide input by using the input() function. Furthermore, I will guide on the way to keep your code running using a while loop pending when the condition becomes false. If you can learn how to ask for input from users andcontrol how long a program should run, then you can effectively write interactive programs that will solve many problems.

The simplest means of displaying output on the screen in Python is through the "print" statement, which allows you to pass expression or zero separated by commas. It can also convert expressions passed through a string and returns the results. For instance, consider the string below.

```
Print("Learning is part of Life. Python is life, Does that sound good?")
```

When you run the program, your output will be:

```
Learning is part of Life. Python is life, Does that sound good?
```

Besides this, python provides two means of accepting keyboard input into the program. You can either use the raw_input function or the input() function. Let us begin with the input function, as it is the most widely used input function in Python.

Using the input() Function

Have you ever stopped a moving vehicle? Do you remember what happened? You waved your hand, and the vehicle stopped. The driver opens the door, and you enter before he zoomed off. Yes, as simple as that illustration is, that is what the input() function works. It pauses and waits for an input from the user. In a similar pattern, the driver stops, the car door opens before you hop into it. In Python, the moment the user inputs the information, the value of information is assigned to a variable.

For instance, the program below requests the user to insert their first name and surname. It further displays both names on the screen.

```
full_name = input("Please, what is your first name and surname?")

print(full_name)
```

The input() function here prompts a message on what the user should do. In this situation, it requests the users to enter their first name and surname. The program will wait pending when the user has responded to the prompt, and once the "Enter" key is pressed, the information is assigned to the variable "full_name" before printing the content of the information. Assuming the user's inputs, "Amanda Norman," the output will be:

```
Please, what is your first name and surname?

Amanda Norman
```

As simple as this, you have created your first program that requests input from the user. Whenever you use the input() function, endeavor to include an understandable prompt a message on what the user should do or what particular type of information you want. Additionally, it should be as brief as possible and very instructive.

Compare the Two Programs Below

full_name = input("Enter Name:") print(full_name)	full_name = input("Please what is your first name and surname?") print(full_name)

If you observe clearly, the first program on the left hand requires a name, but doesn't explain what type of name. It could be the full name of a street, football team, business, or drink. The instruction isn't concise. However, the code on the right hand clearly states what is required from the user. This makes it easy for the user to input the needed information from him or her.

Multi-Line String When Using input() Function

At times, when writing a program, the prompt you wanted to write may exceed a line. For instance, you may decide to tell your user why you are requesting the specific information from them. In this situation, you can assign the message to a variable before passing the variable to the input() function. With this method, you can build numerous prompts through different lines. Let us use an example to illustrate it:

```
message = "Please tell us your full name, to enable us to provide a personalized message."
message += "\nWrite your full name"


full_name = input(message)
print("Welcome," + full_name + "!")
```

This example, simply shows you a way of building a multi-line string. In the first line, we assign the variable message with the information we want the user to respond to. However, the second line included the += operator to take the first string stored in a message and attach it with this second one. With this, our message spans two lines. When you run the program, you should have something like this, depending on the name you insert.

```
Please tells us your full name to enable us to provide a personalized message.
Write your full name
Welcome, Amanda Norman!
```

You can include as many messages you want on different lines. You can begin by practicing this little exercise. Create a Python program that allows you to write a multi-line string with input requests for the names of your family members.

Accepting Numerical Input in Python

The input() function is used when you want the user to input string; however, if you want to input numerical value from the user, then you have to use the int() function. Let us consider the program below that requires the user to input their age.

```
my_age = input ("Please, What is your current age?")
```

When you write this code, the interpreter will wait until it gets a response from you. Assuming your age is 45, the program will look like this:

```
>>>my_age = input ("Please, What is your current age?")

Please, What is your current age? 45

>>>my_age

"45"
```

The users enter 45; however, when we request for the value of the age from the interpreter, it returns "45," which is an illustration of the string value we inputted. As we already know, Python interprets the input() function as a string since the number has double-quotes. Notwithstanding, if you decide to print only the input, that will work well. However, printing the input as a number when it is in string format will generate an error.

```
>>> my_age = input ("Please, What is your current age?")

Please, What is your current age? 45

>>> my_age

40
```

If you run this program, you will get an error. This is what you will see.

```
>>> my_age = input ("Please, What is your current age?")

Please, What is your current age? 45
```

```
>>> my_age >=40

Traceback (most recent call last):

    File "<stdin>", line 1, <module>

TypeError: unorderable types: str() >= int()
```

What happened in this code is that you try to use the input() function to perform a numerical evaluation in line 3. Python generates an error message because you are trying to compare a string with an integer type. The string in this situation is 45, which is assigned to the variable my_age, which can't be compared to the number value of 40.

To solve this issue, we have to use the int() function then informs the Python interpreter to accept it as a numerical value. Therefore, it then converts the "number string" into a numerical value, as shown below.

```
>>> my_age = input ("Please, What is your current age?")

Please, What is your current age? 45

>>> my_age >=int(my_age)

>>>my_age >= 40

True
```

In the code above, when prompted to enter how old the person is, we joined 45. However, the number is interpreted as a string, helps to convert the number string to a numerical value. With this, the interpreter then runs a conditional test to compare the age to see if it is greater than or equal to 40. Inthis case, our age "45" returns true because it is greater than 40.

How then can we use the int() function in a real program? Well, let us use a program that checks if people are tall enough to participate in a basketball match.

```
basketball_height = input("What is your current height? It should be in feet's:")

basketball_height = int(basketball_height)
```

```
if basketball_height>=7:

print( "\nYou have what it takes to participate in a basketball match!")

else:

print("\nYou do not meet up with the requirement for this match!")
```

This program compares the height of the person to 7 inches because we already convert as a numerical value. If the user inserts anything below 7, themessage "You do not meet up with the requirement for this match!" will display. However, let us assume the user input 8, the output will be as follow:

```
What is your current height? It should be in feet's: 8

You have what it takes to participate in a basketball match!
```

Modulo Operator

Already, you should know that we have an important operator to use in manipulating numerical values. Besides the popular addition, subtraction, multiplication, and division, we also have a unique operator called the "modulo operator." It is represented by the percentage (%) sign and returns the remainder of a number divided by another.

```
>>> 10 % 4
2
>>> 7 % 4
3
>>> 20 % 5
0
>>> 5 % 4
1
>>> 3 % 3
0
```

Note: The operator does not tell us the number of times the number fits in the other number, rather it tells us the reminder of the operator. For instance, the first example, which is 10 divided by 4, what the module operator does here is to return the reminder when the division takes place. In this situation, it returns the value 2 because 4 can only go into 10 twice and with 2 remaining. Interestingly, you can use this to ascertain if a particular number is odd or even. Let see how that works out:

```
num = input("Key in a number of your choice, and I will let you know if it is odd or even: ")

num = int(num)


if num % 2 == 0:

        print ("\nThe number you enter is an even number.")

else:

        print("\nThe number you enter is an odd number. ")
```

Even numbers are numbers we can divide by two. Therefore, when a number modulo and two are equivalent to zero, then the number is even. However, if it turns out otherwise, let us run the program and assume that you insert 46.

```
Key in a number of your choice, and I will let you know if it is odd or even: 46

The number you entered is an even number
```

Closing and Opening Files

Since you have learned how to use the input and output functions to display output on the screen, it is time to learn how to use data files when writing a program. Python has basic methods and functions, which are essential to manipulate files without you performing any operation on them. We will explore some of these functions:

Open Function

Before you think of writing or reading a file in Python, you have to open it through the inbuilt open() function. This creates a file object, which you can use to call other methods related to it. The syntax is as follow:

file object = open(file_name [, access_mode][, buffering])

- file_name: This is a string value, which contains the particular file you want to access

- access_mode: This determines the mode by which the file in question will be opened. For instance, append, write, or read.

- Buffering: If you set this value to 0, nothing will take place. However, setting the buffering value to 1 will perform line buffering when accessing the file. For buffering values greater than 1, the action will be performed alongside the indicated buffer size.

Modes for Opening a File in Python

Modes	Meaning
r	This opens a file for reading purposes only. The default mode is to place the file pointer at the beginning of the file
r+	This opens a file for both writing and reading. Similar to the r mode, the pointer is at the beginning of the file
rb	If you want to open a file in binary format, then you have to use the rb mode. Furthermore, you place the point at the starting point of the file
rb+	Open files for both writing and reading in binary format
w	Open files for writing purposes only. if the file doesn't exist, it will create a new file, but if it does exist, it will overwrite the file

wb	This opens a file for writing in binary format. It also overwrites and creates new files depending on the existence of the file
w+	This opens a file for both writing and reading purposes. It also overwrites and creates new files depending on the existence of the file.
wb+	Both write and read files in binary format. Overwrites and create new files based on the existence of the file.
a	This opens a file for appending. If the file exists, the pointer is positioned at the end of the file
a+	Opens file for both reading and appending purposes.
ab	Opens file for appending in binary format.
ab+	If you want to read and append files in binary format, then the ab+ mode is relevant. If the file exists, the pointer is positioned at the file end.

Exercise to Try

- Write a program, which requests a particular user to insert the choice of their rental car. Print a message that displays the choice of their rental car.

- Write another program, which requests for a number and print if the number is a multiple of 9 or not.

- Write a simple program that asks a user the number of a person in a queue in a bank. If the user's reply is above 8, it should print a message that they have to wait or go home and return tomorrow.

Introduction to While Loops

Initially, I have introduced you to "for loop" in the chapter on lists. The purpose of the "for loop" is to execute a line of code once for every item in a list. However, the while loop is different because it runs continuously pending when a particular condition returns true. I hope that is clear enough for you to understand the basic difference that exists between the "for and while loops."

Using While Loop

As stated already, the while loop is used to repeat a block of lines pending when the condition is true. For instance, here is a while loop that counts from 10 to 20:

```
i = 10
while i <= 20:
        print(i)
        i += 1
```

Before generating the output of how the program will be, let me explain what happens in each line of code. In the first line, we assigned the variable i with the value 10. This is where the number begins counting. In the second line, the while loop takes operation and runs pending when the number is less thanor equal to 20; in each loop, it prints the number to the screen. However, the last line adds 1 to the number and returns to the loop. In Python, to perform increment, we can use the "+=" operator. It is akin to saying number = number + 1.

Therefore, the loop repeats because the first number 10 is less than 20. It then prints 10 and adds 1 to test the next line. It continues this process up to the tenth number before stopping. Finally, our output becomes:

```
10
11
12
```

```
13
14
15
16
17
18
19
20
```

The various programs you use nowadays involves the use of while loops. For instance, the game you play contains or uses a while loop to continue playing pending when you want to quit it. It would be awkward and painful when playing a game, and it abruptly stopped without you making any request.

Giving the Users a Choice

We can write a program that runs continuously, depending on the choice of the user. We can do this by putting the program inside the while loop.However, we will define an exit value that will quit the program. If the user doesn't input that number, the program will continue to run. Consider the program below:

```
request = "\nSay something to me, and I will rephrase it perfectly:"
request += "\nIf you want to exit, Enter 'stop' to terminate the program!"
prompt1 = ""
while prompt1 != 'stop' :
        prompt1 = input(request)
print(prompt1)
```

In the first line, we define a variable request and give them two options on what to do. The first is to enter a message, whereas the second is to exit the program by entering stop. Them in line three, we defined any variable "prompt" with an empty string. During the first time, the interpreter checks on the variable and compare the value of the prompt1 to see if the user has input "stop." However, the user hasn't inputted any value yet. The while loop will continue to run as long as the prompt isn't equal to 'stop.'

During the first loop, a prompt1 is just a string without any value, so the loop begins. Then at prompt1 = input(request), it shows the request and waits on the user to respond. Whatever message the user enter is printed out on the screen, and the interpreter reevaluates the condition to ascertain that thecondition is still within the while loop statement. Since the user hasn't entered the word 'quit,' the program further asks the user to make an input. However, once the user enters "stop," the program stops executing the loop and halts the program.

Let assume the users in his interaction with the program entered the following statements.

- I am new to Python Programming!

- Programming in Python is the best for beginners!

- I am in an advanced learning phase in Python Programming!

- My Python course will soon end!

- Stop

Then the output will be as follows:

Say something to me, and I will rephrase it perfectly:

If you want to exit, Enter 'quit' to terminate the program!

I am new to Python Programming

Say something to me, and I will rephrase it perfectly:

If you want to exit, Enter 'quit' to terminate the program!

Programming in Python is the best for beginners!

Say something to me, and I will rephrase it perfectly:

> If you want to exit, Enter 'quit' to terminate the program!
>
> I am in an advanced learning phase I Python in Python Programming!
>
>
> Say something to me, and I will rephrase it perfectly:
>
> If you want to exit, Enter 'quit' to terminate the program!
>
> stop

If you observe, the program included the "quit" word. Naturally, we don't want that word printed out on the screen. Well, to avoid such a situation, we can use the simple if statement to fix it.

```
request = "\nSay something to me, and I will rephrase it perfectly:"
request += "\nIf you want to exit, Enter 'stop' to terminate the program!"

prompt1 = ""
while prompt1 != 'stop' :
        prompt1 = input(request)

if prompt1 != 'stop':
print(prompt1)
```

Now reenter the statements you entered the first time and observed the difference. If properly done, your output will be as follow

> Say something to me, and I will rephrase it perfectly:
>
> If you want to exit, Enter 'stop' to terminate the program!
>
> I am new to Python Programming
>
>
> Say something to me, and I will rephrase it perfectly:
>
> If you want to exit, Enter 'stop' to terminate the program!

> Programming in Python is the best for beginners!
>
> Say something to me, and I will rephrase it perfectly:
>
> If you want to exit, Enter 'stop' to terminate the program!
>
> I am in an advanced learning phase I Python in Python Programming!
>
> Say something to me, and I will rephrase it perfectly:
>
> If you want to exit, Enter 'stop' to terminate the program!

Flag in a Program

In our last example, we performed a task pending when the condition is true. However, what if it is a more complicated program, which has numerous events that can make the program stop?

For instance, a game can have several exit points. Do you remember the famous snake game in Nokia phones? Remember, each time the snake touches the wall or touches itself, the game terminates. The game can alsoend if you intentionally or mistakenly exit the game application. All of these come with different possible events that might terminate the games. Therefore, in testing these different conditions using a while loop statement becomes difficult and complicated.

If you want to run a program that continues running, pending when the condition is false, then you have to define a variable, which will determine if the program is active or not. This kind of variable is known as a flag because it acts as a pointer to the program. With this, we can create codes that run while the variable "flag" is positioned to be True and stops when any of the different event's value of the flag is False. All of these sound complicated, however, let us upgrade our previous example by using the flag in the program.

```
request = "\nSay something to me, and I will rephrase it perfectly:"

request += "\nIf you want to exit, Enter 'stop' to terminate the program!"

start = True
```

```
while start:

prompt1 = input(request)

if prompt1 == 'stop' :

start = False

else:

print(prompt1)
```

In the program above, we set "start" to be "True," and this is where the program begins. This makes the while loop easier because there is no comparison tested within our while statement. However, the logic of the program is done in another part of the program. The loop will continue to runpending when the expression becomes false.

The if a statement is contained within the while loop, which checks the value of the prompt1 whenever the user enters their request. However, once someone enters "stop," we set the variable "start" to False, thereby triggering the loop to stop. Notwithstanding, anything besides the quit statement will print the request, which the user enters.

The program here will produce the same output as the previous one, where we directly test the condition inside the while loop. However, with the flag, we indicate when the program is an inactive state and makes it simpler to include additional, conditional tests.

Exiting a Loop

Well, Python allows us to use the break statement to direct the flow of our program. For instance, let us look at a program, which asks the user about the country they have visited in their life. In our previous program, we can use the "break" statement to halt the program once the user enters 'quit.' Let see how that works.

```
request = "\nPlease enter the country you have visited recently:"

request += "\nIf you want to exit, Enter 'quit' to terminate the program!"
```

```
while True

country = input(request)


if country == 'quit' :

break

else:

print(f" I have visited {country.title()}.")
```

The loop begins with the "while True" statement, which runs continuously pending when it reaches the break statement. The loop will continue to ask the user to input the country they have visited pending when they enter "quit." The break statement takes effect when the user enters "quit" and causes the program to exit the loop. Our output will be as followed if the userentered Canada, Hungry, and Portugal.

```
Please enter the country you have visited recently:

If you want to exit, Enter 'quit' to terminate the program!

I have visited Canada.


Please enter the country you have visited recently:

If you want to exit, Enter 'quit' to terminate the program!

I have visited Hungry.


Please enter the country you have visited recently:

If you want to exit, Enter 'quit' to terminate the program!

I have visited Portugal.
```

Using "continue" in a Loop

Instead of using the break statement to exit a loop without executing the remaining code completely, the continue statement can be used to return to the starting point of a loop. However, this depends on the outcome of the conditional test in question. For instance, let us look at the program, which counts from 10 to 20 but display only the even numbers.

```
even_number = 10
while even_number < 20:
even_number +=1
if even_number %2 == 0:
continue
print(even_number)
```

Firstly, we assigned an even_number to 10. However, since the number is less than 20, it goes through the while loop. In the loop, we increase the value of the number by 1, which now becomes 11. Then the if statement verifies if the modulo of the number is 0. This means there is no remainder when we divide the number by 2. Nevertheless, the continue statement informs the interpreter to overlook the loop while returning to the starting point of the statement. However, if the number isn't divisible by 2, the remaining part of the program is executed and displays the number:

```
10
12
14
16
18
20
```

Avoiding Endless Loop

Have you ever encountered a situation where your phone cannot respond irrespective of what you do? You even allowed it to stay for hours, yet no solution. You decided to charge it, yet to no avail. Finally, you have the instinct to remove the battery of the phone. And you pressed the power button and "boom" the phone came alive and responded perfectly. At least, you had a way out.

What if after writing your program and decides to run it and suddenly your key developed a fault? Or you forget the particular word to enter to exit the program. Besides this, you can even face one of the worst challenge most beginner face when using conditional statement – an endless loop. How do you override this situation?

In a while loop, you must have a way of stopping it from running continuously. For instance, the loop below counts from 10 to 15:

```
number = 10
while number <= 15:
print(number)
number +=1
```

When this program is run, you will get the output as follow:

```
10
11
12
13
14
15
```

However, let us assume that you accidentally forget to include the line "number+=1) in the program. What will happen when Python encounters this program?

```
number = 10
while number <= 15:
print(number
```

The program will run continuously and never stop. The value of the number will start at 10, but it won't change. Because of this, the conditional statement number <=15 will evaluate to True at all times. Additionally, the while loop will not stop because it will be printing 1o upon 10 throughout the program.

Don't beat yourself up if you face such an issue because virtually all programmers have accidentally written an infinite loop. If you find yourself stuck in such a situation, take a glass of cooled water and quench your taste. There is nothing to stress yourself about; you can use the **CTRL+C** button to escape from this endless loop. Additionally, you can close the Python program. To avoid such an endless loop, you should test each while loop and ensure the loop ends where it should.

Exercises to Try

- Write a simple looping program, which asks the user to input the names of their family members pending when the user input a "stop" value to halt the program. In each name, it should printwhat makes that person special.

- Write a program that offers four different meals to customers depending on their choice. If a person decides to take water, then the meal should be $20. If the meal is a plate of rice, then the ticket is $30; but if the meal is a chicken pile, then the ticket is $40. If the person doesn't choose anything, then the ticket should be $0. Write a loop to ask the user what meal they want and print the price of the meal on the screen.

- Use a conditional statement on the above program within the while statement to halt the loop

- When writing the second program, use a break statement to stop the loop whenever the users enter "stop."

Using While Loop Condition with Dictionaries and Lists

So far, you have only worked on the user requests for information at a time. Once the user enters their response, the response is printed out. However, how can you keep track if we have numerous users and information? Well, in this situation, you will need to use the while loop in dictionaries and lists.

An effective way of looping through a list is using a "for loop" conditional statement. However, don't try to change a list contained in a "for loop" because it will be hard for Python to keep track of the items on your list. Nevertheless, if you want to change a list while working on the items, you need a while loop test. With this, you can collect, store, and arrange different inputs to report or examine later.

How to Move Items from a List to Another

Let us consider a list comprising of students registered, but not approved to participate in the upcoming campus queen. Once we verify their registration, we can transfer them to the list of registered students. To do this, we can use a while loop test to move users from our unapproved lists to approved lists. Let us see how the code will be:

```
#starts with students that should be approved,

# and an empty list to store approved students

unapproved_student = ["Moses," "Sarah," "Abigail," "Benson"]

approved_student = []

#check if the user pending when there are no more unapproved students

#transfer each approved students to the approved list.


while unapproved_student:

user = unapproved_student.pop()


print(f "Checking student: {user.title()}")

approved_student.apend(user)


#Prints all the list of approved student

print("\nThe following students have been approved:"

for approved_students in approved_student:

print(approved.title))
```

Let us analyze the program before giving a sample of the output. We declare a variable unapproved_student with values as Moses, Sarah, Abigail, and Benson. Then we also declared another variable as approved_student but with an empty list. Furthermore, we use the while loop, which runs as far as our unapproved_student list isn't empty. Insider the loop, we use the pop() function, which removes any unapproved_student starting from the end of the list.

Here, because Benson is the last name in our unapproved_student list, his name will be taken off from the list before assigned to a user before it isadded to our approved list. Then it will go back to the while loop andcontinue the process from Abigail, to Sarah and finally to Moses.

We check each student to ascertain their approval statues before adding them to our list of approved students. As the unapproved student list decreases, so do the approved list increases. However, once the unapproved student list becomes empty, the loop stops and the approved student list is printed. Let us check our output:

Checking student: Benson

Checking Student: Abigail

Checking Student: Sarah

Checking Student: Moses

The following students have been approved:

Benson

Abigail

Sarah

Moses

How to Remove Instances of Particular Values from a List

At times, you may decide to remove a particular value from a list. Well, you remember the remove() function we talked about? This works perfectly well; however, what if we want to remove values that appear twice in a list. That also is possible to do in Python.

For instance, here is a list of footballers' names with "Oscar" repeated thrice. You can use a while loop to remove all instances of the name pending when there is no "Oscar." Check the code to see as that is possible.

```
footballers = ["Oscar," "Messi," "Vardy," "Oscar," "Ronaldo," "Oscar," "Fred," "Lampard," "Terry"]

print(footballers)


while "Oscar" in footballers:

footballers.remove("Oscar")

print(footballers)
```

The logic of the program is very easy to understand. We assign the variable footballers with various values, but "Oscar" repeated thrice. It prints the names of the footballers. Then the code enters the while loop because wehave Oscar in our list in more than one instance. Inside the loop, the first instance of Oscar returns to the while line before it reenters the loop to ascertain if there is another Oscar. It continues in such a manner until the list is empty. The output for our program will be":

```
["Oscar," "Messi," "Vardy," "Oscar," "Ronaldo," "Oscar," "Fred," "Lampard," "Terry"]

["Messi," "Vardy," "Ronaldo," "Fred," "Lampard," "Terry"]
```

Using User Input to Fill a Dictionary

You can request for input as much as required from a user to pass through a while loop. The program below is a polling program whereby whenever we pass through the while loop, it requests input from the user. We will then store the information we gather from the users in a dictionary. The idea behind this is to enable us to link each response we get to a particular user's input.

```
remarks ={}
```

```
# let set a flag to indicate that the polling is active
poll_active = True

while poll_active
# request for the name of the user and their remark
fullname = input("\Enter your full name:")
remark = input("What is your country of residence?")

#store the remark in the dictionary.
remarks[fullname] = remark

#Let us know if someone is still available to take the poll.
next = input("Is there anyone else available to answer a question? (yes/
no)")
if next == "no":
poll_active = False

# Our Poll is complete. Therefore, display the results.
Print("\n**** Poll Results ****")
for fullname, remark in remarks.item():
print (f "{fullname}, [remark] is my country of residence. ")
```

In the program above, we defined an empty dictionary (remarks) while setting a flag to indicate when the poll is active. The program will continue to run within the while loop as long as the poll_active is True.

Inside the while loop, the user is requested to enter their full name and their current country of residence. The information inserted by the user is then stored in the remarks dictionary. Additionally, the program then asks the user if they are any person available to take the poll. If the response is yes, the programs go back to the while loop. However, if it is no, the poll-active flag becomes false with the loop stops. The final line is the code that will display the results of the program. Let us run the program with the following input:

- Luis Gracious

- Herbert Franklin

- Lilian Cosmos

Enter your full name: Luis Gracious

What is your country of residence? South Africa

Is there anyone else available to answer a question? (yes/ no) yes

Enter your full name: Lilian Cosmos

What is your country of residence? Turkey

Is there anyone else available to answer a question? (yes/ no) yes

Enter your full name: Herbert Franklin

What is your country of residence? Canada

Is there anyone else available to answer a question? (yes/ no) no

**** Poll Results ****

Luis Gracious, South Africa is my country of residence.

Lilian Cosmos, Turkey is my country of residence.

Herbert Franklin, Canada is my country of residence.

Exercises to Try

- Write a simple program that polls teachers about their best subject to teach in class. Use a prompt to request for their best subject. Then use the print statement to display their response to the question.

- Make a list of famous places to visit before you reach 50 years. Write the names of different places. Make an empty list called Places_visit. Use a while loop to go through the list of places visited and display the result of their choice.

Summary

In this User's input and loop, you have learned how Python language accepts inputs from users by using the input() function. Furthermore, you have been equipped with the knowledge of how to work with both numerical and text inputs. Additionally, with the looping lessons you learned in this chapter, you could easily write programs to control a decision. With the while loop conditional test, you can move items from a particular list to another. Then, you learned how to create your own dictionary using the while loop.

In the next chapter, you will learn about functions in Python. Functions give you the opportunity to break your programs into parts; each of these parts carries out a specific job. Additionally, functions can be called as many as you want in the program. I know you are excited, so see you in the next chapter.

Functions

In this chapter, you will know how to write functions easily in Python. Functions are a line of codes, which are designed to perform a particular job. When you want to write a program that will perform a specific task, then you have to define the function and call the function. Furthermore, I will teach you how to pass information to functions and display them on the screen.

Defining a Function

At times, the best way to explain a thing is to provide an example. The program below is a welcome program that prints a message.

```
def welcome_user():

#Transmit a Welcome Message

        print("Welcome to Learning Python Programming.")


welcome_user()
```

In this example, it shows the simplest structure of how a function works. The first line uses the keyword "def" to tell the interpreter that you want to define a function. Therefore, whenever you see the word "def" and the word following it, it signifies a function definition. The parenthesis does the job of holding the information you need. Then after the parentheses, the function definition ends with a colon.

Whenever you see an indented line after defining a function, which is the body of the function, the second line is known as a docstring, although it is a comment and describes the purpose of the function. Docstring is usually enclosed with three quotes. Furthermore, the third line prints the statement "Welcome to Learning Python Programming." This line contains the main message of the function. This means welcome_user has the primary job of printing "Welcome to Learning Python Programming."

If you want to call a function, you have to write the function name before following it with parentheses and a colon. Our program output will be as follow:

> Welcome to Learning Python Programming.

How to Pass Information to a Function

We will modify our previous example to explain how you can pass information to a function. We can do it in such a way that the program will not only say "Welcome to Learning Python Programming" but also include the user name. To do that, we have to request a user to enter their name.

```
def welcome_user(name):

#Transmit a Welcome Message.

        print("Welcome to Learning Python Programming, " + name.title()
+ " !")


welcome_user("thomas")
```

When we enter welcome_user("Thomas") it calls the function welcome_user() and passes the name "Thomas" to the function to execute the print command. With this, our output will be:

> Welcome to Learning Python Programming, Thomas!

Arguments and Parameters

In our previous example, we defined a function, which requires the user to input a value for the variable username. Immediately, you call the function and assign a value to it; it prints the message in the print() function. Our function has a variable inside it. The variable is an example of what a parameter is in Python, whereas Thomas is the argument. Arguments are values that contained information and pass from a function call to the function. For instance, when we call the function, we placed a value inside the function. In this scenario, our argument is "Thomas," and we passed the information to the function.

Note: People interchangeably use both terms. Therefore, when you see a definition of a function referred to as an argument or vice-versa.

How to Pass an Argument in Python

Since a function definition can have several parameters, a function call may also require several arguments. It means you can pass your argument to a function in multiple ways. You can use either keyword argument or positional arguments. In the latter, the argument must be of the same order as your parameter, whereas, in the former, each argument comprises a variable name and its equivalent value.

Positional Arguments

This argument is the simplest way of passing an argument in Python because each argument in the function must match with a parameter in the function declaring section. To see how this works, let us write a program that shows information about animals. The function in this situation tells us the particular type of animal and the name of the pet.

```
def animal_list(animal_kind, pet_name):

#Display Details About Animal

print(f "\nThis is a {animal_kind}.")

print (f "My {animal_kind}'s name is {pet_name.title()}.")


animal_list ("Cat," "lucy")
```

The first block of line defines a function. It indicates that the function requires a particular animal's type and its pet name. After defining the function, we provided the animal kind and pet name. For instance, in the function call (animal_list), we assign Cat as an animal kind while Lucy is the pet's name. Our output will display the detail about the animal Cat with the pet name Lucy.

```
This is a Cat.
```

My Cat's name is Lucy.

Calling Multiple Functions

We can call the function as many times as we want. All we need is to add another parameter to our function. Check the code below:

```
def animal_list(animal_kind, pet_name):
""" Display Details About Animal."""
print(f "\nThis is a {animal_kind}.")
print (f "My {animal_kind}'s name is {pet_name.title()}.")


animal_list ("Cat", "Lucy")
animal_list ("Dog," "Bruce")
animal_list ("Rat," "Chase")
```

The program follows the same sequence and performs the output. However, in this situation, we added two more parameters to the list. Therefore, our output will look like this:

```
This is a Cat.
My Cat's name is Lucy.

This is a Dog.
My Dog's name is Bruce.

This is a Rat.
My Rat's name is Chase.
```

Calling a function several times is an efficient way when you have several parameters. The code about the details of the animal is written once inside the function. However, whenever you want to describe a new animal, all you need is to call the function by providing information about the animal.

Keyword Arguments

This is a name/value pair, which you pass to a function. You have to directly link the value and the variable name inside the argument. With this, there won't be any confusion when you pass the argument to the function. Let's rewrite our previous code using the keyword arguments to call our animal_list()

```
def animal_list(animal_kind, pet_name):
""" Display Details About Animal."""
print(f "\nThis is a {animal_kind}.")
print (f "My {animal_kind}'s name is {pet_name.title()}.")

animal_list (animal_kind ="Cat", pet_name= "Lucy")
animal_list (pet_name= "Chase", animal_kind ="Rat")
```

Our first four lines haven't changed. However, there is a difference between the last two lines. When the interpreter reads the fourth line, it calls the function and assigns the parameter Cat to animal_kind and Lucy to pet_name, respectively. For the next line, it will perform the same operation because the order doesn't matter when dealing with keyword arguments. Therefore, the last two lines of codes are equivalent and produce the same output. Our program above will display:

```
This is a Cat.
My Cat's name is Lucy.

This is a Rat.
My Rat's name is Chase.
```

When using keyword arguments, ensure that the right parameter names are used in the function definition to avoid any error.

Default Value

Besides using the keyword parameter and position argument, each parameter can have a default value in a function. If you provide a parameter that is providing in the function, Python uses the value. However, if there is no parameter value, then Python uses a default value for the parameter.

```
def animal_list(pet_name, animal_kind = "Cat"):
""""" Display Details About Animal."""""
print(f "\nThis is a {animal_kind}.")
print (f "My {animal_kind}'s name is {pet_name.title()}.")

animal_list (pet_name= "Lucy")
```

Compare this program with the previous code. Did you notice anything from the first and last line? Well, animal_list function is used to describe a particular animal kind where we set the default value as Cat.

```
I have a Cat.
My name is Lucy.
```

Observe that the parameter order inside the function definition must be changed since the default value makes it pointless to stipulate the particular animal kind as an argument. Therefore, the only argument available in the function is the name of the pet.

Classes in Python

O ne of the effective methods of writing software is object-oriented programming. It allows you to write classes, which represent real-world situations and things. Furthermore, you create these objects based on these classes. In writing a class, you define the overall behavior of the entire object in that program. Perhaps you may have heard of the term "instantiation" if you haven't, it means making an object from a class. The knowledge of classes is very important in programming, and in this chapter, you will learn how to write and create instances of a class. Furthermore, you will learn how to specify the kind of information you want your instance to store.

Having a comprehensive knowledge of object-oriented programming will fine-tune your learning process as a programmer. It will help you understand your entire code instead of what is happening on each line. Once you understand the logic behind classes, you can think logically to write effective programs that will address any problem you face in life.

Creating a Class

You can model anything you want using classes. The best way to explain it is to show you an example. Let us write a simple class, Cat, which represents a cat. Note this is not just a particular cat in question, but also any cat. What information do you want to know about the cat? Cats all have a name; some can sit while others can spit. With this, we have important information such as their names, ages, and behaviors (sitting and spitting). We can use this to create a class since it is common with most cats. Once we write our class, we can use it to make individual instances.

Example – Creating the Cat Class

Every instance, we create from the Cat class will have a name and age. Additionally, we will give their behavior as spit() and sit():

```
class Cat:
```

```
""" A Sample Program to Model a Cat."""
def __int__(data, name, age):
""" Let us initialize the age and name attributes of the Cat."""
data.name = name
data.age = age
def spit(data):
""" Stimulate the Cat to spit saliva."""
print(f"{data.name} is spitting saliva."
def (sit):
""" Make the Cat to sit."""
print(f"{data.name} is sitting on the floor."
```

There are many things you will notice in this program, but don't worry because, at the end of this chapter, you will be familiar with this structure. The first line of code is a class definition called Cat. The second line is a docstring, which describes the role of the class.

__int__() Method

You may be surprised because this is the first time we are using this method in this book. Well, a function that is part of a class is called a method. All you have learned about functions applies to methods. Notwithstanding, the primary difference between them is how a method is called. The _int_() method is a unique method, which runs automatically once an instance is created in a class. A method has the keyword "int" being preceded and succeeded by two underscores. It is important to use two underscores on bothsides because if Python sees only one, the method won't be automatically called when you need to use the class. As a result, it may cause errors in your program.

Our __int__() method has three parameters, which are data, name, and age. We need the data parameter, and it must come before other parameters. You have to include it in the definition because when the software calls this method, it will automatically pass the data argument. In our program, we will pass Cat() a name and an age argument. With this, whenever we make an instance of the Cat class, we will only provide values for the name and age parameters.

The line "data.name=name and data.age=age" contains two variable definitions, with each having the prefix data. Any variable that is prefixed with data is available to all methods in the class and can access them through any instance we create in the class. What happens in "data.name=name" is that it takes the value connected with the parameter name and assigns it to the variable name. The same thing happens to the data.age=age. Our cat class contains two methods – spit() and sit().

```
class NewClass:

    "This is another example of a class"

    area = 15

    def room(size):

    print('To ascertain the size of a room')


# Output: 15

print(NewClass.area)
```

The output will be:

15

Exercises to Try

- Write a function known as Television(), which accepts different television names and the names of the television to be printed. Additionally, use a positional argument to make the television. Also, use the keyword argument to call the function

- Write a function called country() that accepts the capital and country name. Your function must print a simple sentence such as

New York is in the United States of America. Call at least four different cities

General Exercises to Try

- Which tool will you use in Python to find any bug in a program?

- Does Python have a double data-type?

- Is string in Python mutable or immutable?

- Is python platform-dependent?

- How can you get the length of a list in Python?

Key Terms

Learning a new programming language comes with the knowledge of new terms as it relates to this language. Understanding these terms will help fast track your learning process. This section contains some important but common Python programming terms that will equip you in his quest. Toavoid any form of confusion, and help you kick-start your learning process,let us begin with the key terms.

- **Dictionary** - A dictionary is a group of key-value pairs. Every single key in the dictionary has its corresponding value; the key enables you to have access to the value, and it can be a list, string, number, or dictionary.

- **Floating point** - A float is a number with a decimal.

- **Function** - Functions are a line of codes, which are designed to perform a particular job.

- **Keywords** - Keywords are reserved words that are used specifically by the programming language. Each programming language has its unique keyword, which is meant for a particular purpose.

- **List** - A list refers to a data type that contains a collection of items in an orderly manner.

- **String** - This is a series of characters, which is enclosed in quotes.

In Python, anything in quotes is regarded as a unique character.

- **Tuple** – A tuple is similar to the list I explained earlier; however, we use parentheses for tuple as an alternative to square brackets used in a list. You can access each element after defining a tupleby using each index.

- **Variable** - A variable is a storage location, which has a name assigned to it. In Python, we can assign a value to a variable and recall these variables.

General Exercises to Try

- Which tool will you use in Python to find any bug in a program?

- Does Python have a double data-type?

- Is string in Python mutable or immutable?

- Is python platform-dependent?

- How can you get the length of a list in Python?

Conclusion

Congratulations on completing this book – **Python Crash Course: The Ultimate Guide for Beginners to Coding with Python Accompanied by Useful Tools**. You have learned the fundamentals of the language and can apply this knowledge in various meaningful projects. Firstly, don't rush into allprojects, but only those which interest you because programming is moreappealing when it is aimed at solving relevant and important problems. I amconvinced you can apply your skills to various projects. Furthermore, I believe

- You have a comprehensive knowledge of Python.

- You can install Python on various operating systems.

- You can create your own first program.

- You can use Python to create a calculator program.

- You can use control flow tools such as elif statement, if-else, and if statements effectively.

- You can easily manipulate various loops – for, while, and while true loop.

- You understand what a function is and how to use it in a program.

- You know how to pass a statement in a program.

Congratulations on the sleepless night and mistakes you had to accomplish this feat. However, continuous learning is important to sharpen your skill to become a more efficient and productive programmer with Python. One of the best choices you can ever make is to learn Python programming language because it is the simplest language for anyone to learn without requiring a tutor. As simple as it is, it has great power behind it to generate massive programs that will revolutionize the programming world. There are a thousand things you can do when writing Python programs. Additionally, youcan integrate with some programming languages to create web applications orgames.

Programming is easy, but we all get stuck as time goes on. This is even stressful when you are just starting new. Therefore, don't despair because the best programmers have learned to unstuck themselves from any code that gives them a headache.

If you find yourself stuck, the first step is to assess your current situation. Ensure to reevaluate your situation by asking these three important questions:

- What is my goal? (What am I trying to achieve?)

- What steps have I taken? (What have I tried and haven't tried?)

- What result am I getting?

Before thinking of giving up, try one more. Take a step backward to retrace where you got it wrong. If you are trying to write a program to achieve using "for loop," it won't harm you to check through similar examples. Go through your codes, perhaps you have omitted a colon, inserted a single quote where there should be double. Review your work carefully.

If, after this, there is no solution, it is time to take a break. Maybe, you are stressed and cannot stay focus when looking for the solution. When we work for a long period, our brain gets tired, and we need to refresh or reboot the brain. In this situation, take a nice shower, nap, or have fun. Most programmers take a long break because once they resume, they become filled with enthusiasm to find what the problem was. Programming is interesting and shouldn't stress the hell out of your life.

Machine Learning with Python

The Complete Beginner's Guide to Understand Machine Learning with Python from Beginner to Expert

Steve Blair

Introduction

Congratulations for purchase *Machine Learning with Python: The Complete Beginner's Guide to Understand Machine Learning with Python from Beginner to Expert.* At this point, I would like to take a moment to thank you for doing so. There are many people out there who would love to learn Machine Learning with Python and its many features. Hopefully, this book will help them do so. At first, this book might be a bit freighting to most, with all its talk about Algorithms, Decision Trees, Pandas, and so forth. You might be saying to yourself now, "What is all this talk about Trees and Pandas?" By the end of this book, I guarantee that you will fully understand if you follow the steps in this book. Machine Learning with Python should become as easy as tying your shoes and Decision Trees and Pandas will become like your second language.

The first couple of chapters will cover the topics of what Machine Learning is, with a brief history. The Machine Learning types like supervised, unsupervised, semi-supervised machine learning, etc. This book will go over Conditional Statements in Python, using Loops in Python, what is NumPy and how to use it, and many more. Lastly, this book uses a step-by-step process on how to do many programming projects of Machine Learning and Python.

There are lots of different books on Machine Learning and Python out on the market, so thanks again for picking this one as your go-to for all things Python! Every effort was made to ensure that this book was full of as much useful information as possible, so please enjoy it!

CHAPTER 1:

Machine Learning

M achine Learning is made up of many different segments that can retrieve, store and process data in a human fashion. By being able to do this, it brings its self from an uncertain position to a self-learn mode. So, when giving new information in a series of digits between 0 and 1, these electronic device programs are authorized to enlarge, learn, and develop to a high state of intelligence by themselves.

Machine Learning History

Deep Blue was an intelligent electronic device that defeated the titleholder of chess at his game in 1997. Did this happen by chance? No, this electronic device was programmed to do this and this alone. If given a different challenge, this electronic device probably would have malfunctioned. So, it was time to go back to the drawing board with a new program, new sense, and with new regulations. With that in mind, you can use algorithms that master new prototypes with proficiency, rather than depending on harshcoded regulations. You can say that this is truly the definition.

Machine Learning Types

The thought of using this type of learning came about years ago, but the qualification to independently give difficult mathematical thoughts (such as measurements or statistics) to an electronic device is a fresh idea that came to completion in this profession a few years ago. Likewise, there are different kinds of machine learning that work with algorithms with a fixed type of machine learning. Throughout this chapter, we will discuss these types.

Supervised Machine Learning

Supervised machine learning can only handle simple tasks and algorithms that it recognizes. These tasks can only be carried out if the electronic device has access to preprogrammed data of input-output duos.

```
iris = datasets.load_iris()
X = iris.data[:, :2]
Y = iris.target
```

Summary

- Projecting Prototype
- Categorized data
- Classification Problems and Regression

Algorithms

- SVM's
- DT's
- K-NN
- Naïve Bayes
- Linear Reversion
- Neural Networks

K-Nearest Neighbours is a statistical style that can be employed for resolving classification and regression problems. This is also called kNN. Now, let us talk about the different examples of categorizing an unrecognized object employing kNN. Think about the arrangement of objects picturedbelow:

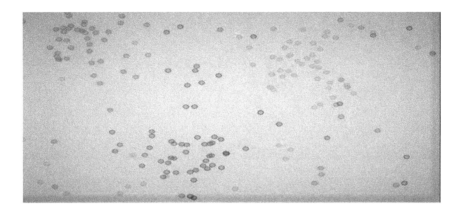

The illustration shows three different objects labeled in green, blue, and red hues. When you employ the kNN classifier to the above data set, the limits for each will be labeled as pictured below:

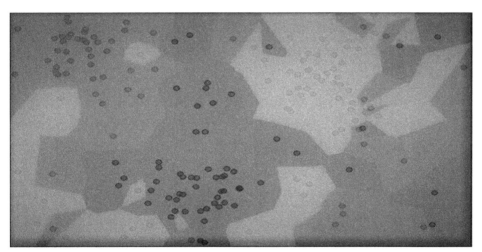

Now, imagine a new unrecognized object that you want to label as red, blue, or green. This is shown in the illustration below:

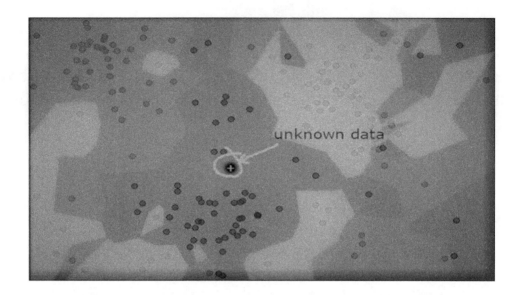

As you have noticed, the unrecognized data belongs to the group of blue objects. Mathematically, this can be completed by measuring the length of this unrecognized point with each different point in the data set. By doing so, you will see that every point close to it has a blue hue. The mean length to green and red objects would be certainly more than the mean length to the blue objects. Hence, this unrecognized object can be labeled part of the blue class.

The kNN algorithm can be employed for regression problems as well. The kNN algorithm can be found in most ML libraries as a ready to use application.

Naïve Bayes is employed for generating classifiers. It is called Naïve Bayes because the computation of the chances for each theory is clarified to make their computations manageable. Instead of striving to compute the figures of each characteristic figure P(d1, d2, d3|h), they are claimed to be self-dependent granted that the target figure can be computed as P(d1|h)*P(d2|H) and so on.

Assume you want to put fruits of different kinds in order in a fruit basket. You may employ attributes like hue, dimensions, and the form of a fruit. For instance, any fruit that is circular in form, red in hue, and is 10 cm in dimension could be labeled as an apple. You would employ these attributes and test the likelihood that a used attribute meets the desired conditions to teach the model. The likelihood of distinct attributes is then conjoined to come to a likelihood that a given fruit is surely an apple. Naïve Bayescommonly requires a fine amount of training data for classification.

Decision Trees have three major portions: branches, foliage, and root nodes. The roots are at the beginning of the tree, and the foliage and root nodes alike have inquiries or properties to respond to. The branches are actually the lines and arrows that bring them together, demonstrating how it leads from question to answer. This is usually demonstrated by two or more nodeswhether it be root or foliage nodes. For instance, if the inquiry in the first node needs a "yes" or "no" response, there will be one leaf node for a "yes" response and another node for "no."

A plain decision tree in a diagram form is pictured below:

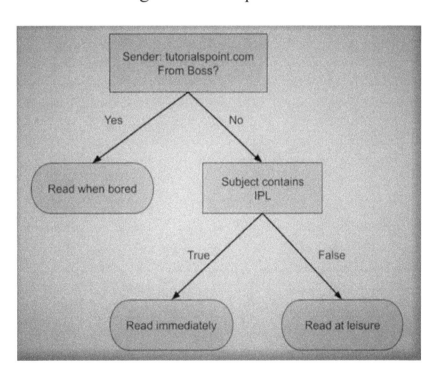

You would draft a code to categorize your input data based on this diagram. The diagram is self-illustrative and ordinary. In this text, you are trying to categorize an email you have received and choose when to open it.

In reality, the decision trees can be much grander and challenging than the one in the diagram. There are a few more algorithms accessible to develop and navigate these trees. As a machine learning addict, you need to comprehend and ace these styles of developing and navigating decision trees.

Linear Regression

The word "linearity" in algebra implies a linear connection between two or more variables. If we draw this connection in a two-dimensional space (amongst two variables), we get a conservative line.

Linear regression completes the duty to foresee a dependent variable rate (y) built on a certain independent variable (x). So, this regression method finds out a linear connection between x (input) in addition to y (output). Thus, they term it the Linear Regression. If we plot the dependent and independent variable (y and x) on their axis, linear regression gives us a conventional line that fits the information plugs as revealed in the picture below. We then recognize that the equation of a conventional line is essential.

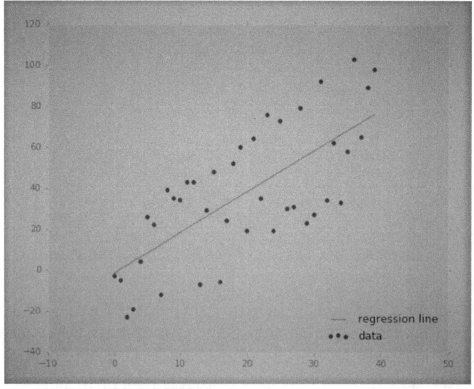

The equation of the overhead line is:

Y= mx + b

Where b is the advert and m are the hills of the line. So, essentially, the linear regression algorithm gives us the greatest ideal rate for the advert and the hill (in two magnitudes). Although the y and x variables produce the result, they are the data structures and cannot be altered. The figures that we can switch are the advert(b) and hill(m). There can be numerous conventional lines relying upon the figures of the advert and the figures of the hill. Essentially, what the linear regression algorithm ensures is it fits numerous lines on the data points and yields the line that results in the slightest mistake.

This similar idea can be stretched to cases where there are additional variables. This is termed numerous linear regressions. For example, think about a situation where you must guess the price of the house built upon its extent, the number of bedrooms, the regular income of the people in the area, the oldness of the house, and so on. In this situation, the dependent variable (target variable) is reliant on numerous independent variables. A regression model including numerous variables can be signified as:

y = b0 + m1b1 + m2b2 + m3b3 + ... mnbn

This is the comparison of a hyperplane. Recall that a linear regression model in two magnitudes is a straight line; in three magnitudes it is a plane, and in additional magnitudes, a hyperplane.

Support Vector Machines (SVM)

A managed algorithm used for machine learning which can mutually be employed for regression or classification challenges is Support Vector Machines. Nevertheless, it is typically employed in classification complications. In this algorithm, we design each data entry as a point in n-dimensional space (where n is many structures you have) with the rate of each feature being the rate of a coordinate. Then, we complete the classification by finding the hyper-plane that distinguishes the two classes very well. Look at the image below:

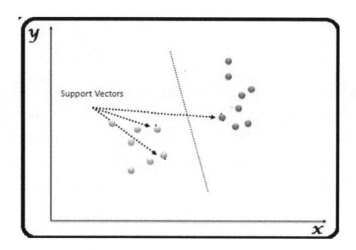

Support Vectors are the coordinates of separate thoughts. Support Vector Machine is a borderline that best isolates the two classes (hyper-plane/ line).

Neural Networks

A neural network is more appropriately mentioned as an 'artificial' neural network (ANN). The ANN was presented by the inventor of one of the very first neurocomputers, Dr. Robert Hecht-Nielsen.

ANNs are configuring devices (actual hardware or algorithms) that resembles the way neurons are constructed in a human's cerebral cortex on a smaller measure. A very large artificial neural network can hold hundreds or even thousands of supercomputer parts, however, a human brain can hold billions of neurons with an equivalent growth in the size of total collaboration and developing conduct. Although artificial neural network scholars are not worried about whether their networks correctly bear a resemblance to genetic structures, some are consumed. For instance, scholars have correctly replicated the use of the retina and reformed the eye to satisfactory.

Being that the calculations that are involved with ANN's are not a small task, they are still relatively simple for a user to gain at least a working tolerance of their construction and purpose.

(1943 model) McCulloch-Pitts Model of Neuron

This prototype was put together with a simple component called Neuron. The core illustration of their Neuron prototype is that a weighted quantity of input indicators is in contrast to a portal to regulate the neuron output. When the quantity is larger than or equivalent to the portal, the output is 1. When the quantity is lower than the portal, the output is 0. This can be put into the equations like the ones shown below:

$$Sum = \sum_{i=1}^{N} I_i W_i \quad\text{...........................}\ (1)$$

$$Output\ (y) = f(Sum) \quad\text{......................}\ (2)$$

Unsupervised Machine Learning

Unsupervised machine learning requests designs from a data set of amended answers. This is useful in learning dissection.

```
X = np.array([[1, 2], [1, 4], [1, 0], [10, 2], [10, 4]])
kmeans = KMeans(n_clusters=2, random_state=0).fit(X)
kmeans.predict([[0, 0], [12, 3]])
```

If the algorithm does not employ training information but immediately operates on the data set, it's an unsupervised algorithm.

Summary

- Expressive Model

- Clustering

- Association rule learning algorithms

Algorithms

- K-means clustering, Association rules

K-means Clustering

The 2000 and 2004 Constitutional determinations in the United States were closed. The highest percentage received by any runner from a general ballot was 50.7% and the lowest was 47.9%. If a proportion of the electorates were to have their sides swapped, the result of the determination would have been dissimilar. There are small clusters of electorates who, when appropriately enticed, will change sides. These clusters may not be gigantic, but with such close competitions, they might be big enough to change the result of the determination. By what means do you find these clusters of individuals? By what means do you petition them with an inadequate budget? To do this, you can employ clustering.

Let us recognize how it is done.

- First, you gather data on individuals either with or without their permission: any kind of data that might give an approximate clue about what is vital to them and what will affect how they vote.

- Then you set this data into a clustering algorithm.

- Next, for each group (it would be very nifty to select the principal one first), you create a letter that will appeal to these electorates.

- Lastly, you send the campaign and measure to see if it's employed.

Clustering is a category of unsupervised learning that routinely makes clusters of comparable groups. It is like an involuntary classification. Youcan cluster nearly everything, and the more comparable the objects are in the cluster, the enhanced the clusters are.

Semi-Supervised Learning

In the prior examples, moreover, there are no labels for all the data sets observed or the observations have labels. Semi-supervised learning places its self in the middle of the previous examples. The dollar sign for labels is extremely high. The reason is that it requires human experts that are very talented. Hence, the presence of labels in most of the observations, which makes them the best algorithms applicants for the prototype building. This approach utilizes the thought that the data transports important information through group elements even though the assemblage of memberships for the unlabeled data is unbeknown.

Reinforcement Learning tenders to the machine a plan to measure its readings by using incontestable reinforcement. This is positively parallel to the ways in which humans or animals master certain duties. It is due to the reality that the machine tries dissimilar ways of resolving a problem and it gets rewarded with a signal if it is flourishing. Reinforcement learning has algorithms that are normally called agents. They learn from the elements they are surrounded by in a hands-on style. Throughout this process, the agent begins to adapt to its surroundings and begins to masters the full range of the possible states.

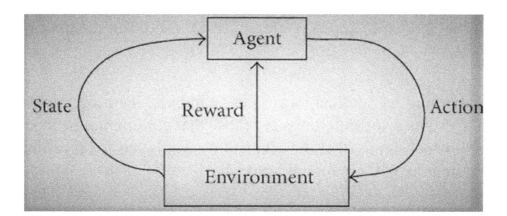

Deep Learning is modeled after Artificial Neural Networks (ANN), but to be more particular, it is more like Convolutional Neural Networks (CNN)'s. Deep Learning has a few configurations that are employed such as deep belief, recurrent, convolutional, and regular neural networks.

These networks, when flourishing, can solve problems of medical image analysis, speech recognition, natural language processing, computer vision, drug design, bioinformatics, and games. There are countless different areas in which deep learning is perceptively used. Deep learning warrants large processing power and enormous data, which is commonly accessible these days.

Deep Reinforcement Learning (DRL) merges the styles of both deep and reinforcement learning. Reinforcement learning algorithms such as Q- learning are now merged with deep learning to make a significant DRL model. This style has been a huge winner in the area of robotics, videogames, finance, and healthcare. Lots of hopeless problems now have hope by making DRL models.

Operations

Machine learning operations are astronomic and apply to different domains.

Data security is one of the domains where machine learning is very serviceable due to the reality that malware is a serious problem that will always exist as long as electronic devices exist. Generally, when it comes to distinguishing malware, machine learning is used for designs and signal monstrosities.

Financial trading is another way that machine learning algorithms are employed. Designs and foretellings are those that commemorate stock markets in the game, which imply that the algorithms employed for machine learning assist in foretelling and implementing deals.

Marketing personalization likewise employs machine learning algorithms in array to demonstrate a targeted customer endurance depending on how they conduct themselves or locality-based information.

Healthcare also employs machine learning algorithms. Scientists and researchers have substantiated different designs to teach machines to determine cancer by clearly observing cell images. This can be accomplished with an astronomic amount of great quality image data and machine learning algorithms to foretell the capability of a patient getting cancer.

Therefore, machine learning is an operation that continuously develops and remodels, which might revolve to be additionally helpful for our everyday duties. Machine learning defines a tool that essentially automates the procedure of analytical model building and allows machines to adjust to anew set-up's self-supporting.

Applied Machine Learning Process

There has been a lot printed about the procedure of applied machine learning. There is a 6-step procedure for the organization and regression sort difficulties. The common difficulty sorts at the core of most machine learningdifficulties are as follows:

1. Problem Definition: Comprehend and visibly define the problem that is being explained.
2. Analyze Data: Comprehend the obtainable data that will be employed to make a prototype.
3. Prepare Data: Learn and expose the building in the dataset.
4. Evaluate Algorithms: Grow a healthy test harness and starting point exactness from which to advance and check the algorithms
5. Improve Results: Influence outcomes to grow more precise prototypes.
6. Present Results: Label the situation and answer so that it can be understood by 3rd parties.

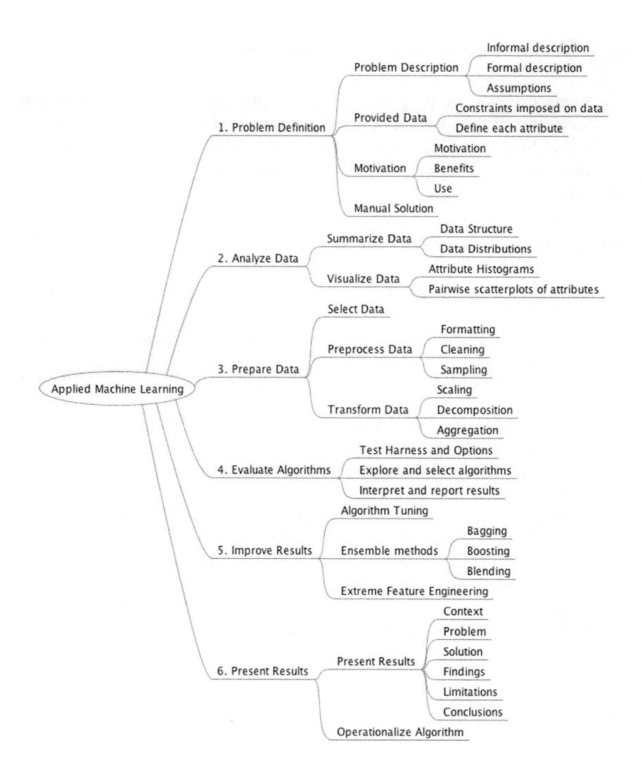

Applied Machine Learning Process Overview

Using this organized procedure on each situation you can work through, you apply a minimum level of rigor and intensely upsurge the probability of receiving good (or more likely outstanding) outcomes.

Use the Weka Machine Learning Workbench

The software stage for novices to study is the Weka Machine Learning Workbench. The decision to use Weka when beginning is a no-brainer because:

- It delivers a meek graphical user interface that summarizes the procedure of applied machine learning charted above.

- It helps with algorithm and dataset examination as well as rigors trial strategy and examination.

- It is free and open-source and is certified under the GNU GPL.

- It is used over different platforms and can be run on the major computer systems (it needs a Java computer-generated machine).

- It covers advanced algorithms with an imposing profusion of Decision Trees, Rule-Based Algorithms, and Ensemble techniques as well as others.

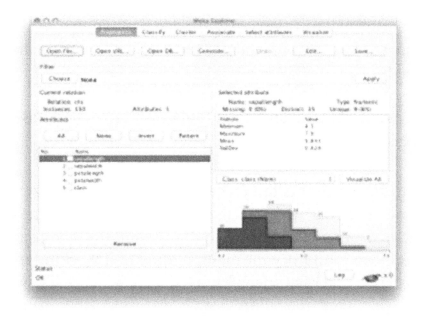

Practice, Practice, Practice on Datasets

When you are up and working with Weka, you must train by employing the 6-step procedure of applied machine learning.

The Weka download contains an information manual with numerous typical machine learning datasets; most are reserved from real systematic situation domains. Likewise, there is a treasure of outstanding datasets to experiment and study from the UCI Machine Learning Repository. These datasets are an outstanding dwelling for you to begin educating and practicing.

- The datasets are minor and effortlessly fit into memory.

- The small size of the datasets likewise means that algorithms and trials are rapid to run.

- The difficulties and information are real, as well as the noise. Prejudices in sampling and information groups are something that you want to contemplate.

- The information is very well understood so that you can influence what has recognized and flexibly deliberate the information with peers.

- There are recognized "good outcomes" for you to associate to and reconstruct.

You can select your level of detail on each stage of the organized procedure. It is recommended spending no more than 1-hour on each stage when you are first getting started. You can do and study a whole lot about a problem in 1 hour with Weka, especially if your manipulating and working trials. This will retain your incentive and plan speed high.

Lots of Data

The organized procedure inspires you to give explanations and keep record outcomes and results as you go through a certain problem. It is intelligent to retain these explanations and results organized, maybe in a plan almanac or GitHub plan.

It is recommended blogging about each of your plans, maybe even every stage of a plan, as you finish it. You can do this on your blog (if you have one) or on Facebook or Google+ forms (that now provides descriptions and text configuring). The idea of blogging plans is very encouraging. It can likewise deliver an indicator to your professors and classmates that you are a very attentive person, and you are serious about cracking down and developing some jaws in applied machine learning.

What is Python?

Python is an advanced machine learning application that can store, retrieve, and process data. In specialized terms, Python is object-familiarized, lofty-level programming that includes vigorous significations solely for web and app expansions. It is enormously appealing in the plot of fast rate application development since it tenders to energetic typing and energetic binding choices.

Python is fairly easy. With that being said, it's simple to master since it warrants a particular syntax that centers on legibility. Developers can peruse and restate Python code substantially easier than other languages. In return, this brings down the cost of the program preservation and expansion because it permits teams to work jointly without eloquent languages and proficiency barricades.

How is Python Used

Python is a common-goal oriented programming language, which is a different way to say that it can be employed for almost everything. Most significantly, it is a decyphered language. Although, most programming languages do this change before the program is exactly running. This class of language is likewise related to as a Scripting Language because it was originally meant to be employed for trivial projects.

The generality of a Scripting Language has revised astronomically since its beginning; because Python is now employed to write grand marketable applications, rather than unexciting ones. This dependence on Python has matured as the internet accumulated popularity. A grand number of web applications and platforms bank on Python, including Google, Youtube, and the web-initiated transaction network of the New York Stock Exchange (NYSE). The language must be considered severe when it is commanding a stock exchange system.

NASA uses Python to program their equipment and space machinery. Python is employed behind the scenes to operate a lot of components you might need or run into on your tablets, laptops, desktops including your mobile phones.

Benefits of Learning Python

Many benefits come with learning Python, particularly as your first language. If you're just an outright beginner, and this is your first time employing any type of coding language, then you need to start with Python.

Python is broadly employed by a grand number of huge companies, as spoken about earlier in this book. These companies are Google, Pinterest, Instagram, Disney, Yahoo, Nokia, IBM, and the list goes on. Raspberry Pi, which is a mini electronic device and a Do It Yourself lovers' dream, depends on Python as its go-to programming language, too. Now, you're probably thinking to yourself why any of this matter. Once you start learning Python, that puzzle will start to come together. You will never run out ofways to use this skill. Not to mention, all the cash you can make since a lot ofgrand companies depend on the language.

Other benefits of Python include:

- Python can be employed to make prototypes very fast because it is so easy to learn.
- The majority of automation, data mining, and huge data platforms depend on Python. The reason for this is because Python is the ideal language to learn for the general-purpose task.
- Python permits a more constructive coding atmosphere than huge languages like C# and Java. Educated coders tend to be a lot more orderly and constructive when they work with Python.
- Python is simple to understand, even if this is your first time trying to program. The average Joe can start working with this language, all it takes is applying yourself and tolerance.
- It contains a huge support platform because it is actually an open-source and community enhanced. Millions of developers who are like-minded work with the language every day and persist to better core functionality. Python's latest rendition continues to welcome improvements and updates as time advances.

CHAPTER 2:

Terminology and Notations for Machine Learning & Python

Notation

Whatever you do, you cannot dodge math notations when analyzing the explanations of machine learning techniques.

Frequently, to spoil the perception of the complete process, one piece of notation in an equation or one term out of place is all it takes. This can be maddening, for machine learning beginners approaching these methods for the first time.

One can make excessive advancements if you know a basic thing or two about math and some skills for functioning through the many explanations of electronic database learning procedures in documents and files.

The Hindrance with Math Notation

You will come across mathematical notation as soon as you are beginning to read about most topics pertaining to electronic database learning.

For instance, math might be used to:

- Express a procedure
- Express information research
- Express outcomes
- Express test control
- And express inferences

These depictions will possibly be in research papers, workbooks, blog columns, and in other places.

Frequently, these findings are well-understood, but there are also math rules that you possibly will not be acquainted with.

If one term or one equation that you do not comprehend pops up, your comprehension of all the techniques you just learned will be out the window. Living through this unruly situation many times can be extremely maddening!

In this chapter, we will take our time and go over some uncomplicated mathematical notation that will benefit you in the long run when reading explanations of electronic database learning procedures.

Mathematics

In this segment, we will go over understandable elementary mathematics as well as a limited amount of philosophies you might have disregarded since school.

Minimal Mathematics

The symbolization for simple math is as you would write it. For instance:

Adding: $2 + 2 = 4$
Subtracting: $4 - 2 = 2$
Multiplying: $4 \times 3 = 12$
Dividing: $5 / 6 = 30$

Arithmetical processes have a parallel process that works the opposite of the process; for instance, the deduction is the opposite of adding and separation is the opposite of increase.

Algebra

Frequently, we need to define processes hypothetically to detached them from certain information or certain operations.

Algebra is used for this substantial motive. Characters are used in algebra either in upper or lower case to signify terms or thoughts in precise symbolization. We also use characters in the Greek alphabet for symbolization.

Respectively, sub-sets of mathematics will possibly have set aside characters, which are words or characters that sometimes represent something similar. However, algebraic terms must be identified as part of the explanation and if not, it might just be a bad explanation.

Multiplication Symbolization

Multiplying is a common symbolization and has some short ways to be done.

Frequently, an "x" or a symbol "*" is employed to signify the operation of increasing:

$d = c \times c$
$d = c * c$

It may be a dot representation employed; for instance:

$d = c.c$

This is similar to:

$d = c*c$

Interchangeably, there might not be anything at all, and no split area amongst formerly expressed terms; for instance, which is similar yet again:

$d = cc$

Exponents and Square Roots

Exponents are sums elevated to power.

Notations are penned as the initial sum, for instance:

4^4

That should be considered as 4 increased by 4, or raised to its cube:

4 x 4 x 4= 64

A sum elevated to the power of 4 is said to be square:

4^4 = 4x 4 = 16

The quad of a sum can be reversed by computing the quad root. This is exposed by using the symbolization of a sum and by using the "sqrt ()" operation for easiness:

sqrt(8) = 4

We see the outcome and the proponent, and we want to find the bottom.

The radicle function can be employed to reverse any proponent. It just so occurs that the defaulting quad radicle adopts a proponent of 2, characterized by a 2 printed above the line in front of the quad radicle tick.

For instance, we can reverse the raising of the cube of a given sum by taking the cuboid (please take heed to the fact that the 4 is not being multiplied here. It is a symbolization before the tick of the radicle sign):

3^4 = 81
4 sqrt(81) = 3

$$2^3 = 8$$

$$\sqrt[3]{8} = 2$$

E and logarithms

Increasing 20 to a number proponent is called an order of degree:

20^3= 20 x 20 x20 or 8000

An additional way to change this process around is using the computing logarithm of the outcome 300 supposing a base of 10; in symbolization, this is inscribed as log10():

$\text{Log}_3(8000) = 8.180\ldots$

Now, we know the outcome and the bottom and want to find the proponent.

This permits us to navigate through orders of degree very easily. Using the logarithm and supposing the bottom is 3 and also frequently employed,assume the use of two mathematic components used in computers.

For instance:

$3^5 = 243$

$\text{Log}_3(243) = 5$

Additional to the common logarithm, you can suppose the normal bottom is E. The E is kept as a specific sum or a coefficient known as Euler's number (pronounced "oy-ler") that relates to a figure with nearly endless accuracy.

$E = 2.71828\ldots$

Raising E to a power is called a normal exponential purpose:

$e^2 = 7.38905\ldots$

It can be reversed by employing a natural logarithm, which is symbolized as ln ():

$\ln(7.38905\ldots) = 2$

The natural proponent and natural logarithm confirm to be useful all over calculations to theoretically define the constant growing of some structures, for example, structures that produce rapidly such as complex interest.

Greek ABC's

Greek characters are employed all through arithmetical notations for constants, variables, meanings, and furthermore.

For instance, in the science of collecting and analyzing numerical information in big numbers, we convert about the norm employing the small letters in the Greek character mu, and the normal nonconformity as to the smaller case Greek character sigma. In lined reversion, we covert about the coefficients as the smaller case character beta and so forth.

It is valuable to know all the bigger and smaller case Greek characters and how to articulate them.

The full Greek alphabet is pictured below:

Greek letters														
Name	TeX	HTML	Name	TeX	HTML	Name	TeX	HTML	Name	TeX	HTML	Name	TeX	HTML
Alpha	$A\alpha$	A α	Digamma	$Ϝϝ$	Ϝ ϝ	Kappa	$K\kappa\varkappa$	K κ ϰ	Omicron	Oo	O o	Upsilon	$\Upsilon\upsilon$	Y υ
Beta	$B\beta$	B β	Zeta	$Z\zeta$	Z ζ	Lambda	$\Lambda\lambda$	Λ λ	Pi	$\Pi\pi\varpi$	Π π ϖ	Phi	$\Phi\phi\varphi$	Φ φ φ
Gamma	$\Gamma\gamma$	Γ γ	Eta	$H\eta$	H η	Mu	$M\mu$	M μ	Rho	$P\rho\varrho$	P ρ ϱ	Chi	$X\chi$	X χ
Delta	$\Delta\delta$	Δ δ	Theta	$\Theta\theta\vartheta$	Θ θ ϑ	Nu	$N\nu$	N ν	Sigma	$\Sigma\sigma\varsigma$	Σ σ ς	Psi	$\Psi\psi$	Ψ ψ
Epsilon	$E\epsilon\varepsilon$	E ε ε	Iota	$I\iota$	I ι	Xi	$\Xi\xi$	Ξ ξ	Tau	$T\tau$	T τ	Omega	$\Omega\omega$	Ω ω

Order Representation

Machine learning representation frequently defines an action on an order.
Some orders might be a collection of information or a group of words.

Indexing

A vital way to analyzing representations for orders is the representation of indexing foundations in order.

Frequently, the representation will stipulate the order from beginning to end, such as 2 - O, where O will be the degree or distance of the order.

Objects in the order are indexed by a constant such as k, l, m. This is just like the range representation.

For instance, o_u is the u^sb part of the order a.
If the order is two-sided, two directories may be employed. For instance:

$c_{k,l}$ is the o,u^sp element of the sequence c.

Order Processes

Mathematical processes can be done in order. Two processes are done in order so frequently that they partake in their own method of abbreviations: multiplying and the quantity.

Order Summary

The quantity over an order is symbolized as the capital letters in the Greek character sigma. It is stated with the variable and started with the order summary below in the sigma (for example. $j = 2$) and the index of the end of the summary above the sigma (foe example. m).

Sigma $j = 2$, n b_j

This is the quantity of the order b beginning in section 2 to section O.

Multiplug Order

The multiplication over an order is represented as the capital letter in Greek character pi. It is stated in the same way as the order summary with the start and conclusion of the process underneath and directly exceeding the letter separately.

Pi $i = 2$, m b_j

Above is the outcome of the order b starting at section 2 to section m.

Group Representation

A group is a cluster of exceptional objects. We might see a group of representations employed when decyphering words in electronic database learning.

Group of Figures

A regular group you might see is a group of sums, such as a word identified as being contained by the group of numbers or the group of actual sums.

Several regular groups of sums that you might see contain:

- A group of all numbers: Z
- A group of all-real sums: N
- A group of all real numbers: R

Frequently, we talk about factual sums or factual figures when decyphering terms instead of fluctuating-point standards, which are separate formations for processes in electronic devices.

Group Association

It is unvarying to see group association in meanings of words. Group association is signified as a figure that appears like a Capital "E".

a E R

$$a \in \mathbb{R}$$

This results is being decyphered and relates to group R or the group of natural sums.

Likewise, there is a group of set processes; two joint set processes that contain:

- Mixture, or accretion: A U B
- Linking, or intersection: A ^ B

Other Notations

There are additional notations that you might come past. It is common to explain an intangible system, and then explain it again as a precise application with detached representation.

For instance, say we are guessing a variable x, we can portray it using a representation that changes the x; for instance:

- x-bar $(\bar{x})$

- x-prime $(\grave{x})$

- x-hat $(\hat{x})$

- x-tilde $(\tilde{x})$

A similar representation might use a dissimilar sense in a dissimilar setting, such as employed on dissimilar items or a few different subjects of mathematics. For instance, $|x|$ can often be misunderstood depending on the setting which can be sometimes taken as:

$|x|$: Whole or assured worth of x.

$|x|$: Span of the course x.

$|x|$: Cardinality of the group x.

Terminology

The succeeding chart portrays an abstract of a collection of data on an Iris plant, which is an example that is always used in electronic database learning. This collection of information covers the shapes and sizes of over 150 different blooms of Iris's from dissimilar classes like the Virginica, Sentosa, in addition to Versicolor. Here, each bloom example signifies one line, and the bloom's shapes and sizes in centimeters are kept as columns in ourdataset. These are likewise called the structures of the dataset:

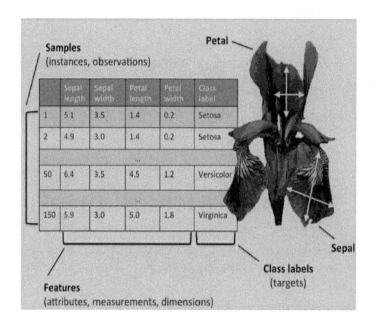

Representation and processes should be kept in a well-organized and meek order. We can do this by attaining the use of the fundamentals of linear algebra. In the succeeding sections, course representation and matrix are used to describe our information. Shadowing the regular agreement to signify each example in an isolated line in a character matrix X. Keeping the character in an inaccessible line is how we will do this.

The 150 examples and four characters of the Iris dataset can then be inscribed as a 150×4 matrix : $X \in \mathbb{R}^{150 \times 4}$

$$\begin{bmatrix} x_1^{(1)} & x_2^{(1)} & x_3^{(1)} & x_4^{(1)} \\ x_1^{(2)} & x_2^{(2)} & x_3^{(2)} & x_4^{(2)} \\ \vdots & \vdots & \vdots & \vdots \\ x_1^{(150)} & x_2^{(150)} & x_3^{(150)} & x_4^{(150)} \end{bmatrix}$$

We employ lowercase, bold-aspect attributes to signify vectors $\left(x \in \mathbb{R}^{n \times 1} \right)$ and uppercase, bold-aspect attributes to signify matrices $\left(X \in \mathbb{R}^{n \times m} \right)$. To signify solo components in a course or matrix, we inscribe the typescripts in a typeface called italics ($x^{(n)}$ or $x_{(m)}^{(n)}$, respectively).

For instance, x_1^{150} signifies the first shapes and sizes of the 150 bloom samples, the parts of the calyx of a flower span. Therefore, each line in this feature matrix signifies one bloom example and can be inscribed as a four-sided line course $x^{(i)} \in \mathbb{R}^{1 \times 4}$:

$$x^{(i)} = \begin{bmatrix} x_1^{(i)} & x_2^{(i)} & x_3^{(i)} & x_4^{(i)} \end{bmatrix}$$

And each individual dimension is a 150-sided line vector $x_j \in \mathbb{R}^{150 \times 1}$.

For instance:

$$x_j = \begin{bmatrix} x_j^{(1)} \\ x_j^{(2)} \\ \vdots \\ x_j^{(150)} \end{bmatrix}$$

Likewise, we accumulate vital factors as a 150-sided line course:

$$y = \begin{bmatrix} y^{(1)} \\ \dots \\ y^{(150)} \end{bmatrix} \left(y \in \{\text{Setosa, Versicolor, Virginica}\} \right)$$

Roadmap for Building Machine Learning Systems

Now, let's backtrack a bit about the roadmap to all of this machine learning. This roadmap consists of four major blocks which are the preprocessing, learning, evaluation, and prediction.

➢ Preprocessing – moving information into a form

Fresh unique information seldom arises in the form of new methods that are needed for the best presentation of an electronic database procedure. Therefore, the re-examining of the information is one of the greatest important phases in all electronic database applications. Think about the Iris plants' collection of information from the earlier segment in this chapter as a model. We might think of the fresh data as an arrangement of the plants' descriptions from which we want to remove momentous descriptions. Appropriate descriptions may perhaps be the type, the shade, the tallness, the greatness of the plants, and the plant's spans and widths. Numerous machine learning algorithms likewise need these descriptions on the identical measure for optimum functions, which is regularly reached by changing the descriptions in the assortment [1, 2] or a normal ordinary dispersal with a 0 average and unit alteration.

Some of these certain descriptions might be extremely consistent and consequently unnecessary to a particular level. In these circumstances, span decreasing methods are valuable for squeezing the structures onto a low measure of space. Decreasing the span of our attributed space may have the benefit that minimal storing volume is very mandatory and makes the procedure run much quicker.

To govern whether or not our algorithm not only implements well on the drill set but likewise, abridges well to fresh information, we also need to carefully separate the collection of information into a sole drill and test group. We employ the drill group to teach and expand our electronic database example. The test set up is held pending the definite finish to assess the last example.

➢ **Teaching and choosing a prognostic prototype**

Numerous distinctive machine learning algorithms have been created to explain diverse problematic responsibilities. A chief fact that was summed up well came from a famous computer scientist that is well-known for his No Free Lunch Theorems which means that we can't get learning "for free" (D.H. Wolpert and W.G. Macready, 1997). Spontaneously, this concept can be connected as well to this admired saying, "I suppose it is tempting, if the only tool you have is a hammer, to treat everything as if it were a nail" (Maslow, 1966). For instance, an individually methodical algorithm contains its built-in prejudices, and no sole methodical example relishes on dominance if we don't make any theories about the job. In preparation, it is consequently important to contrast the smallest number of diverse algorithms to educate and choose the best implementing example. Nevertheless, before we can associate diverse examples, we initially must choose upon a metric to evaluate functionality. Classification accuracy is a solitary and frequently employed metric, which can be defined as the segment of suitable classified examples.

A single appropriate inquiry to ask yourself is: in what way can we identify which example does good on the concluding test dataset and practical information if we do not employ this trial set for the example collection but preserve the dataset for the concluding example assessment? To concentrate on the matter rooted in this inquiry, a diverse model evaluation method can be employed where the drill dataset is additionally detached into drill and verification subdivisions to guess the simplification act of the example. Lastly, we likewise cannot assume that the neglected limits of the assorted algorithms offered by program collections are best for our exact unruly task. Thus, we will have to make regular use of prior distribution optimization methods that will assist us to perfect the production of our examples in later sections of this book. Spontaneously, when we look back on those prior distributions as limits that are not deliberated from the information but indicate the handles of an example that where we can turn its functions to advance.

➢ Assessing Replicas and Predicting Unseen Data Instances

When we have carefully chosen an example that has been tailored to the drill dataset, we can employ the trial dataset to guesstimate how fine it does on this concealed information to guesstimate the full inexactness. If we are very contented with its presentation, we can now employ this example to foresee fresh information much later. It is very vital to know that the limits for the formerly specified activities—for example, dimensionality reduction and variables range normalizing — only originated from the drill collection of information, and the undistinguishable limits are later submitted to alter the trial collection of information, as well as any other fresh information examples—the operations measured on the trial information may be oversold otherwise.

#### CHAPTER 3:

Employing Python for Machine Learning

Employing Python

This chapter's purpose is to take a novice from little to no familiarity with machine learning in Python to a well-informed expert in only 7 steps while using generously available resources along the way.

Please continue reading this book, especially this chapter, if you are still lacking the skills mentioned below:

- Python
- Electronic Database Learning

You will perhaps be obliged to partake in nearly all necessary comprehension of one or each individual subject; nevertheless, that will not be required. You only have to a lot enough time to thoroughly understand the topic, especially with mathematics to help you in creating your own program or whatever you will need Python. Below are some of the steps that you can follow in order for you to fully understand Python.

➢ Step 1: Simple Python Skills

If your purpose is to use Python to do machine learning, having some foundation in knowing Python is very important. Luckily, because it is widely accepted as an over-all targeted programming language, in addition tobeing accepted in mutual electronic database learning and scientificcomputing, being a beginner programmer of Python is not hard at all. Your extent of knowledge in mutual software design and Python is highly important in knowing where you should begin.

Foremost, Python must be ultimately set up on your computer. The reason is that in order to employ systematic computing and machine learning platforms, it is suggested that you program your computer to run Anaconda.

Anaconda is an industrialized-intense Python application for Windows, Linux, and OSX filled with the needed suites for electronic databases that contain Matplotlib and NumPy. It also contains Scikit-learn and a Notebook in IPython, a communicating place for several lessons. It is likewise recommended to have Python 2.7, for no added motive than that it is still, to this day, the leading most connected version.

If you are lacking in the familiarity with programming, my advice is to gain access to this free book, then shift to the succeeding resources:

- Zed A, Shaw: Python the Hard Way

And for those who have prior familiarity in program writing but none in Python particularly, or if your knowledge in Python is minimal, it is in your best interest to indulge in one or both as follows:

- Google Developer's Python Course (extremely suggested for graphic learners)
- M. Scott Shell: An Introduction to Python for Scientific Computing

Those who are just rummaging and feel that they know everything there is to know about Python, have a look at this reference book:

- (X =Python) Learn X in Y Minutes

➢ **Step 2: Foundational Machine Learning Skills**

Is it essential to comfortably comprehend kernel methods to professionally make and increase awareness from a support vector apparatus example? The answer to this is no. Like nearly everything in this day and age, it is extremely vital to have concrete knowledge in Python Programming and Machine Learning, because it can be applied to various applications. For a more advanced knowledge in these two programming languages, a closestudy in algorithms is much required and usually needs a considerable amount of time and full concentration to learn.

The great news is that it doesn't really require you a diploma or pursue a specific degree for you to be able to have the basic, even the advanced, knowledge of Python and Machine Learning. Nowadays, it is easier for students as well as learners to gain knowledge of every topic they wanted to learn. There are already many resources out there, especially on the internet, that they could look up to. They must only find the right resources that will suit their specific needs. There is almost nothing impossible now because of our fast-advancing technology.

One great example is Andrew Ng's online courses discussing Python and other programming languages. Many aspiring students of data science have turned into his courses for the full understanding of scipy, numpy, Python, and others and they are very satisfied with the course syllabus. Not only are they able to learn while in class, but they are also able to learn while doing their assignments when their classes end. There are many topics that Ng's course has to offer so it will be up to you which topic you really want tofocus on. The more topic you want to learn, the better it will be for you.

Aside from that, there are also audiovisual lessons that are offered on the internet and some of them are the courses offered by Maria-Florina Balcan and Tom Mitchell. Both of these courses are very welcoming to data scientist aspirants and very accommodating. It is also good for learning since you can see and hear videos of their lessons and how they do programming.

Remember that you should take your time taking all those lessons up if you prefer to. The best suggestion is to focus on one subject at a time and enhance your knowledge of it. You can use one reference such as those of Mitchell, and then switch up to Ng's lessons for further knowledge. Taking them all at once will be too much for you.

➢ **Step 3: Technical Python Bundles Rundown**

Good. We've consumed a lot about this Python database. We also now have a grip on Python program writing and an understanding of machine learning.

Aside from Python, there are a lot more sources to check out and employ to simplify practical machine learning. Overall, these are the major technical Python collections we employ when implementing straightforward machine learning skills:

- **NumPy** - mostly beneficial for its collection of N-shaped magnitudes objects
- **Pandas** - Python information studies citation collections that include configurations such as information frames
- **Matplotlib** - 2D plotting collections that help create book quality images
- **Scikit-learn** -These are mostly algorithms that are employed for information studies and information withdrawing responsibilities

The best way to learn and be knowledgeable about the topics enumerated above is to go over the references below:

- 10 Minutes to Pandas
- Gael Varoquaux, Emmanuella Gouillart, and Olav Vahtras: SciPy Lecture Notes,

You will discuss other platforms in the following lessons as well as illustrations of Seaborn, which is a piece of information-imagining library grounded on matplotlib platforms. These platforms are essential in the extensive collection of machine learning responsibilities in Python. Nevertheless, studying them fully will help you familiarize with the additional platforms that you will eventually learn in the upcoming chapters

Without further ado, let's talk about them now.

➤ **Step 4: Python: Developing Your Knowledge**

- Python. Score.
- Matplotlib. Score.
- Pandas. Score.
- NumPy. Score.
- Machine learning fundamentals. Score.

It is now time to put all those knowledge and hard work to test. Let's begin submitting all of our Python knowledge of Machine Learning algorithms to the standard electronic database learning collection, Scikit-learn.

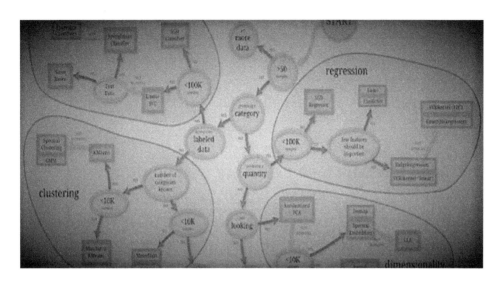

Diagram of Scikit-learn

Numerous succeeding lectures and pieces of training will be influenced by the notebook in iPython, which is a collaborative setting for performingPython. These notebooks in iPython can be found all throughout the internet, you can copy or downloaded in your computer so that you can study it more.

Our first lectures for getting down to the nitty-gritty with Scikit-learn is as follows. It is highly recommended that you do all of these in the correct order before progressing on to the next step.

- Notebooks in iPython Synopsis from Stanford

A wide-range overview of Scikit-learn that has a highly-employed all- purpose Python collection. This also contains procedures for k-nearest neighbors.

- Jake VanderPlas: An Intro to Scikit-learn

This offers a more detailed and extended overview together with the first-course plan with a familiar dataset:

- Randal Olson: Example Machine Learning Notebook

This emphasizes on approaches for assessing diverse examples in Scikit-learn and encompasses teach/trial dataset splits.

- Kevin Markham: Model Evaluation

➢ **Step 5: Topics on Machine Learning with Python**

We have established a good footing in Scikit. We can now move on to a more detailed analysis of the many useful and common algorithms. Let's begin with k-means clustering, which is one of the utmost recognized algorithms. Using this algorithm is the easiest and often the most successful technique for explaining unsupervised learning difficulties:

- Jake VanderPlas: K-means Clustering

This will help us review a little about classifications and have a deeper look at the common classification techniques.

- The Grimm Scientist: Decision Trees

After looking at classification, we will now look at endless numeric projections.

- Jake VanderPlas: Linear Regression

We can now veer over to regression for classification difficulties, by means of an arithmetical prototype, that in its simplest form, uses a logistic curve to model a two contingent adjustable.

- Kevin Markham: Logistic Regression

➢ Step 6: Topics on Advanced Electronic Database Learning

Now that we've gotten down to the nitty-gritty details of Scikit-learn and we placed our minds on some ground-breaking subjects, let's now discuss support vector machines. This is an undeviating classifier banking on multifaceted alterations of information divided into advanced 4-sided spaces.

- Jake VanderPlas: Support Vector Machines

Next, we have the random decision forests, which is a collective classifier. They are inspected through a Kaggle Titanic Competition tread-over:

- Donne Martin: Kaggle Titanic Competition

Decreasing shapes and sizes is a practice for reducing the sum of elements being thought about in an obstacle. A method of unsupervised dimensionality reduction is Principal Component Analysis.

- Jake VanderPlas: Dimensionality Reduction

We are now approaching the last and final steps in the Python roadmap. Now, let's take a deep breath and reflect on the fact that we have done a lot of research into this topic and its been a long hard road to travel. Employing Python and its many citations collections, we've consumed some of thehighly used and recognized algorithms (K-NN's, KMC, SVM's), examined an authoritative collective method (random decision forests), and inspected several added maintenance tasks (model validation methods, dimensionality reduction). Accompanied by several introductory aptitudes, we've begun to consume a satiating much-appreciated box of tools.

For the road, let's add one more must-have instrument to that box before concluding.

➢ Step 7: Python and Deep Learning

One topic that is far and wide is Deep Learning. It is a topic that fabricates on neural network studies and which goes back a few eras. However, increased development over the past decades has intensely improved the apparent power of deep neural networks.

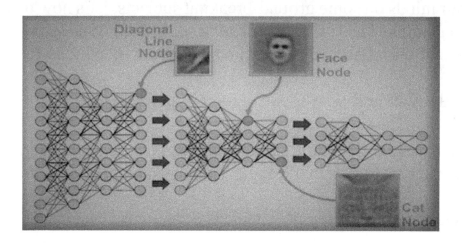

Deep Learning

There are two major deep learning libraries that novice coders should familiarize themselves with. They are the Theano and Caffe collections. These two libraries will be briefly discussed below. If you want to have a more thorough study, the references indicated below can be looked into. Note that the mentioned books are free to use.

- Michael Nielsen: Neural Systems and Deep Learning

Theano

Theano is a Python collection that permits you to improve, describe, and evaluate scientific terms concerning several 4-sided shapes in a systematic arrangement professionally.

The succeeding preliminary lecture on computational thinking in Theano is very extensive, but it is very explanatory, a good read, and deeply-remarked:

- Colin Raffel: Theano Deep Learning Tutorial

Caffe

The next set of collections is a trial run in Caffe. Caffe is another computer thinking program outline made with swiftness, manifestation, and modularity. This collection was published by the Berkeley Vision and Learning Center (BVLC).

This chapter is just icing on the cake. Despite the fact that we have taken on several stimulating samples above, none of them can compare with the following, which is applying Googles#DeepDream using Caffe. Have fun with this one! When you fully get the hang of things, go crazy on whatever programs you can do on your computer.

- Dreaming Deep with Caffe via Googles GitHub

Variables in Python

➢ **Variables**

A variable is a component that holds a value that may change. In modest words, a variable is just a cube that you can put things in. You can manipulate variables to stock all types of things, but for now, we are only going to look at saving sums in variables:

```
gold = 9
print (gold)
9
```

This encryption makes a variable called gold and gives to it the integer sum of 9 When we question Python to tell us what is deposited in the variable gold, it yields that sum once more.

We can likewise alter what is within a variable. For instance:

```
varying = 9
print (varying)
9
```

```
shifting =12
print (shifting)
12


dissimilar = 15
print (dissimilar)
15


fluctuating = 18
print (fluctuating)
18
```

We state a variable called <u>varying</u>, enter the integer <u>9</u> in it, and confirm that the task was correctly done. Then, we allocate the integer <u>12</u> to <u>shifting</u> and enquire once more what is deposited in <u>shifting</u>. Python has gotten rid of the <u>9</u> and has swapped it with <u>12</u>. Next, we make an additional variable, which we call <u>dissimilar</u>, and put <u>15</u> in it. Now, we have two self-governing variables, <u>dissimilar</u> and <u>shifting</u>, that hold different data. Giving a new valueto one of them will not disturb the other.

You can likewise allocate the quantities of a variable to be the quantity of the additional variable. For instance:

```
pink =10
navy = 15
print (pink, navy)
10 15


beige = pink
print (beige, pink, navy)
10 10 15


pink = navy
```

print (beige, pink, navy)

10 15 15

To comprehend this encryption, keep in mind that the **title** of the variable is always on the left adjacent of the (=) symbol (the task worker) and the **worth** of the variable on the right adjacent of the (=) symbol. First is the term, and then the worth.

We begin by stating that pink is 10, and the navy is 15. As you can now tell, you can permit numerous disputes to print to tell it to print many things on one line, untying them by places. As projected, Python states that pink stores 10, and navy holds 15.

Now, we make a 3rd variable called beige. To establish its value, we express to Python that we want beige to be whatever pink is. (Recall: term to the left, worth to the right.) Python distinguishes that pink is 10, so it likewise sets beige to be 10.

Now, we are going to take the pink variable and set it to the value of the navy variable. Do not get disordered — term on the left, worth on the right. Python examines the value of the navy and discovers that it is 15. So, Python tosses away pink's old value (10) and substitutes it with 15. After this task, Python states that beige is 10, pink is 15, and the navy is 15.

But hold up, didn't we say that beige should be whatever the value of pink is? The case for beige still being 10 when pink is 15 is because we only said that beige should be whatsoever pink is at the time of the task. After Python has found out what pink is and allocated that value to beige, beige does not care about pink any longer; beige has a worth now, and that worth is going to stay the same with no question on what happens to pink.

Essential Operators for Python

Operatives are the concepts that can handle the value of an operation.

Think about this statement $5 + 6 = 11$. At this point, 5 and 6 are described as the operations and plus symbol is described as the operative.

➤ Operator Types

Python linguistics supports the succeeding sorts of operatives.

- Mathematics Operatives
- Contrast (Interpersonal) Operatives
- Task Operatives
- Rational Operatives
- Bitwise Operatives
- Membership Operatives
- Identity Operatives

We are now going to go over these operatives one by one.

➤ Python Mathematics Operatives

Suppose variable b controls 20 and variable c controls 40. See the table below.

Operator	Explanation	Examples
+ Adding	Enhances quantities on each side of the operative.	b + c = 60
- Deduction	Deducts right-hand operation from left-hand operation.	b – c = -20
* Multiply	Multiplies quantities on each side of the operative	b *c = 80
/ Separation	Divides left adjacent process by right adjacent process	c /b = 2
% Modulus	Divides left adjacent process by right adjacent process and yield a balance	c% b = 1
** Advocate	Transfers out continuous (powers) calculation on operatives	c**b =20 to the power 40
//	Floor Division - The separation of operations where the outcome is the proportion in which the figures after the number point are removed. But if one of the operations is negative, the outcome is floored, resonant away from zero (in the route of a negative infinitude).	19//4 = 4 and 19.0/4.0 = 4.0, -12/4 = -5, -12.0//4 = -5.0

➢ Comparison Operators in Python

These operatives contrast the figures adjacent to them and choose the figure between them. Likewise, they are called Interpersonal operatives. Suppose adjustable b controls 20 and adjustable c controls 40. Let us see the following table.

Operator	Explanation	Examples
==	If the quantities of the two processes are equivalent, then the disorder is factual.	b ==c) is false.
!=	If the quantities of the two processes are not equivalent, then the disorder is factual.	(b! = c) is factual.
<>	If the quantities of the two processes are not equivalent, then the disorder is factual.	(b<>c) is factual. This is the same as to!= operative.
>	If the quantity of the right process is lower than the quantity of the left process, then the state turns out to be factual.	(b>c) is factual.
<	If the quantity of the right process is higher than the quantity of the left process, then the state turns out to be factual.	(b < c) is factual.
>=	If the quantity of the right process is lower than or equivalent to the quantity of the left process, then the state turns out to be factual.	b >=c) is false.
<=	If the quantity of the right process is higher than or equivalent to the quantity of the left process, then the state turns out to be factual.	(b<= c) is factual.

Operator

➢ Assignment Operators in Python

Suppose variable c controls 20 and variable d controls 40. Take a look at the table below.

Operator	Explanation	Examples

=	Allocates quantity from right adjacent processes to left adjacent process	f=d+deallocates quantity of d + d into f
+= Add AND	It adds the right adjacent process to the left adjacent process and then allocates the outcome to left adjacent process	f+= dis corresponding to f=f + cb
-= Subtract AND	It subtracts the right adjacent process from the left adjacent process and allots the outcome to left adjacent process	f-= d is corresponding to e= e- c
*= Multiply AND	It multiplies the right adjacent process with the left adjacent process and allots the outcome to left adjacent process	f *= d is corresponding to g= g* e
/= Divide AND	It divides the left adjacent process with the right adjacent process and allots the outcome to left adjacent process	f /= d is corresponding to f = f / d f /= d is equivalent to f = f / d
%= Modulus AND	It requires modules using two processes and allots the outcome to left adjacent process	f %= d is corresponding to f= f% d
**= Exponent AND	Carry's out exponential (power) calculations on operatives and allots quantities to the left adjacent process	f **=d is corresponding to f = f** d
//= Floor Division	It carries out floor division on processes and allots quantities to the left adjacent process	f //= d is corresponding toe= f // d

➤ Bitwise Operators in Python

Operators called Bitwise works on bits and carry out bit by bit processes. Suppose $b = 70$, and $c = 14$. Now, in a dualistic format, they will look like the following:

b = 011 110
c = 000 111

----

b & c = 000 110
b|c = 011 111
b^c = 011 001
~b = 110 011

The following Bitwise operatives are warranted by Python linguistic.

Operator	Explanation	Examples
& Binary AND	Operative copies a bit to the outcome if it befalls in both processes.	(b & c) (by way 000 110)
| Binary OR	It copies a bit if it befalls in each process.	(a | b) = 78 (by way 011 111)
^ Binary XOR	It copies a bit if it is set in one process but not both.	(a ^ b) = 72 (by way 011 001)
~ Binary One Complement	It is solitary and has the effect of 'overturning' bits.	(~a) = -71 (by way 110 011 in 2's accompaniment form due to an indicated binary number.
<< Binary Left Shift	The left adjacent processes quantity is moved left by the sum of bits stated by the right adjacent process.	a << 2 = 340 (by way 111 000)
>> Binary Right Shift	The left adjacent processes quantity is moved right by the sum of bits stated by the right adjacent process.	a >> 2 = 16 (by way 000 111)

➤ Rational Operatives

The succeeding logical operators are reinforced by Python language. Suppose variable b controls 20 and variable c controls 40. Please see the table below.

Operator	Explanation	Examples
and Rational AND	If the mutual processes are found to be true, then the disorder is true.	(b and c) is factual.
or Rational OR	If any of the binary operations are not equal to zero, then the disorder is true.	(b or c) is factual.
not Rational NOT	Employed to converse the rational status of its process.	Not(b and c) is untrue.

➤ Association Operatives

Python's association assesses the operator in order, such as list, tuples, or strings. Here are the binary association operatives. Please see the table below.

Operator	Explanation	Examples
in	Assesses to factual if it determines an adjustable in the stated order, and untrue if not.	Here, the outcome is a -1 if -x turns out to be in association with -y.
not in	Assesses to factual if it does not determine an adjustable in the stated order, and untrue if not.	Here, the outcome is not in association with a -1, if -x is not an association of order -y

➤ **Individuality Operatives**

Individuality operatives contrast the holding places of two substances. There are binary Individuality operatives such as shown in the table below:

Operator	Explanation	Examples
is	Assesses to factual if the adjustable on each are adjacent to the operative directed to a similar item and untrue if not.	Here, the outcome is in association in -1, if id (-x) totals up to id (-y)- totals id(-y)
is not	Assesses to untrue if the adjustable on each are adjacent to the operative directed to a similar item and factual if not.	Here, the outcome is not in association in -1 if id (-x) is not totaling up to id (-y

➤ **Operatives Superiority**

The succeeding index covers every operative from the uppermost superiority to the lowermost.

Sr.No.	Operative & Explanation
1	** Raises one quantity to the power of another.
2	~ + - Brings to perfection the single components of positive and negative (technique titles if the previous two are -@ and +@)

3	* / % //
	Multiplication, division, floor division, and modulo

4	+ -
	Adding & deduction

5	>> <<
	Right adjacent and left adjacent bitwise shift

6	**&**
	Bitwise 'AND'

7	^ |
	Bitwise high-class `OR' and ordinary `OR'

8	<= < > >=
	Contrast operatives

9	<> == !=
	Fairness operatives

10	= %= /= //= -= += *= **=
	Obligation operatives

11	**is is not**
	Individuality operatives

12	**in not in**
	Association operatives

13	**not or and**
	Rational operatives

Functions

Functions deliver improved modularity used for products and a high grade of cypher recycling.

By now, you should already know how this works. Python offers numerous incorporated functions like print (), but likewise, you can make any function.

Made up functions are referred to as producer-distinct functions.

➢ Describing a Function

Here are a few guidelines to explain Python functions.

- We start with the concept **def** in Function chunks followed by the function term and digressions (( )).
- Influences or input limits should be put inside these digressions. Likewise, you can explain limits within these digressions.
- The first remark of a function is capable of being elective. This is the docstring or the documents string of the function.
- The function inside a colon (:) is concave and called the cypher block.
- The comment reoccurrence [statement] leaves a purpose, voluntarily giving a statement to the visitor. A reoccurrence remark without influences is like reoccurrence Nothing.

➢ Syntax

def function name(limits):

"function_docstring"
function_group
reoccurrence [statement]

Through failure, limits use location and you essentially have to notify them in the identical control that they were outlined.

➢ Example

This is an input function which uses a thread as a token in limit and copies it out on a normal computer screen.

def copyme(thr):

"This copies an accepted thread into this function"
copy thr

reoccurrence

> **Requesting a Purpose**

Make sure it has a title, stipulates the parameters that should be contained in this function, and assembles the chunks of a cryptogram.

When and if the main assembly of a purpose is confirmed, it may be performed by requesting it through an additional purpose or straight through the results. The code below follows an illustration to visit copyme() purpose:

```
#!/usr/bin/Python

# Purpose denotation is here
def copyme( thr ):
"This copies an accepted thread into this purpose"
copy thr
reoccurrence;
 # Here you can visit copyme purpose
copyme("I am the first visitor to use explained purpose!")
copyme("Once more, a second visit to the similar purpose")
```

Once the above cryptogram is performed, you will see the results as shown below:

I am the first visitor to use explained purpose!
Once more a second visit to a similar purpose

> **Value vs Pass by Citation**

Limits (influences) in the Python language are approved by citation location.

These limits express if you exchange what a limit refers to within a purpose. The exchange likewise imitates back in the visiting purpose. For instance:

```
#!/usr/bin/Python

# Purpose denotation is here
def exchangeme( mylist ):
" Exchanges an approved list into this purpose"
mylist.attach([5,6,7,8]);
copy "Quantities within the function: ", mylist
reoccurrence

# Here you can visit exchangeme purpose
mylist = [40,50,60];
exchangeme( mylist );
copy "Quantity beyond the purpose: ", mylist
```

At this point, we're upholding the citation of the approved item and attaching quantities in a similar item. This would result in the following:

Quantities within the function: [40, 50, 60, [6, 7, 8, 9]]
Quantities beyond the function: [40, 50, 60, [6, 7,8, 9]]

Now, look at this illustration where the disagreement has clearly been accepted by the citation and the citation has clearly been written over within the visiting purpose.

```
#!/usr/bin/Python

# Purpose denotation is here
def exchangeme( mylist ):
```

```
" Operation exchanges an accepted list into this purpose"
mylist = [6,7,8,9]; # This operation would allocate a fresh citation in mylist
copy "Quantities within the purpose: ", mylist
reoccurrence

# Here you can visit exchangeme purpose
mylist = [40,50,60];
exchangeme( mylist );
copy "Quantities beyond the purpose: ", mylist
```

This limit in mylist is local to the purpose exchangeme. Altering mylist inside the purpose will make mylist untouchable. The purpose achieves non-entity and lastly, this results in the following:

Quantities within the function: [6, 7, 8, 9]
Quantities beyond the function: [40, 50, 60]

➢ **Arguments of Functions**

Likewise, you can visit a purpose employing the following kinds of official influences:

- Obligatory influences
- Computing influences
- Evasion influences
- Adjustable-span influences

➢ **Obligatory influences**

Obligatory influences are the influences accepted to a purpose in precise location instruction. At this juncture, the sum of influences in the purpose visited must equal precisely with the purpose denotation.

Visiting the purpose copytme(), you certainly are required to permit one influence, or else, it sends a syntax oversight like the one below:

```
#!/usr/bin/Python
# Purpose denotation is here
def copyme(thr ):
" Operation copies an accepted thread within this purpose"
copy thr
reoccurence;

# Here you can visit copyme purpose
copyme()
```

If the previous cryptogram is performed, it results in the following:

```
Extract (greatest current visit at the end):
File "test.py", line 22, in <unit>
copyme();
TypeError: copyme() takes exactly 2 argument (1 given)
```

➢ Computing influences

Computing influences are closely connected to the purpose visits. When you employ computing influences in a purpose visit, the visitor classifies the influences by the limit time.

This permits you to hop influences or store them out of order since the translator can use the given computing to contest the quantities with limits. You can likewise permit compute visits to the *copyme()* purpose in the following actions:

```
#!/usr/bin/Python
```

```
# Purpose denotation is here
def copyme( thr ):
" Operation copies an accepted thread within this purpose"
copy thr
reoccurrence;

# Here you can visit copyme purpose
copyme( thr = "My thread")
```

If the cryptogram pictured above is performed, it results in the following:

My thread

The succeeding illustration produces a richer image. Observing the order of limits doesn't mean a thing.

```
#!/usr/bin/Python

A # Purpose denotation is here
def copyinfo( title, stage ):
" Operation copies accepted info within this purpose"
copy "Title: ", title
copy "Stage ", stage
reoccurrence;

# Here you can visit copyinfo purpose
copyinfo( stage=60, title="Niki" )
```

If the cryptogram pictured above is performed, it results in the following:

Title: Niki
Stage: 60

➢ Evasion influences

An evasion influence is an influence that undertakes a failure quantity if a quantity is not given in the purpose visit. The following code portrays an impression on evasion influences. It copies the evasion stage if it is not approved.

```
#!/usr/bin/Python

# Purpose denotation is here
def copyinfo( title, stage = 45 ):
"This operation copies accepted info within this purpose"
copy "Title: ", title
copy "Stage ", stage
reoccurrence;

#Right here you can visit copyinfo purpose
copyinfo( stage=60, title="Niki" )
copytinfo( title="Niki" )
```

If the cryptogram pictured above is performed, it results in the following:

Title: Miki
Stage 60
Title: Miki
Stage 45

➢ Adjustable-span influences

You might need to make a purpose for additional influences than you stated while labeling the purpose. These influences are named adjustable-span influences and are not termed in the purpose of denotation, unlike obligatory and evasion influences.

The syntax made for a purpose with non-computing adjustable influences are pictured below:

def purposetitle([formal_args,] *var_args_tuple):

"purpose_docthread"
purpose_group
reoccurrence [statement]

A symbol (*) is located ahead of the adjustable time that controls the quantities of all non-computing adjustable influences. The tuple order stays unfilled if no extra influences are stated throughout the purpose visit. The following is a mere representation:

#!/usr/bin/Python

# Purpose denotation is here
def copyinfo(arg1, *vartuple):
" Operation copies adjustable accepted arguments"
copy "Output is: "
copy arg1
for var in vartuple:
copy var
reoccurrence;

# Here you can visit copyinfo purpose
copyinfo(20)
copyinfo(80, 70, 40)

If the cryptogram pictured above is performed, it results in the following:

Production is:
20

Production is:

80

70

40

> **The Unidentified Purposes**

Since they are not processed in the normal way by employing the def computing purpose, they are named unidentified. The 'I' computing purpose can be employed to make minor unidentified purposes.

- 'I' methods can take any sum of influences but yield just one quantity in the formula of an expression. They can't hold instructions or numerous statements.
- An unidentified function can't be a straight call to print because 'I' needs a statement
- 'I' functions consume their residents that are used to organize objects of various kinds and can't retrieve variables except for the ones in their limit list and the ones in the worldwide namescope.
- Even though it seems that 'I' are an internet form of a function, they aren't equal to aligned declarations in C or C++, whose drive is bypassing purpose pile distribution throughout supplication for presentation motives.

> **Syntax**

The syntax of 'I' purposes shelter only solitary statements, that you will find illustrated below:

'I' [arg1 [,arg2, ... argn]]:statement

The following is an illustration to demonstrate how 'I' procedures of purpose facilitate:

#!/usr/bin/Python

```
# Purpose denotation is here
sum = 'I' arg3, arg4: arg3 + arg4;

# Here you can visit amount as a purpose
copy "Quantity of a whole: ", amount( 20, 30 )
copy "Quantity of a whole: ", amount( 30, 30)
```

If the cryptogram pictured above is performed, it results in the following:

Quantity of a whole: 50
Quantity of a whole: 60

➢ **The return Report**

The report revenues [statement] withdrawals a function, by choice, giving a former statement to the visitor. A reoccurrence statement without influences is like reoccurrence Nothing.

The previous illustrations don't give back any quantity. You can give back a quantity from a function like the one illustrated below:

```
#!/usr/bin/Python

# Purpose denotation is here
def amount( arg3, arg4 ):
# Buildup each of the limits and resumes them."
full = arg3 + arg4
copy "Within the purpose: ", full
reoccurrence full;

# Here you can visit amount purpose
full = amount( 20, 40);
copy "Beyond the function: ", full
```

If the code pictured above is performed, it results in the following:

Within the purpose: 60
Beyond the purpose: 60

➤ Extent of Adjustable

Extent adjustable in a database might not be available at all settings in that database. It entirely rests on wherever you consume or professed an adjustable.

The extent of an adjustable controls the percentage of the database wherever you can retrieve a specific object. There are 2 main extents of an adjustable in Python:

- Worldwide adjustable
- Resident adjustable

Worldwide vs. Resident adjustable

Adjustables that are well-described within a purpose frame contain a resident extent, and those well-described beyond have a worldwide extent.

Hence, resident variables can be retrieved solely within the function in which they're professed, while worldwide variables can be retrieved all over the database frame by just about every function. When you call a function, the variables professed within it are guided to an extent. The following codes are an example:

```
#!/usr/bin/Python

full = 1; # This is worldwide adjustable.
# Purpose denotation is here
def amount( arg3, arg4 ):
#Buildup each of the limits and resumes them."
```

full = arg3 + arg4; # Here a whole is resident adjustable.
copy "Within the purpose resident full: ", full
reoccurrence full;

# Here you can visit amount purpose
amount(30, 40);
copy Beyond the purpose worldwide full: ", full

If the cryptogram pictured above is performed, it results in the following:

Within the purpose resident full: 70
Beyond the purpose worldwide full: 1

CHAPTER 4:

Conditional Statements

Conditional statements

In software design, very often we want to check the circumstances and do modifications to the behavior of the program.

➤ Using Conditional Declarations

Conditional Declarations are inscribed files that carry additional choice actions varying on a variable's quantity. The if declaration may be the greatest recognized declaration form. Employing the if declaration works like this; if you want something to do one act, you add if to the item to make it true, or any sum of further actions if another thing is true. We need to employ notches to explain the code that is being performed, based on whether demand is kept. To associate information in Python, we can employ the comparison operators.

➤ Syntax as the If Declaration

The syntax is the if declaration:

if expression:
declaration(s)

➤ Elif Declaration

Occasionally, there are a lot more than 2 options, in this case, we can employ the
elif declaration.

It means "else if", which entails that if the first if declaration is untrue and the elif declaration is factual, perform the following section of cryptogram of the elif declaration.

The syntax of the if...elif declaration is:

if staement2:
declaration(s)
elif staement3:
declaration(s)
elif staement4:
declaration(s)
else:
declaration(s)

➤ Else Declaration

You can join an else declaration with an if declaration.

An else declaration covers the section of cryptogram that performs if the temporary statement in the if declaration does not settle to 1 or an untrue quantity.

The else declaration is an elective declaration and there might be, at maximum, only one else declaration succeeding if.

The syntax of if...else is:

if statement:
declaration(s)
else:
declaration(s)

Example 1

The characters below will associate 2 strings depending on the input from the user.

```
# This database associates 2 threads.

# Acquire a PIN from the user.
PIN = raw_input('Enter the PIN: ')

# Govern whether that was the accurate PIN
# was entered.

if PIN == 'hello':
  print'PIN Accepted'

else:
  print' Sorry, that is the incorrect PIN.'
```

Example 2

Now, let's give one more illustration where we will likewise put to use the elif statement.

```
#!/usr/bin/Python

number = 30

guess = int(input('Enter a number : '))

if guess == amount:
  print('Cheers, predicted it.')
```

```python
elif guess < amount:
  print('No, no, no, it is slightly higher than that')

else:
  print('No, no, no. it is slightly lower than that')
```

Using Loops in Python

Labeling the different types of loops in Python will be discussed in this part of the chapter.

For Loop

Once you consume a part of the cryptogram that you wish to recap "n" number of times, the for loop is employed to recapitulate over the components in order.

- Its purposes are like this: "for all elements in a group, do this"

Now, imagine you have stored this list:

```python
processer_makes = ["Asus", "Apple", "Samsung", "Dell"]
for makes in processer_makes:
  copy makes
```

This recites for each component that we allot the adjustable makes.
In the list processer_makes, copy out the adjustable makes:

```python
figures = [2,60,70,80,90,100]
amount = 2
```

```
for quantity in quantities:
amount = amount + quantities
copy amount
for i in variety(2,60):
 copy i
```

➤ The Split

To split away from a loop, one can employ the computation "split".

```
for i in variety(2,20):
 if i ==4:
 split
 copy i
```

➤ The Resume

To tell Python to bounce over the rest of the declarations in the present loop sections and to keep on to the succeeding statements of the loop, the resume declaration is employed.

```
for i in variety(2,20):
 if i ==4:
 resume
 copy i
```

➤ Throughout Loop

The throughout loop expresses to the processer to do a task if the stipulation is met. Its concept contains a section of a cryptogram and a stipulation.

- It functions like this: " If throughout this is true, do this "

```
processer_makes = ["Asus", "Apple", "Samsung", "Dell"]
```

```
i = 1
though i < len(processer_makes):
 copy processer_makes(i)
i = i + 2
```

This tells that if the quantity of the adjustable *i* is a lesser amount than the span of the

list (processer_makes), copy out the adjustable title.

```
though Factual:
response = rare_contribution("Start typing...")
 if response == "quit":
 split
 copy "Your response was", response
```

Now, let us go over an additional illustration.

- We customize the adjustable pawn to a 1.

- Now, for each time the though loop rounds, the quantity of the pawn is amplified by 3.

- The though loop will continue to make rounds if the adjustable pawn is fewer or equivalent to 200.

```
pawn = 1
though pawn <= 200:
 copy pawn
pawn + 3
```

➢ **Nested Loops**

- In certain scrawls, you might need to employ nested loops. A loop within another loop is called a nested loop.

```
for x in variety(2, 12):
 for y in variety(2, 12):
 copy '%d * %d = %d' % (x, y, x*y)
```

How to use NumPy and what it is?

NumPy delivers a more efficient way to detect objects in numerous shapes and sizes and the tools used in working with these objects. That is why it is a range-wide signal-processing bundle. It covers numerous topographies and is the central bundle for technical calculating in Python. Below are a few of these different topographies:

- Valuable lined algebraic equations, Fourier transform, and by chance, sum abilities
- Refined (distribution) purposes
- A robust N-shaped array item
- Tools for mixing C/C++ and Fortran cryptogram

Random informational-categories can be clearly described employing this database which permits NumPy to flawlessly and quickly mix with an extensive diversity of files.

The same as its clear technical usages, NumPy can be employed as a well-organized, multi-shaped vessel of general information.

➢ **Installation:**

- **Linux and Mac** operators can connect to NumPy through a pip instruction:

pip connect NumPy

- **Windows** don't consume suite administrator matching like in Mac or Linux.
- You must transfer the already built-in windows computer

programmer for NumPy (giving your structure arrangement and Python type, and then program the suites physically).

Note: The illustrations shown below **will not** be able to run on an **internet IDE.**

1. **NumPy Arrays:** NumPy's main part is the comparable multi-shape collection.

   - In this database, scopes are named axes. The sum of the axes is called the total.
   - This databases collection lecture is called **NDarray or the code-name (array)**
   - It is a chart of all similar kind components (typically factors), put together by order by a tuple of + integers.

Example :

[[2, 3, 4],

 [5, 3, 6]]

Here,

total = 3 (it is 3-sided, or consumes 3 axes)

key shapes, and sizes(axis) span = 3, secondary shapes, and sizes have a span = 4

general form can be stated as: (3, 4)

clean_nothing

correct

perform_bolt

glare_5

Python package to prove

simple arrangement features

Bring in numpy as np

```
# Making arrangement item
arr = np.arrangement( [[ 2, 3, 4],
[ 5, 3, 6]] )

# Coping kinds of arr item
copy("Arrangement is of kind: ", kind(arr))

# Coping arrangement scopes (axes)
copy("No. of scopes: ", arr.ndim)

# Coping Form of an arrangement
copy("Shape of arrangement: ", arr.form)

# Coping scope (full sum of components) of arrangement
copy("Scope of arrangement: ", arr.size)

# Coping group of components in arrangements
copy("Arrangements keeps components of kind: ", arr.dtype)
```

Production:

The arrangement is of the sort:
No. of shapes, and sizes: 3
the shape of an arrangement: (3, 4)
Scope of an arrangement: 7
the object keeps components of type: int74

2. **Formation of Arrangement:** There are numerous methods to make objects in NumPy.

- Let's say, you are making an object from a normaldatabase list or **tuple** employing the **object** task Paine. The kinds of consequent objects are concluded from the kinds of components

in the arrangements.
- Frequently, the rudiments of an object are initially unidentified, but its magnitude is known. Therefore, NumPy suggests numeroustasks to make objects with **original placeholder content**. These reduce the need for increasing objects, which is a luxurious process.

For example: np.full, np.empty, np.ones, np.zeros.

- Generating orders of statistics in NumPy delivers an action similar to a range that yields objects as an alternative of lists.
- **arrange:** yields evenly spread out quantities inside a specified break. **step** size is detailed.
- **linspace:** yields evenly spread out quantities inside a specified break. **num** no. of rudiments are given back.
- **Redesigning array:** We can employ the **redesign** technique to redesign an object. Think of an object with a shape (b3, b4, b5, …, bO). It can be redesigned and changed into an alternative object with a design (c3, c4, c5, …, cN).

B3x b4 x b5 … x cN = c3 x c4 x c5 … x cN . (The normal scope of the object stays unaffected.)

- **Compressed array:** We can employ the **compressed** technique to get a reproduction of the object distorted into **one measurement**. It takes an order influence. The Default quantity is 'B' (for line- key order). Use 'G' for article-key order.

Note: This Sort of object is openly well-described while making an object.

clean_nothing
correct
perform_bolt
glare_5

```python
# Python database to prove
# arrangement formation methods
Bring in numpy as np

# Making arrangement from list with form drift
b = np.arrangement([[2,3, 5], [6, 9, 8]], dtype = 'drift')
copy ("arrangement made employing accepted list:\n", a)

# Making arrangement from tuple
c = np.arrangement((2 , 4,3))
copy ("\n.arrangement made employing accepted tuple:\n", b)

# Making a 4X5 arrangement with all 0's
d= np.0's((4, 5))
copy ("\nAn arrangement prepared with all 0's:\n", c)

# Make a continuous worth arrangement of multifaceted sort
e= np.full((4, 4), 7, dtype = 'multifaceted')
copy ("\nAn arrangement prepared with all 7s."
"Arrangement type is multifaceted:\n", d)

# Make an arrangement with by chance figures
e = np.by chance,bychance((3, 3))
copy ("\nA by chance arrangement:\n", e)

# Make an order of numbers
# from 1to 40 with stages of 6
f = np.arange(1, 40, 6)
copy ("\nA consecutive arrangement with stages of 6:\n", f)

# Make an order of 11 figures in variety 1 to 6
```

```
g = np.linspace(1, 6, 11)
copy ("\nA consecutive arrangement with 11 figures amongst"
"0 and 6:\n", g)

# Redesigning 4X5 arrangements to 3X3X4 arrangements
arr = np.arrangements([[2, 3, 4, 5],
[6, 3, 5, 3],
[2, 3, 1, 2]])

newarr = arr.reshape(3, 3,4)

copy ("\nOriginal array:\n", arr)
copy ("Reshaped array:\n", fresharr)

# Crush arrangement
arr = np.arrangement([[2, 3, 4], [5, 6, 7]])
crarr = arr.crushed()

copy ("\nOriginal array:\n", arr)
copy ("crushed arrangement:\n", crarr)
```

Production:

An object-shaped employing a passed list:

```
[[ 2. 3. 5.]
 [ 6. 9. 8.]]
```

An object-shaped employing a passed tuple:

```
 [2 4 3]
```

An object set with all ones:

[[1. 1. 1. 1.]
 [1. 1. 1. 1.]
 [1. 1. 1. 1.]]

An object set with all 7s. Object categories is multifaceted:

[[7.+1.k 7.+1.k 7.+1.k]
 [7.+1.k 7.+1.k 7.+1.k]
 [7.+1.k 7.+1.k 7.+1.k]]

An accidental object:

[[1.579310677 1.7818104910]
 [1.11018109510 1.106521575]]

A consecutive object with steps of 6:

[1 6 11 16 21 26]

A consecutive object with 11 quantities between 1 and 6:

[0. 0.55555556 1.11111111 1.66666667 2.22222222 2.77777778
 3.33333333 3.88888889 4.44444444 5. .666]

Original object:

[[2, 3, 4, 5]
 6 3 5 3]
 [2 3 1 2]]

Reformed object:

[[[2 3 4]
[5 6 3]]

[[5 3 2]
[3 1 2]]]

Original object:

[[2 3 4]
[5 6 7

Fattened object:

[2 3 4 5 6 7]

3. **Categorizing of Arrangements:** Identifying the fundamentals of categorizing of arrangements is significant for examining and operating the arrangement article. NumPy provides numerous habits to perform categorizing arrangements.

   - **Number categorizing arrangements:** In this technique, lists are accepted in categorizing for individual scopes. One-to-one charting of reliable components is completed to make a freshrandom object.
   - **Cutting:** Like the groups in Python, NumPy objects can be cut. As objects can be multi-shaped, you need to stipulate a cut for each scope of the object.
   - **Boolean categorizing arrangements:** The technique is employed once we essentially choose rudiments from objects which satisfy most conditions.

clean_nothing
correct
perform_bolt

```
glare_5
# Python database to prove
# categorizing in numpy
Bring in numpy as np

# Example arrangement
arr = np.arrangement([[-2, 3, 1, 5],
[5, -1.6, 7, 1],
[3.7, 1, 8, 9],
[4, -8, 5, 3.1]])

# Cutting arrangement
fill-in = arr[:3, ::3]
copy ("Array with first 3 rows and alternate"
"columns(1and 3):\n", fill-in)

# Number arrangement categorizing illustration
fill-in = arr[[1, 2, 3, 4], [4, 3, 2, 1]]
copy ("\ncomponents at indices (1,4), (2, 3), (3, 2),"
"(3,1):\n", fill-in)

# boolean categorizing arrangement illustration
diso = arr > 1 # diso is a boolean arrangement
fill-in = arr[diso]
copy ("\ncomponent larger than 2:\n", fill-in)
```

Production:

Object with first two rows and alternate columns (1 and 3):

[[-2. 1.]

[5. 7.]]

Rudiments at directories (1, 4), (2, 3), (3, 2),(4, 1):

[5. 7. 1. 3.]

Rudiments larger than 1:

[3. 5. 5. 7. 3.7 8. 9. 4. 5. 3.]

4. **Operation basics:** Overabundance of integral mathematic functions are given in NumPy.

- **Single array operations:** You can employ encumbered mathematic operatives to do component-wise processes on objects to make a fresh object. In the case of +=, -=, *= operatives, the current object is altered.

```
clean_nothing
correct
perform_bolt
glare_5
# Python database to prove
# rudimentary processes on sole array
Bring in NumPy as np

a = np.arrangement([2, 3, 6, 5])

# add 3 to each component
copy ("Accumulation 2 to each component:", a+2)

# deduct 4 from each component
print ("Deducting 4 from each component:", a-4)
```

```python
# increase each component by 11
print ("Increasing each component by 11:", a*11)

# shape each component
print ("Shaping each component:", a**3)

# regulate current arrangement
b *= 3
copy ("Folded each component of original array:", b)

# move of arrangemet
b = np.arrangement([[2, 3, 4], [4,5, 6], 10, 7, 1]])

copy ("\nOriginal array:\n", b)
copy ("Transpose of array:\n", b.T)
```

Production:

Totaling 2 to each component: [3 4 7 5]
Deducting 4 from each component: [-3 -2 3 1]
Increasing each component by 11: [11 21 51 31]
Shaping each component: [2 5 26 10]
Folded each component of original object: [3 5 11 7]

Original array:

 [[2 3 4]
 [4 5 6]
 [10 7 1]]

Transpose of an array:

```
[[2 4 10]
[3 5 7]
[4 6 1]]
```

- **Unary operatives:** Numerous unary processes are given as a technique of **ndarray** class. These classes contain max, min, and sum. These tasks can likewise be placed in line-wise or article- wise by situating an axis limit.

clean_nothing

correct

perform_bolt

glare_5

Python database to prove

unary operatives in numpy

Bring in numpy as np

arr = np.arrangement([2, 6, 7],

[5, 8, 3],

[4, 2, 10]])

maximum component of arrangement

copy ("Chief component is:", arr.highest())

copy ("Row-wise supreme componets:",

arr.highest(axis = 2))

least component of arrangement

copy ("Column-wise least componets:",

arr.least(axis = 2))

amount of arrangement componets

```
copy ("Amount of all array componets:",
arr.amount())

# increasing amount along each row
copy ("Increasing amount along each row:\n",
arr.cumsum(axis =3))
```

Production:

```
Chief component is: 10
Line-wise supreme components : [7 8 10]
Article-wise least components: [2 2 3]
Amount of object components: 40

Increasing the amount lengthwise in each line:

[[ 2 7 23]
 [ 5 22 24]
 [ 4 5 24]]
```

- **Binary operatives:** Processes operate on an arrangement component-wise and an original object is shaped. You can employ all rudimentary mathematic operatives like /, +, -
- In the case of -=, =, + = operatives, the current arrangement is altered.

```
clean_nothing
correct
perform_bolt
glare_5
# Python database to prove
```

```
# binary operatives in Numpy
Bring in numpy as np

b = np.arrangement([[2, 3],
[4, 5
c = np.arrangement([[5,5],
[4, 3]])

# enhance arrangements
copy ("Array amount:\n", c + d)

# increase arrangements(component-wise increase)
copy ("Array increase:\n", c*d)

# medium increase
copy ("Medium increase:\n",b.point(c))
```

Production:

Array quantity:

[[6 6]
 [6 6]]

Array growth:

[[5 7]
 [7 5]]

Matrix growth:

[[9 6]
 [21 14]]

- **Worldwide purposes:** NumPy offers acquainted arithmetical purposes such as exp, sin, and cos. Tasks likewise work component-wise on an object, creating an array as output.

Note: The processes we went through previously all states that employing overloaded operatives can be made through worldwide purposes like sum, multiply, divide, subtract, and add.

clean_nothing

correct

perform_bolt

glare_5

Python database to prove

worldwide purposes in numpy

Bring in numpy as np

make an arrangement of sine figures

b = np.arrangement([1, np.pi/3, np.pi])

copy ("Trigonometric figures of arrangement components:", np.tri(b))

increasing figures

c = np.arrangement([5, 6, 7, 8])

copy ("Advocate of arrangement components:", np.adv(b))

square-shaped bottom of arrangement figures

copy ("Square root of array components:", np.sqrt(b))

Production:

Sine values of array components: [1.11111111e+11 2.11111111e+11 2.33575791e-27]

Exponent of array components: [2. 3.82939294 8.4991672 31.19664793]

Square root of array components: [1. 2. 2.52532467 2.84316192]

5. **Organizing arrangements:** Presently, there is a meek **np.sort** technique for the organization of NumPy arrangements.

clean_nothing

correct

perform_bolt

glare_5

Python database to prove organization in numpy

Bring in numpy as np

a = np.arrangement([[2, 5, 3],

[4, 5, 7],

[1, -2, 6]])

organized arrangement

copy ("Array basics in organized order:\n",

np.organize(a, axis = Nothing))

organize arrangemet line-wise

copy ("Line-wise organized arrangement:\n",

np.organize(a, axis = 2))

stipulate organize procedure

copy ("Column wise sort by applying merge-sort:\n",

np.organize(a, axis = 1, sort = 'combineorganize'))

Sample to demonstrate organization of planned arrangement

set code-titled titles for dtypes

```
dtypes = [('name', 'S11'), ('graduation_time', int), ('cgpa', drift)]
# Standards placed in arrangement
figures = [('Mark', 2008, 9.6), ('Lee', 2009, 9.8),
('Mira', 2009, 8.8), (Kesha', 2008, 8.1)]

# Making arrangement
arr = np.arangement(figures, dtype = dtypes)
copy ("\nArrangement organized by titles:\n",
np.category(arr, series = 'titles'))

copy ("Array sorted by graduation year and then dhqb:\n",
np.category(arr,series = ['graduation_time', 'dhqb']))
```

Output:

Array components in prearranged order:

[-2 1 2 3 4 5 5 6 7]

Row-wise prearranged array:

[[2 3 5]

[4 5 7]

[-2 1 6]]

Column wise categorize by applying merge-sort:

[[1 -2 3]

[2 5 6]

[4 5 7]]

Array prearranged by terms:

[('Kesha', 2008, 8.1) ('Lee', 2009, 9.8) ('Mark', 2008, 9.6)

('Mira', 2009, 8.8)]

Array prearranged by graduation year and then CGPA:

[('Mira', 2009, 8.8) ('Lee', 2009,9.8) ('Mark', 2008, 9.6)

('Kesha', 2009, 8.1)]

CHAPTER 5:

Pandas

Introduction to Pandas

Pandas is an unclosed-branch in Python's Orientation collections offering elevated-adaptations in information handling and examination tools to use its influential information constructions. The term Pandas is copied from Econometrics Multi-shaped information called Panel Data-information.

In the year 2008, a designer named Wes McKinney began building Pandas to become the most important program in Python and the best for high-level performance and supple tools for examination of information.

Before Pandas, Python was excessively employed for information manipulation and planning. Back then, it had a very slight influence in the direction of information examination. Pandas fixed this problematic issue. Employing Pandas, we can achieve 5 characteristic stages in the production and examination of information, irrespective of the source of information. They are the make, operate, model, weight, and examine.

Pandas is employed in an extensive range of subjects when used with Python that includes theoretical and marketable areas like economics, business investments, analytics, Statistics, analytics, etc.

➢ **Pandas Key Features**

- Quick, well-organized DataFrame objects with non-remittance and modified indexing.
- Tools for filling information into in-recall information items from dissimilar file arrangements.
- Information placement and combined treatment of lost information.
- Redesigning and turning of period groups.

- Indexing, label-founded slicing, and subsetting of big information groups.
- Pieces from an information assembly can be erased or introduced.
- Group by information for combination and alterations.
- Elevated presentation integration and connection of information.
- Time Sequence serviceability.

Standard Python delivery does not come tied together with the Pandas module. An insubstantial substitute is to download and install NumPy, utilizing a general Python database downloader, **pip.**

- ### Pip download Pandas

If you download and connect the Anaconda Python database, Pandas will be connected automatically with the following:

- ## Windows

- **Anaconda** is a way to get Python for free from SciPy stack. This is also obtainable for Mac and Linux. It is downloadable for free.
- **Canopy** is also obtainable for free as a marketable delivery with full programs.
- **Python** (x,y) is free from Python delivery with SciPy stack and Spyder IDE for Windows OS.

➢ **Linux**

Database administrators of individual Linux supplies are employed to connect one or more databases in the SciPy stack.

➢ **Data Constructions**

Pandas works with the following 3 data constructions:

- Series
- Panel
- DataFrame

Data constructions are as fast as lighting because they are built on to the top of Numpy arrangements.

➤ **Measurement & Explanation**

When you are thinking of these data constructions, the best way to think about it is the more advanced a 4-sided shape is, the more the data construction is a craft of its lower-4-sided shaped data structure. For instance, an Information Frame is a craft of Series, and A Panel is a craft of an Information Frame.

Information Construction	Dimensions	Explanation
Series	2	2D categorized consistent array, scope unchangeable.
Data Frames	3	Over-all 3D categorized, scope-changeable tabular construction with possibly consistent typed columns.
Panel	4	Over-all 4D categorized, scope-changeable array.

Constructing and managing two or a few additional dimensional objects is a tiresome job. A load is put on the operator to contemplate the location of the information set in inscription functions.

For instance, if you use the tabular information frame (DataFrame), it is more rhetorically accommodating to reflect on the **directory** (the lines) and the articles; preferably axis 1 and axis 2.

➤ **Changeability**

Each one of Pandas' information constructions is quantity changeable (you can change them). Apart from Series, all are magnitude changeable. Series is magnitude unchangeable.

Note: An Information Frame is extensively employed and one of the highly significant information constructions. The panel is employed for a considerably reduced amount.

➢ Series

This is a one-sided object like construction with equal data. For instance, a subsequent chain in a group of integers 11, 24, 57, …

| 11 | 24 | 57 | 18 | 53 | 62 | 74 | 91 | 27 | 73 |

➢ Key Points

- Magnitude Immutable
- Equivalent information
- Quantities of Information Mutable

➢ DataFrame

DataFrame is a two-sided object with equal information. For instance:

Term	Time of life	Gender	Score
Tyree	18	Male	4.46
Anita	17	Female	5.7
Lee	42	Male	4.9
Mary	4	Female	3.79

The chart above signifies the information of a trades' squad of an association with their general operation score. This information is signified in lines and articles. Each article signifies quality and each line signifies an individual.

➢ **Articles in Data Type**

The information categories of the 4 articles are as follows:

Article	Group
Title	Line
Time of life	Number
Sex	Line
Score	Drift

➢ **Key Points**

- Magnitude Changeable
- Equivalent information
- Information Changeable

➢ **Panel**

A Panel is a 3-sided information construction with equal information. It is tough to signify the panel in a pictured image. But a panel can be demonstrated as a vessel of an Information Frame.

➢ **Key Points**

- Magnitude Changeable
- Equivalent information
- Information Changeable

A Series is a one-sided characterized object that is able to maintain information of all sorts (line, drift, article, number, Python, etc.). The axistags are mutually called an index.

- **Pandas.Series**

A Pandas Series can be shaped by employing the following builders:

Pandas.Series (index, dtype, data, copy)

The parameters of the builders are as follows:

Sr.No	Limit & Explanation
1	**index** Index quantities must be limited and hashable, similar in length as information. Neglect **np.arrange(n)** if no index is passed.
2	**data** data receives numerous kinds like constants, ndarray, list
3	**copy** Copy data. Neglect
4	**dtype** the data type (information type). If Nothing, the data type will be deduced.

A series can be shaped utilizing numerous contributions. For instance:

- Magnitude value or continuous
- Dict
- Array

➢ Bare Series Creation

A simple series that can be shaped is a Bare Series.

For Example

#bring in the Pandas collection and misidentification of a signal frequency as pd
Bring in Pandas as pd
t = pd.Sequence()
copy t

Its **production** is as follows:

Sequence([], dtype: float74)

➢ Ndarray Series Creation

If the information is a ndarray, then the index accepted should be of the identical span. If no index is accepted, then by evasion categorizing, it will be a **range(n),** where **n** is arrangement span. For instance:

 [5,6,7,8…. **range(len(arrangement))-2].**

For Example

#bring in the Pandas collection and misidentification of a signal frequency as pd
Bring in Pandas as pd
Bring in numpy as np
information = np.arrangement(['f','g','h','i'])
t = pd.Sequence(information)

print t

Its **production** is as follows:

1 f
2 g
3 h
4 i
dtype: article

We didn't permit any index, so by evasion1., it allotted the indexes ranging from 1 to **len(data)-2**, f.i., 1 to 4.

Example

#bring in the Pandas collection and misidentification of a signal frequency as pd
Bring in Pandas as pd
Bring in numpy as np
information = np.arangement(['f','g','h','i'])
t = pd.Sequence(information,category=[212,213,214,215])
copy t

Its **production** is as follows:

212 f
213 g
214 h
215 i
dtype: article

We accepted the categorizing quantities here. Immediately, we can see the modified categorized quantities in production.

➢ **Dict Series Creation**

A **dict** can be accepted as a contribution and if no category is stated, then the lexicon solutions are taken in an organized order to construct a category. If **the category** is accepted, the quantities in information consistent with the tags in the category will be dragged outward.

Example 1

#bring in the Pandas collection and misidentification of a signal frequency as pd

Bring in Pandas as pd

Bring in numpy as np

information = {'c' : 2., 'd : 3., '3' : 4.}

t= pd.Sequence(information)

print t

Its **production** is as follows:

b 2.1
c 3.1
d 4.1
dtype: float74

Note: Lexicon solutions are employed to make a category.

Example 2

#bring in the Pandas collection and misidentification of a signal frequency as pd

Bring in Pandas as pd

Bring in numpy as np

information = {'c' : 2., 'd' : 3., 'e' : 4.}

t = pd.Sequence(information,category=['d','e','f','c'])

copy t

Its **production** is as follows:

d 3.1

e 4.1

f NaN

c 2.1

dtype: float74

Note: Category order perseveres, and the lost component is occupied with NaN (Not a Sum).

➢ **Magnitude Series Creation**

If information is a physical quantity, a ncategory must be given. The quantity will be recurring to be equal to the span of **category.**

#bring in the Pandas collection and misidentification of a signal frequency as pd

Bring in Pandas as pd

Bring in numpy as np

t= pd.Sequence(6,category=[1, 2, 3, 4])

copy t

Its **production** is as follows:

1 6

2 6

3 6

4 6

dtype: int74

> **Retrieving Information from Sequence with Location**

Information in the sequence can be retrieved like that in a **ndarray.**

Example 1

Recover the primary component. As we previously talked about, the calculating begins from 1 for the object, which means the primary component is kept at a 0th place and so forth.

Bring in Pandas as pd

t = pd.Sequence([3,4,5,6,7],index = ['c','d','e','f','g'])

#recover the primary component

copy s[2]

Its **production** is as follows:

3

Example 2

Recover the primary 4 components in the Sequence. If b: is added in its opposite, all substances from that category will be removed. If 3 limits are employed, substances amid the 3 categories (not containing the halt category).

Bring in Pandas as pd

t = pd.Sequence([3,4,5,6,7],category = ['c','d','e','f','g'])

#recover the primary 4 components

copy t[:4]

Its **production** is as follows:

c 3

d 4

e 5

f 6

dtype: int74

Example 3

Recover the previous 5 components:

Bring in Pandas as pd

t = pd.Sequence([3,4,5,6,7],category = ['c','d','r','f','g''])

#recuperate the previous 3 components

copy t[-3:]

Its **production** is as follows:

c 3

d 4

e5

dtype: int74

➢ **Retrieve Information Using Label (category)**

A Sequence is just like a steady-magnitude **dict** in that you can acquire and place quantities by category labels.

Example 1

Recover a sole component employing category labels quantity.

Bring in Pandas as pd
t = pd.Sequence([3,4,5,6,7],category = ['c','d','e','f','g''])
#recuperate a sole component
copy t['b']

Its production is as follows:

3

Example 2

Recover numerous components employing a list of category label quantities.

Bring in Pandas as pd
t = pd.Sequence([3,4,5,6,7],category= ['c','d','e','f','g''])
#recover numerous components
copy t[['c','e','f']]

Its production is as follows:

c 3
e 5
f 6
dtype: int74

Example 3

If a label is not controlled, an exclusion is elevated.

Bring in Pandas as pd

t = pd.Sequence([3,4,5,6,7],category = ['c','d','e','f','g'])

#recuperate numerous components

copy t['h]

Its **production** is as follows:

…

KeyError: 'h'

An Information frame is a 2-sided information construction. The information is ranged in a pictorial style in lines and articles.

➤ **Information Frame Features**

- Magnitude – Changeable
- Possibly columns are of dissimilar sorts
- Can do mathematic processes on lines and articles
- Labeled axes (lines and articles)

➤ **Structure**

Now, let us suppose that we are generating an information frame with the pupil's information.

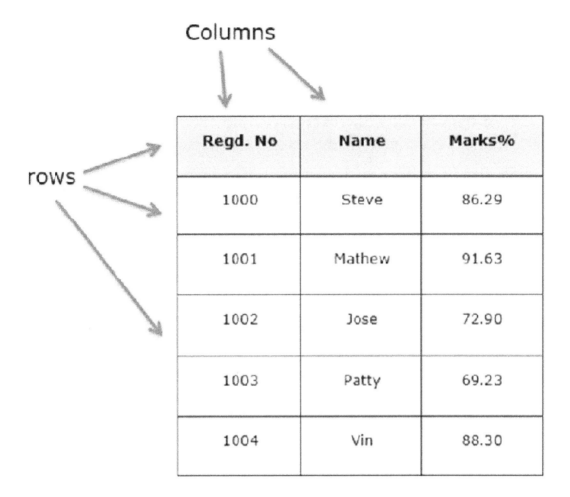

You can think of this as an SQL chart or a database information illustration.

➢ Pandas Information Frame

A Panda's information frame can be shaped by employing the following builder:

Pandas.DataFrame(copy, index, data, dtype, columns)

The limits of the builder are as follows:

Sr.No	Parameter & Explanation
1	**copy**

	This order (or whatsoever it is) is employed for the printing of information if the evasion is False.	
2	**category** For the line tags, the category to be employed for the following frame is Elective Evasion np.arrange(n) if no category is accepted.	
3	**data** data holds numerous types like the map, ndarray, list, series, map, dict, constants, and another DataFrames	
4	**dtype** The data type of both columns.	
5	**articles** For article labels, the optional evasion syntax is np.arrange(n). This is scarcely true if no category is accepted.	

➢ Create DataFrame

A Pandas DataFrame can be shaped employing numerous feed-ins like:

- dict
- Lists
- Numpy ndarrays
- Series
- Another DataFrame

In the following segments, we will visit how to generate a DataFrame employing these feed-ins.

➢ Bare Information Frame

A simple DataFrame, which can be shaped, is an Empty Dataframe.

Example

#bring in the Panda's collection and misidentification of a signal frequency as pd

Bring in Pandas as pd
eg = pd.informationFrame()
copy eg

Its production is as follows:

Bare InformationFrame
Articles: []
Category: []

➤ **Information Frame from Lists**

An Information Frame can be shaped by employing a sole list or a list of lists.

Example 1

Bring in Pandas as pd
information = [3,4,5,56]
eg= pd.InformationFrame(information)
copy eg

Its production is as follows:

1

1 2

2 3

```
3 4
4 5
        5    6
```

Example 2

Bring in Pandas as pd
information = [['Tyree',11],['Tom',13],['Lee',14]]
eg = pd.InformationFrame(information,articles=['Title','Stage'])
copy eg

Its production is as follows:

Title Stage
1 Tyree 11
2 Tom 13
3 Lee 14

Example 3

Bring in Pandas as pd
information = [['Tyree',11],['Tom',13],['Lee',14]]
eg = pd.InformationFrame(information,articles=['Title','Stage'],dtype=drift)
copy eg

Its production is as follows:

Title Stage
1 Tyree 11.0
2 Tom 13.0
3 Lee 14.0

Note: Notice that the **dtype** limit fluctuates the kind of Stage article to drift-point.

➢ Information Frame from Dict of ndarrays / Lists

Ndarrays must be of a similar span. If the category is accepted, then the span of the category must be equal to the span of the arrangements.

If no category is accepted, then by evasion, the category will be a variety(n), where **n** is the arrangement span.

Example 1

Bring in Pandas as pd

information = {'Name':['Tim', 'Jake', 'Tyree', 'Bob'],'Age':[29,35,30,43]}

eg = pd.InformationFrame(information)

copy eg

Its production is as follows:

Stage Title

1 29 Tim

2 35 Jake

3 30 Tyree

4 43 Bob

Note: Notice the quantities 2,3,4,5. They are the evasion category allotted to each employing the purpose variety(n).

Example 2

Now, let us generate a categorized Information Frame employing objects.

Bring in Pandas as pd

information = {'Title':['Tim', 'Jake', 'Tyree', 'Bob'],'Age':[29,35,30,43]}

eg = pd.InformationFrame(information, category= ['rank3','rank4','rank5','rank6'])

copy eg

Its production is as follows:

```
 Stage Title
Rank3 29 Tim
Rank4 35 Jake
Rank5 30 Tyree
Rank6 43 Bob
```

Note: Notice that the **category** limit allots a category to every line.

➤ **Information Frame from List of Dicts**

Directory of Lexicons can be passed as feed-in information to generate an Information Frame. The lexicon keys remain by evasion occupied as column terms.

Example 1

The following illustration demonstrates how to generate an Information Frame by passing a directory of lexicons.

Bring in Pandas as pd

information = [{'c': 3, 'd': 4},{'c': 7, 'd': 22, 'd': 32}]

eg = pd.InformationFrame(information)

copy eg

Its production is as follows:

b c
d
1 2 3
NaN
2 6 2 1
31.1

Note: Notice that NaN (Not a Number) is added in absent ranges.

Example 2

The following illustration demonstrates how to generate an Information Frame by accepting a directory of lexicons and the line directories.

Bring in Pandas as pd
information = [{'c':2, d': 4},{'c': 7, 'd': 22, 'e': 32}]
eg = pd.InformationFrame(information, category=['second', 'third'])
copy eg

Its production is as follows:

d e
e
second 3 4
NaN
third 7 22
42.2

Example 3

The succeeding illustration demonstrates how to generate a DataFrame with a directory of lexicons, line directories, and articles directories.

Bring in Pandas as pd

information = [{'c': 3, 'd': 4},{'c': 7, 'd': 22, 'e': 32}]

#With 3 articles directories, quantities similar as lexicon keys

Eg2 = pd.InformationFrame(information, category=['third', 'fourth'], articles= ['c', 'd'])

#With 2 article directories with 3 categories with other term

Eg 3= pd.InformationFrame(information, category=['third', 'fourth'], articles= ['c', 'd2'])

copy eg2

copy eg3

Its production is as follows:

#eg2 output

b c

second 2 3

third 6 11

#eg3 output

b c 2

third2 NaN

fourth 6 NaN

Note: Notice that the eg3 InformationFrame is shaped with an article category other than the lexicon key; therefore, adding the NaN's in location. While the eg2 is shaped with article directories similar to lexicon keys, so NaN's are added.

➢ **Information Frame from Dict of Series**

Lexicon of Series can be accepted to form an Information Frame. The subsequent category is the blending of all the sequence categories accepted.

Example

Bring in Pandas as pd
e = {'two' : pd.Sequence([2, 3, 4], category=['c', 'd', 'e']),
'three' : pd.Sequence([3, 4, 5, 6],category=['c', 'd', 'e', 'f'])}
eg = pd.InformationFrame(e)
copy eg

Its production is as follows:

two three
c 2.1 2
d 3.1 3
e 4.1 4
f NaN 5

Note: Notice that for series two, there is not one label 'e' accepted, nevertheless in the outcome, for the **f** label, NaN is added with NaN.

Let us now understand article collection, adding, and removal through examples.

➢ **Selecting Article**

We will comprehend this by choosing an article from the Information Frame.

Example

Bring in Pandas as pd
e = {'three' : pd.Sequence([3, 4, 5], category=['c', 'd', e']),

'four' : pd.Sequence([3, 4, 5, 6], category=['c', 'd', 'e', 'f'])}

eg= pd.InformationFrame(e)

copy eg['three']

Its production is as follows:

c 3.2

d 4.3

e 5.4

f NaN

Name: one, dtype: float74

➢ Column Addition

We will comprehend this by totaling a fresh article to a current information frame.

Example

Bring in Pandas as pd

e = {'three' : pd.Sequence([3, 4, 5],category=['c', 'd', 'e']),

'four' : pd.Sequence([3, 4, 5, 6], category=['c', 'd', 'e', 'f'])}

eg= pd.InformationFrame(e)

Totaling a fresh column to a current InformationFrame object with article label by passing fresh sequence

copy ("Totaling a fresh article by accepting as Sequence:")

eg['five']=pd.Sequence([11,21,31],category=['c','d,'e'])

copy eg

copy ("Totaling a fresh article employing the current articles in InformationFrame:")

eg['six']=eg[three']+eg['four']

copy eg

Its production is as follows:

Totaling a fresh column bypassing as Series:

```
three four five
c 3.1 3 11.1
d 4.1 4 21.1
e 5.1 5 31.1
f NaN 6 NaN
```

Totaling a fresh column by employing the current articles in Information Frame is as follows:

```
three four five six
c 3.1 3 11.1 12.1
d 4.1 4 21.1 23.1
e 5.1 5 31.1 34.1
f NaN 6 NaN NaN
```

➤ **Deleting an Article**

Articles can be erased or exploded. Now, let us look at the illustration to understand what it means.

Example

```
# Employing the earlier Information Frame, we will erase an article
# employing del purpose
Bring in Pandas as pd
e = {'three' : pd.Sequence([3, 4, 5], category=['c', 'd', 'e']),
'four' : pd.Sequence([3, 4, 5,6], category=['c', 'd', 'e', 'f']),
'five' : pd.Sequence([11,21,31], index=['c','d','e'])}
```

```
eg= pd.InformationFrame(e)
copy ("Our Informationframe is:")
copy eg
# employing del purpose
copy ("Deleting the 2nd article employing DEL purpose:")
del eg['three']
copy eg
# using pop purpose
copy ("Deleting an additional article employing POP purpose:")
eg.pop('three')
copy eg
```

Its production is as follows:

Our Information frame is:

```
  three four five
c   3.1 11.1    3
d   4.1 21.1    4
e   5.1 31.1    5
f   NaN NaN     6
```

Deleting the 3rd article employing DEL purpose:

```
  four five
c 11.1    3
d 21.1    4
e 31.1    5
f NaN     6
```

Deleting an additional column employing POP purpose:

four

c 11.1

d 21.1

e 31.1

f NaN

➢ Line Assortment, Adding, and Removal

Now, we will checkout comprehending line assortment, adding, and removal within illustrations. The first one will be the idea of selection.

➢ Label Assortment

Lines can be nominated by accepting line label to a **loc** purpose.

Bring in Pandas as pd
e = {'three' : pd.Sequence([3, 4, 5], category=['c', 'd', 'e']),
'four' : pd.Sequence([3, 4, 5, 6], category=['c', 'd', 'e', 'f'])}
eg= pd.InformationFrame(e)
copy eg.loc['c']

Its production is as follows:

three 4.1

four 4.1

Title: b, dtype: float74

The outcome is a series with labels as article terms of the Information Frame. And, the Term of the series is the label with which it is recovered.

➢ Number Location Assortment

Lines can be nominated by accepting a numeral place to an **iloc** purpose.

Bring in Pandas as pd
e = {'three' : pd.Sequence([3, 4, 5], category=[c, 'd', 'e']),
'three' : pd.Sequence([3, 4, 5, 6], category=['c', 'd', 'e', 'f'])}
eg = pd.InformationFrame(e)
copy eg.iloc[3]

Its production is as follows:

three 5.1
four 5.1
Title: d, dtype: float74

➢ **Line Slices**

Numerous lines can be nominated employing ':' operative.

Bring in Pandas as pd
e= {'three' : pd.Sequence([3, 4, 5], category=['c', 'd', 'e']),
'three' : pd.Sequence([3, 4, 5, 6], category=['c', 'd', 'e', 'f'])}
eg = pd.InformationFrame(e)
copy eg[3:5]

Its production is as follows:

three four
e4.0 4
f NaN 5

➢ **Lines Addition**

Increase fresh lines to an Information Frame employing the **add** task. This task will append the lines after the list.

Bring in Pandas as pd

```
eg = pd.InformationFrame([[3, 4], [5, 6]], category = ['c','d'])
eg3 = pd.InformationFrame([[7, 8], [9, 10]], category = ['c','d'])
eg = eg.add(eg3)
copy eg
```

Its production is as follows:

```
c d
2 3 4
3 5 6
2 7 8
3 9 9
```

➢ **Lines Removal**

Utilize the index tag to erase or descent lines from an Information Frame. If the label is repeated, then numerous lines will be thrown down.

If you have noticed in the previous illustration, the tags are matching. Now, let us descent a tag and we will see how numerous lines will get thrown down.

Bring in Pandas as pd

```
eg= pd.DataFrame([[2, 3], [4, 5]], articles = ['b','c'])
eg3 = pd.DataFrame([[6, 7], [8, 9]], articles = ['b','c'])
eg = eg.append(eg3)
# descent lines with label 1
eg = eg.drop(1)
print df
```

Its production is as follows:

```
b c
2 4 5
2 8 9
```

In the previous illustrations, 3 lines were thrown down since those 3 held the similar label 1.

The name **Panel data** results from econometrics and is partly accountable for the term Pandas. A **panel** is a container of information in 3D.

The terms for the three axes are proposed to give some rhetorical sense to detailing processes connecting the panel data. They are as follows:

- **items** − axis 0, every article resembles an Information Frame confined within.
- **main_alignment** − alignment 2, it is the index (lines) of every one of the Information Frames.
- **slight_alignment** − alignment 3, it is the articles of every one of the Information Frames.

➢ **Pandas.Panel()**

A Panel can be shaped by employing the following code:

Pandas.Panel(items, dtype, data, main_axis, slight_axis, copy)

The parameters of the builder are as follows:

Limit	Explanation
data	Data yields numerous characteristics like the map, dict, ndarray, series, lists, constants and likewise an additional DataFrame
items	axis=0
main_axis	axis=1

slight_axis	axis=2
dtype	Data sort of every article
copy	Copy data. evasion, **false**

➢ Panel Creation

A Panel can be shaped by employing numerous customs. For example:

- From dict of Information Frames
- From ndarrays

➢ 3D ndarray

```
# making a bare panel
Bring in NumPy as np
Bring in Pandas as pd
informtion = np.bychance.bychance(3,5,6)
q = pd.Panel(information)
copy q
```

Its production is as follows:

```
< style 'Pandas.core.panel.Panel'>
Sizes: 3 (objects) x 5 (main_axis) x 6(slight_axis)
Items axis: 1to 2
Main_axis axis: 2 to 5
Slight_axis axis: 2 to 6
```

Note: Notice the sizes of the unfilled panel and the exceeding panel; all the items are dissimilar.

➤ **dict of Information Frame Items**

#making an unfilled panel
Bring in NumPy as np
Bring in Pandas as pd
information = {'Item2' : np.InformationFrame(pd.bychance.bychancen(6, 5)),
'Item2' : pd.InformationFrame(np.bychance.bychancen(6, 4))}
q = pd.Panel(information)
copy q

Its production is as follows:

Sizes: 3(items) x 5 (main_axis) x4 (slight_axis)
Items axis: Item2 to Item3
Main_axis axis:1 to 4
Slight_axis axis: 1 to 3

➤ **Bare Panel Creations**

An unfilled panel can be shaped employing the Panel builder as follows:

#generating an unfilled panel
Bring in Pandas as pd
q = pd.Panel()
copy q

Its production is as follows:

<style 'Pandas.core.panel.Panel'>
Sizes: 2(items) x 2 (main_axis) x 2(slight_axis)
Items axis: None
Main_axis axis: None
Slight_axis axis: None

➢ **Selecting Information from Panel**

Choose the information from the panel by employing:

- Main_axis
- Objects
- Slight_axis

➢ **Using Objects**

```
# generating an unfilled panel
Bring in NumPy as np
Bring in Pandas as pd
information = {'Item2' : np.InformtionFrame(pd.bychance.bychancen(6, 5)),
'Item3' : pd.InformationFrame(np.bychance.bychancen(6, 4))}
q = pd.Panel(information)
copy p['Item2']
```

Its production is as follows:

```
       1 2           3
1 1.599335 -1.239748 1.941928
2 1.528598 1.997792 1.687768
3 -3.886377 1.682779 1.390093
4 -1.511649 -1.255345 2.221646
```

Here, we take 3 objects, and we recovered object2. The outcome is a DataFrame with five lines and four articles, which are the **Main_axis** and **Slight_axis** sizes.

➢ **Employing Main_axis**

Information can be retrieved by means of the method **panel.main_axis(category).**

```
# generating an unfilled panel
Bring in NumPy as np
Bring in Pandas pd
information = {'Item2' : np.InformationFrame(pd.bychance.randn(6, 5)),
'Item3' : pd.InformationFrame(np.bychance.bychancen(6, 4))}
q = pd.Panel(information)
copy p.main_xs(2)
```

Its production is as follows:

```
 Item2 Item3
1 1.528598 1.859523
2 1.997792 -1.668433
3 1.687768 NaN
```

➢ **Employing slight_axis**

Information can be retrieved by employing the technique **panel.slight_axis(category).**

```
# generating an unfilled panel
Bring in NumPy as np
Bring in Pandas as pd
information = {'Item2' : pd.InformationFrame(np.bychance.bychancen(6, 5)),
```

'Item3' : pd.InformationFrame(np.bychance.bychancen(6, 4))}
q = pd.Panel(information)
copy p.slight_xs(2)

Its production is as follows:

Item2 Item3
1 -1.239748 -2.158143
2 1.997792 -1.668433
3 1.682779 1.542964
4 -1.255345 2.413377

Note: Notice the deviations in the sizes.

We have learned about the 3 Pandas Information Structures and how to generate them. Now, we will mostly center on the Information Frame items because of its rank in the actual time information processing as well as deliberate on a few other Information Structures.

➢ **Series Basic Functionality**

Sr.No.	Quality or Technique & Explanation
1	**axes** Yields a directory of the line axis labels
2	**dtype** Yields the dtype of the article.
3	**empty** Yields True if series is empty.
4	**ndim**

	Yields the sum of sizes of the original information by explanation 1.
5	**size** Yields the sum of components in the original information.
6	**values** Yields the Series as ndarray.
7	**brain()** Yields the primary n lines.
8	**end()** Yields the previous n lines.

Now, let us generate a Sequence and see all of the above processes.

Example

Bring in Numpy as np
Bring in Pandas as pd
#Generate a series with one hundred by chance figures
s = pd.Sequence(np.bychance.bychancen(6))
copy s

Its production is as follows:

1 1.978963
2 -1.259479
3 -2.496917
4 -2.8569495

dtype: float74

> **Axes**

Yields the directory of the tags of the sequence.

Bring in Numpy as np
Bring in Pandas as pd
#Generate a series with one hundred by chance figures
s = np.Sequence(pd.bychance.bychancen(6))
copy ("The axes are:")
copy s.axes

Its production is as follows:

The axes are:

[BychanceCtegory(begin=2, halt=6, stage=3)]

The exceeding outcome is a dense arrangement of a directory of quantities from 1 to 6 [2,3,4,5,6].

> **Bare**

Yields the Boolean quantity telling whether the Item is unfilled or not. Factual designates that the item is unfilled.

Bring in Numpy as np
Bring in Pandas as pd
#Generate a series with one hundred by chance figures
s = pd.Sequence(np.bychance.bychancen(6))
copy ("Is the Object empty?")
copy s.bare

Its production is as follows:

Is the Item unfilled?
Untrue

➢ **Ndim**

Yields the sum of sizes of the basic item. So, by description, a Sequence is a 1D information construction. It yields:

Bring in Numpy as np
Bring in Pandas as pd
#Generate a series with five by chance figures
s = np.Sequence(pd.bychance.bychancen(6))
copy s
copy ("The sizes of the item:")
copy s.ndim

Its production is as follows:

1 1.185999
2 1.277298
3-1.610823
4 -2.4881111
5 3.5682222
dtype: float74

The dimensions of the item:

2

➢ **Size**

Yields the magnitude(span) of the sequence.

Bring in NumPy as np
Bring in Pandas as pd
#Generate a sequence with five by chance figures
s = np.Sequence(pd.bychance.bychancen(4))
copy s
copy ("The size of the object:")
copy s.scope

Its production is as follows:

1 4.189169
2 -2.318914
3 -3.429925
dtype: float74

The magnitude of the item:

3

➢ **Values**

Yields the real information in the sequence as an object.

Bring in NumPy as np
Bring in Pandas as pd
#Generate a sequence with five by chance figures
s = np.Sequence(pd.bychance.bychancen(6))
copy s
copy ("The actual data series is:")
copy sfigures

Its production is as follows:

1 2.898484
2 -1.706268
3 1.291588
4 -1.251933
5 -2.362844
dtype: float74

The real information series is:

[2.89848413 -1.71626992 1.29258775 -1.2519329 -2.3628439]

➢ **Brain & End**

To see a slight example of a sequence or the Information Frame item, practice the brain() and the end() methods.

brain() yields the primary **n** lines (notice the category quantities). The evasion sum of components to show is 5, but you can accept a practice sum.

```
Bring in Pandas as pd
Bring in numpy as np
#Generate a sequence with five by chance figures
s = pd.Sequence(np.bychance.randn(5))
copy ("The original series is:")
copy s
copy ("The first two rows of the data series:")
copy s.brain(3)
```

Its production is as follows:

The initial series is:

1 1.831986
2 -1.876999
3 1.5893332
4 -1.249658
5 1.359769
dtype: float74

The primary 3 lines of the information series:

1 1.831987
2 -1.876999
3 1.5893332
dtype: float74

end() yields the previous **n** lines (notice the index values). The neglect sum of components to show is 5, but you can permit a practice sum.

Bring in NumPy as np
Bring in Pandas as pd
#Generate a sequence with five by chance figures
s = np.Sequence(pd.bychance.bychancen(6))
copy ("The original series is:")
copy s
copy ("The last two lines of the data series:")
copy s.end(2)

Its production is as follows:

The initial series is:

1 -17666191
2 -19992518

3 -1.719693
4 -3.452523
5 -6. 563633
dtype: float64

The previous 2 rows of the information series:

4 -3.452523

5 -6.563633

dtype: float74

➢ **Basic Functionality of an Information Frame**

Now, let us comprehend what is the basic functionality of an information frame. The chart below shows the vital qualities or methods that help in information frame basic functionality.

Sr.No.	Quality or Technique & Explanation
1	**T** Transpose lines and articles.
2	**axes** Yields a directory with the line axis labels and article axis labels as the individual members.
3	**dtypes** Yields the dtypes in this item.
4	**bare** True if NDFrame is completely unfilled [no objects]; if any of the axes are of span 0.
5	**ndim**

Sum of axes/collection dimensions.

6 **shape**
Yields a tuple representing the dimensionality of the information frame.

7 **size**
Sum of rudiments in the NDFrame.

8 **figures**
Numpy illustration of NDFrame.

9 **brain()**
Yields the primary n lines.

10 **end()**
Yields previous n lines.

Now, let us generate an information frame and see by what methods the previous stated qualities function.

Example

Bring in Pandas as pd
Bring in numpy as np
#Generate a Lexicon of sequence
e = {'Title':pd.Sequence(['Tim','Bill','Miki','Jon',Tyree,'Jackson','Jake']),
'Stage':pd.Sequence([26,27,26,24,31,30,24]),
'Score':pd.Sequence([5.34,4.35,4.99,3.67,4.31,5.7,4.9])}
#Generate an InformationFrame
eg = pd.InformationFrame(e)

copy ("Our data series is:")

copy eg

Its production is as follows:

Our information sequence is:

```
Stage Title Score
1 26 Tim 5.34
2 27 Bill 4.35
3 26 Miki 4.99
4 24 Jon 3.67
5 31 Tyree 4.31
6 30 Jackson 5.71
7 24 Jake 4.91
```

➢ **T (Transpose)**

This yields the transpose of the information frame. The lines and articles will exchange.

```
Bring in Pandas as pd
Bring in numpy as np
# Generate a Lexicon of sequence
e = {'Title':pd.Sequence(['Tim','Bill','Miki','Jon','Tyree','Jackson','Jake']),
'Stage':pd.Sequence([26,27,26,24,31,30,24]),
'Score':pd.Sequence([5.34,4.35,4.99,3.67,4.31,5.7,4.9])}
# Generate a InformationFrame
eg= pd.InformationFrame(e)
copy ("The transpose of the data series is:")
copy eg.T
```

Its production is as follows:

The transpose of the information series is:

1 2 3 4 5 6 7
Stage 26 27 26 24 31 30 24
Title Tim Bill Miki Jon Tyree Jackson Jake
Score 5.34 4.35 4.99 3.67 4.3 5.7 4.9

➢ **Axes**

This yields the directory of line axis tags and article axis tags.

Bring in Pandas as pd
Bring in numpy as np
#Generate a Lexicon of sequence
e = {'Title':pd.Sequence(['Tim','Bill','Miki','Jon','Tyree','Jackson','Jake']),
'Stage':pd.Sequence([26,27,26,24,31,30,24]),
Score':pd.Sequence([5.34,4.35,4.99,3.67,4.31,5.7,4.9])}
#Generate a InformationFrame
eg = pd.InformationFrame(e)
copy ("Line axis tags and article axis tags are:")
copy eg.axes

Its production is as follows:

Line axis tags and column axis tags are:

[BychanceCategory(begin=2, halt=9 stage=3), Category([u'Stage', u'Title', u'Score'],
dtype='itemt')]

➢ **Dtypes**

This yields the information category of every article.

```
Bring in Pandas as pd
Bring in numpy as np
#Generate a Lexicon of sequence
e = {'Title':pd.Sequence(['Tim','Bill','Miki','Jon','Tyree','Jackson','Jake']),
'Stage':pd.Sequence([26,27,26,24,31,30,24]),
'Score':pd.Sequence([5.34,4.35,4.99,3.67,4.31,5.7,4.9])}
#Generate an InformationFrame
eg= pd.InformationFrame(e)
copy ("The data types of each article are:")
copy df.dtypes
```

Its production is as follows:

The information categories in every article are:

```
Stage int74
Title item
Score float74
dtype: article
```

➢ **Bare**

This yields the Boolean quantity stating whether the Item is unfilled or not. Factual designates that the item is unfilled.

```
Bring in Pandas as pd
Bring in numpy as np
#Generate a Lexicon of sequence
e = {'Title':pd.Sequence(['Tim','Bill','Miki','Jon','Tyree','Jackson','Jake']),
'Stage':pd.Sequence([26,27,26,24,31,30,24]),
```

'Score':pd.Sequence([5.34,4.35,4.99,3.67,4.31,5.7,4.9])}

#Generate an InformationFrame

eg = pd.InformationFrame(e)

copy ("Is the item unfilled?")

copy eg.bare

Its production is as follows:

Is the item bare?

Untrue

➤ **ndim**

This yields the sum of the sizes of the item. If by classification, information frame is a 2D item.

Bring in Pandas as pd

Bring in numpy as np

#Generate a Lexicon of sequence

e = {'Title':pd.Sequence(['Tim','Bill','Miki','Jon','Tyree','Jackson','Jake']),

'Stage':pd.Sequence([26,27,26,24,31,30,24]),

'Score':pd.Sequence([5.34,4.35,4.99,3.67,4.31,5.7,4.9])}

#Generate a InformationFrame

eg= pd.InformationFrame(e)

copy ("Our item is:")

copy eg

copy ("The measurement of the item is:")

copy eg.ndim

Its production is as follows:

Our item is:

```
Stage Title Score
1 26 Tim 5.34
2 27 Bill 4.35
3 26 Miki 4.99
4 24 Jon 3.67
5 31 Tyree 4.31
6 30 Jackson 5.71
7 24 Jake 4.91
```

The measurement of the item is:

3

➢ **Form**

This yields a tuple characterizing the shape and size of the information frame. Tuple (c,d) where **c** characterizes the sum of lines and **d** characterizes the sum of articles.

```
Bring in Pandas as pd
Bring in numpy as np
#Generate a Lexicon of sequence
e = {'Title':pd.Sequence(['Tim','Bill','Miki','Jon','Tyree','Jackson','Jake']),
'Stage':pd.Sequence([26,27,26,24,31,30,24]),
'Score':pd.Sequence([5.34,4.35,4.99,3.67,4.31,5.7,4.9])}
#Generate a InformationFrame
eg = pd.InformationaFrame(e)
copy ("Our item is:")
copy eg
copy ("The form of the item is:")
```

copy eg.form

Its production is as follows:

Our item is:

Stage Title Score
1 26 Tim 5.34
2 27 Bill 4.35
3 26 Miki 4.98
4 24 Jon 3.67
5 31 Tyree 4.21
6 30 Jackson 5.71
7 24 Jake 4.91

The form of the item is:

(8, 4)

➢ **Size**

This yields the sum of components in the information frame.

```
Bring in Pandas as pd
Bring in numpy as np
#Generate a Lexicon of sequence
e = {'Title':pd.Sequence(['Tim','Bill','Miki,'Jon','Tyree','Jackson','Jake']),
'Stage':pd.Sequence([26,27,26,24,31,30,24]),
'Score':pd.Sequence([5.34,4.35,4.99,3.67,4.31,5.71,4.91])}

#Generate an InformationFrame
eg= pd.InformationFrame(e)
```

copy ("Our item is:")

copy eg

copy ("The entire sum of components in our item is:")

copy eg.size

Its production is as follows:

Our item is:

```
Stage Title Score
1 26 Tim 5.34
2 27 Bill 4.35
3 26 Miki 4.99
4 24 Jon 3.67
5 31 Tyree 4.31
6 30 Jackson 5.71
7 24 Jake 4.91
```

The entire sum of components in our item is:

22

➤ **Values**

This yields the real information in the information frame as an **NDarray.**

Bring in Pandas as pd

Bring in numpy as np

#Generate a Lexicon of sequence

e = {'Title':pd.Sequence(['Tim','Bill','Miki','Jon','Tyree','Jackson','Jake']),

'Stage':pd.Sequence([26,27,26,24,31,30,24]),

'Score':pd.Sequence([5.34,4.35,4.99,3.67,4.31,5.71,4.91])}

#Generate a InformationFrame

eg = pd.InformationFrame(e)

```
copy ("Our item is:")
copy eg
copy ("The real information in our information frame is:")
copy eg.figures
```

Its production is as follows:

```
Our item is:
Stage Title Score
1 26 Tim 5.34
2 27 Bill 4.35
3 26 Miki 4.99
4 24 Jon 3.67
5 31 Tyree 4.31
6 30 Jackson 5.71
7 24 Jake 4.91
```

The real information in our information frame is:

```
[[26'Tim' 5.34]
[27 'Bill' 4.35]
[26 'Miki' 4.99]
[24 'Jon' 3.67]
[31 'Tyree' 4.3]
[30 'Jackson' 5.7]
[24 'Jake' 4.9]]
```

➢ **Brain & End**

To see a minor example of an information frame item, employthe **brain()** and end() methods. **end()** yields the primary **n** lines (notice the category quantities). The evasion sum of components to show is 6, but you can accept a practice sum.

```
Bring in Pandas as pd
Bring in numpy as np
#Generate a Lexicon of sequence
e = {Title':pd.Sequence(['Tim','Bill','Miki','Jon','Tyree','Jackson','Jake']),
'Stage':pd.Sequence([26,27,26,24,31,30,24]),
'Score':pd.Sequence([5.34,4.35,4.99,3.67,4.31,5.7,4.9])}
#Generate an InformationFrame
eg = pd.InformationFrame(e)
copy ("Our information frame is:")
copy eg
copy ("The primary 3 rows of the information frame is:")
copy ef.brain(3)
```

Its production is as follows:

Our information frame is:

Stage Title Score
1 26 Tim 5.34
2 27 Bill 4.35
3 26 Miki 4.99
4 24 Jon 3.67
5 31 Tyree 4.31
6 30 Jackson 5.71
7 24 Jake 4.91

The primary 3 rows of the information frame are:

Stage Title Score

1 26 Tim 5.34
2 27 Bill 4.35
3 26 Miki 4.99

end() yields the previous **n** rows (notice the index quantities). The evasion sum of components to show is 6, but you can permit a practice sum.

Bring in Pandas as pd
Bring in numpy as np
#Generate a Lexicon of sequence
e = {'Title':pd.Sequence(['Tim','Bill','Miki','Jon','Tyree','Jackson','Jake']),
'Stage':pd.Sequence([26,27,26,24,31,30,24]),
'Score':pd.Sequence([5.34,4.35,4.99,3.67,4.31,5.7,4.9])}
#Generate an InformationFrame
eg = pd.InformationFrame(e)
copy ("Our information frame is:")
copy eg
copy ("The previous 3 rows of the information frame is:")
copy df.end(3)

Its production is as follows:

Our information frame is:

Stage Title Score
1 26 Tim 5.34
2 27 Bill 4.35
3 26 Miki 4.99
4 24 Jon 3.67
5 31 Tyree 4.31
6 30 Jackson 5.71

7 24 Jake 4.91

The previous 3 rows of the information frame are:

Stage Title Score
5 31 Tyree 4.31
6 30 Jackson 5.71
7 24 Jake 4.91

Matplotlib Python Charting

The structure of a plot, pyplot, pylab, and a whole lot more runs you through the fundamentals of Python information visualization through Matplotlib. We, as human beings, are extremely graphical mortals. We understand objects much greater when we see them pictured. On the other hand, the stageof giving studies, outcomes, or understandings can be a blockage. You may not even distinguish where to begin or you may have by now the right plan inmind, but then inquiries like this one pop up, "Is this the right way to imaginethe visions that I plan to give to my spectators?" And believe me, they will certainly come in your mind.

Once you are occupied with the Python charting collection on Matplotlib, the primary stage to responding to the exceeding inquiry is by constructing familiarity on matters like:

- The structure of a Matplotlib plot: What precisely is a figure?What is a subplot? What are the Axes?
- Plot creation, which can elevate inquiries about what unit you precisely want to bring (pylab or pyplot?), precisely how you must start preparing the shape and the lines of your plot, correctly employing Jupyter within matplotlib pads, etc.
- Charting procedures, beginning with meek styles to chart your information to additional progressive styles of imagining your information.
- Basic chart modification, with an emphasis on chart icons and

transcript, names, axes tags, and chart plans.
- Keeping, displaying, erasing your charts: Demonstrating the chart and collecting one or more figures to, for instance, erase the axes, close the chart, pdf files, or clear the figure.
- Finally, you will quickly go over 2 customs in how you can modify Matplotlib: with chic pages and the RC settings.

➢ How Does a Matplotlib Plot Look?

At first sight, it appears like there is a lot of mechanisms to deliberate when you begin plotting with this Python information imagining collection. You will undoubtedly come to an agreement that it's very unclear, and occasionally, a bit unpromising investigating the quantity of cryptogram that is essential for mot plots, not comprehending exactly how to begin and which mechanisms you ought to employ.

Well, fortunately, this collection is very supple and consumes a lot of accessible, feed-in evasions that will surely assist you extremely. As such, you do not need a lot to get going. You need to produce the essential introductions, formulate various sets of information, and you can begin charting with the assistance of the chart() function! Once you are prepared, do not fail to recall showing your plot and employing the show() function.

The illustration below will show how relaxed the procedure is.

script.py	IPython Shell	Plots
1. # Bring in the essential databases and units 2. bring in numpy as np 3. bring in matplotlib.pyplot as plt 4. 5. # Make the information	In [1] :	

```
6. x = np.linspace(1,
20, 100)
7.
8.    #    Plot    the
information
9.    plt.plot(x,    x,
label='linear')
10.10.
11.#  Enhance  the
legend
12. plt.legend()
13.
14. # Display the plot
15. plt.show()
```

It is important to note that the matplotlib collection's pyplot unit should be brought in under the plt code.

Oh, the happy day you have now magnificently shaped your very 1st chart! Below is how the subsequent plot looks like in close-up.

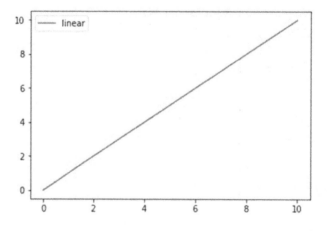

Nice, right?

Here, you cannot tell that, on the outside, you have perhaps involuntarily employed the feed-in evasions that upkeep the formation of the fundamental mechanisms, such as the Numbers and the Axes. Later, we will talk more about these evasions.

Nonetheless, you will start by comprehending that toiling with matplotlib will be a lot simpler when you know how the fundamental mechanisms are epitomized.

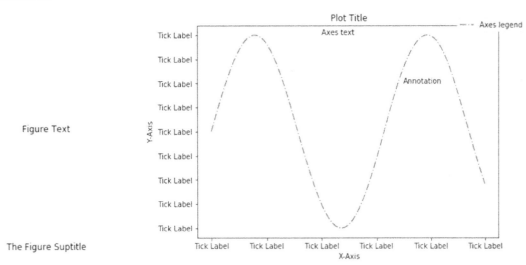

There are 2 large mechanisms that must be taken into reason:

- The **Shape** is the general frame or sheet that, in its entirety, is illustrated on. It's the highest module of all the modules that you will study in the coming sections. You can generate numerous self-governing Figures. A Shape can consume numerous other possessions in it, for example, a subtitle, which is placed in the center of the figure. You will likewise figure out that you can improve an icon and hue bar, for instance, to your Figure.
- You can also add to the figure **Lines**. The Lines are the part on which the information is charted on with purposes such as plot() and scatter() and that can have marks and tags that are connected to the figure. This clarifies why several Axes can be held by Figures.

Tip: ax.set_xlim() should be visited behind the landscapes whenever you come across plt.xlim, for example. All the Axes item's techniques are there as a purpose in the pyplot segment contrariwise. Note that, frequently, you will employ the purposes of the pyplot segment because they are muchfresher at best for simple charts!

By looking at the chart below, you will see just what "clean" stands for in the succeeding bits of cryptogram:

script.py	IPython Shell	Plot
1. bring in matplotlib.pyplot as plt 2. fig = plt.shape() 3. ax = fig.add_subplot(222) 4. ax.plot([2, 3, 4, 5], [40, 50, 36, 60], hue='brightpink',rowthickness=4) 5.ax.sprinkle([1.4, 4.9, 2.3, 3.6], [22, 36, 10, 37], hue='dimjade',indicator='^') 6. ax.set_xlim(1.6, 5.6) 7.plt.show()	In [1] :	

With the portion of cryptogram below:

script.py	IPython	Plot
1. bring in matplotlib.pyplot as plt 2. plt.plot([2, 3, 4, 5], [40, 50, 36, 60],hue='brightpink',rowthickness=4) 3. plt.scatter([1.4, 4.9, 2.3, 3.5], [22, 36, 10, 37], hue='dimjade', indicator='^') 4.plt.xlim(1.6, 5.6)	In [1] :	

5.plt.show()

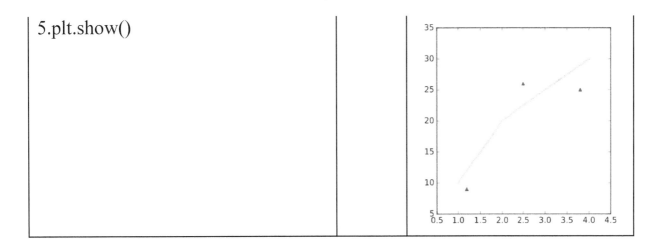

The 2nd chunk of cryptogram is certainly cleaner, isn't it?

Nevertheless, the ax, an Axes item, can be used in these kinds of instances. Using continuously the initial cryptogram hunk is considered to still be better if there are many axes in your possession since it's better to favor clear and understood cryptograms, like the one shown above!

Besides these 2 mechanisms we have previously discussed, there are a few more that you ought to keep in mind:

- Axes are unique objects and can be modified in many ways. They carry an x and y side, which have ticks. These ticks have main and slight impulse lines and impulse labels. They can also have titles, labels, and legends to reflect on when you want to start modifying your axes. Also, bear in mind that you can use axes gages and gridlines to do modifications to your axes as well.
- Spines are what you call the lines connecting the axis impulse marks. It also chooses the limitations of the information area. In short, when no information has been plotted at all, but the axes are initialized. They are the meek black squares that you see, as shown in the bottom illustration:

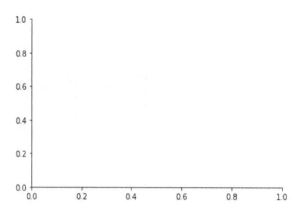

- As seen from the above, the top and right spines are arranged to indiscernible.

Note: Artist is all items that the database must provide to operators, like figures, legends, axes, axis, and other graphical items such as patches, and texts. All of these are drawn employing Matplotlib as part of a unit.

➢ **How are pylot and pylab related?**

This isn't really that surprising. When you talk about "Matplotlib", you talk about the complete Python information imagining database, which you should know by now as Matplotlib.

Furthermore, the reason why you frequently see matplotlib.pyplot in cryptogram is that pyplot is a component in the matplotlib database. This component delivers a margin that allows you to produce axes and figures automatically and indirectly to achieve the plot that you wanted.

If you want to have something plotted swiftly without the need to materialize axes or figures, this can be very accessible. The evasions are adjusted. Also, the current axes and figures will be used whenever you need to do some customizations. As you can notice, these mechanisms are not yet openly stated, but you managed to make a plot that hasn't even undergone modifications!

Finally, pylab is an additional unit, but it gets downloaded together with the matplotlib database. It brings in NumPy and the pyplot collection and is usually recommended when you want to demand access to plotting features, collaboratively does arithmetic, and when you work with arrays.

When you are using the IPython Kernel in Jupyter, you do not need pylab as an additional unit, but you still might see it displayed in the older lessons and illustrations of matplotlib.

As a response to all, the %matplotlib enchantment combined with the correct backend like the qt, inline, and others is best to use. Every so often, employing inline is recommended. The reason is that it ensures the implantation of the plots in the sketchpad.

Note, if you do not want implanted plots, but you would rather want to implant them into web application servers, lot scripts, or graphical user borders, etc., your chosen backend to be employed must be stipulated. However, you need to make sure that you do not work in Jupyter when doing this. Also, depending on the cases and uses, a diverse backend should also be selected.

Matplotlib Plot Data

The Python library for methodical calculating is the key step that you have to take to begin plotting in Python and reviewing NumPy. As explained in the other parts of this chapter, Matplotlib is frequently utilized in envisioning lessons or computations in Python.

Matplotlib's methodical calculation may not seem very interesting, however, you will surely be very busy with lots of data, especially if you are tackling information science. These data can be found stored in the said arrangements. The processes should be done on them, the objects should be reviewed, and they should be operated in order for you to be employed with the data, which is in the right format and will stimulate your studies.

Overall, when you do some work with the collection of information imaging, it is very accessible to use Numpy. You will find that you have the choice to accept Python directories and objects to your plotting purposes along with many other directories.

➢ Generate Your Plot

Ok, you're off to generate your initial plot with Python! Based on our discussions in the previous parts of this book, the key and the first step in controlling and solving the database is the figure. Next, using <u>fig.add_axes()</u>, the figure's axes found in the cryptogram chunk can be reset.

Script.Py	IPython Shell	IPython Shell /when info is imported
1.#Bring in `pyplot` 2.bring in matplotlib.pyplot as plt 3. 4.# Reset a Shape 5.fig = plt.figure() 6. 7.# Rise Axes to the Shape 8.fig.add_axes([0,0,1,1])	In [1] :	Out[1]: <matplotlib.axes._axes.Axes at 0x7fe3b631a240> In [1]:

➢ Subplot

We have gone over all mechanisms of a chart/plot and you have adjusted your first shape and lines. You will sometimes see subplots pop up in a cryptogram to make things a bit more complex.

In some cases, it means that the subplot and the axes are the same and both delegates the same thing. No, you employ subplots to customize and accumulate your Axes on a regular lattice. Also, remember to use the <u>add_subplots()</u> function when calling a subplot, so that your figure can have axes added.

You need to also take note that the add_subplots() function is different from the add_axes(). That topic will be discussed more in the later sections.

Now, let's consider the succeeding illustration:

Script.Py	IPython Shell	Plot
1.#Bring in the essential databases and units 2.bring in numpy as np matplotlib.pyplot as plt 3.bring in matplotlib.pyplot as plt 4. 5.# Make a Shape 6.sha = plt.shape() 7. 8.# Set up Axes 9.ax = fig.add_subplot(111) 10. 11.# Scatter the data 12.ax.scatter(np.rowgap(0, 1, 5), np.rowgap(0, 5, 5)) 13. 14.# Show the plot 15.plt.show()	In [1] :	

Based on the above example, you are positioned with a test because of the add_subplot() purpose. This is because of the add_subplots(111) seen on the cryptogram chunk above.

You may then wonder what the meaning of 111 is.

This only means that the add_subplot() are given 3 influences. To help you visualize, 1,1,1 is the equivalent of 111. The 3 influences elect the plot sum (1), the sum of articles (1), and the sum of lines (1). It only means that only one subplot is actually made.

Note: When you're still a beginner in this collection and always fails to revisit the meaning of the 3 sums, you can actually do whatever you like when you employ this purpose.

Now, think about the succeeding orders. Try imagining how much limitless axes your shape will have and what the plot will look like.

ax = fig.add_subplot(2,2,1).

Did you conjure the picture in your mind, yet?

You're right! A total of four axes will be in your shape arranged in two articles and two rows construction. With the row of cryptograms that you have well-thought-out, you say that the adjustable ax is the primary of the 4 axes to which you need to begin charting. The "1st" in this case means that it will be the primary axes on the left adjacent to the 2 x 2 structure that you have initialized.

➤ **Variances Between add_subplot() and add_axes()**

The variance amongst fig.add_axes() and fig.add_subplot() does not rest on the outcome: they each give an Axes piece. Nevertheless, they do differ in the device that is employed to enhance the axes. You accept a fileto add_axes() which is the inferior left fact, the thickness, and the build. This means that the axes piece is situated in entire equivalents.

In conflict, the add_subplot() purpose does not deliver the choice to put the axes at a sure location. Although, it does permit the axes to be located rendering to a subplot grid, as you have seen in the segment above.

In most instances, you will employ add_subplot() to generate axes. Only in the cases where the insertion matters, you will recourseto add_axes(). Otherwise, you can also employ subplots() if you essentially want to get one or more subplots at the same time. You will see an illustration of how this works in the following segment.

➤ **Modification of Figure Size**

Now that you have seen how to operate a Figure and Axes from a cut, you will likewise want to differentiate how you can swap particular little facts thatthe database put together for you, such as the figure scope.

Now, let's say you do not have the extravagance to go along with the evasions and you want to modify this. How do you go about setting the extentof your figures by hand?

Like all things with this database, it's easy, but you essentially have to know what to modify. Add an argument figsize to your plt.figure() purpose of the pyplot component. You just need to stipulate a tuple with the thickness and stature of your figure in inches, just like this plt.figure(figsize=(3,4)), for this to work.

Note that you can likewise permit figsize to the plt.subplots() purpose of the same component. The inner devices are the same as the figure() purpose that you have just seen.

You can see an example of this below:

Script.py	IPythonPlot Shell	
1. # Bring in`pyplot` from `matplotlib` 2.bring in matplotlib.pyplot as plt 3. 4.# Reset the plot 5.sha = plt.shape(shaextent=(20,10)) 6.ax2 = sha.add_subchart(121)	In [1] :	

7.ax3 = sha.add_subchart(122) 8. 9.# or substitute the three lines of cryptogram above by the succeeding line: 10.#fig, (ax2, ax3) = plt.subcharts(2,3, figsize=(40,20)) 11. 12.# Plot the information 13.ax1.bar([1,2,3],[3,4,5]) 14.ax2.barh([0.5,1,2.5],[0,1,2]) 15.# Show the plot plt.show()	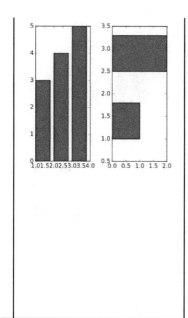

➢ **Plotting Procedures: Pyplot**

Now that everything is customary for you to begin charting your information, it's time to take a closer look at some plotting actions. You will infrequently come across purposes like plot() and scatter(), which also tie points with lines or pointers connecting them, or draw separate points, which are mounted or tinted.

But, as you have previously seen in the illustration of the first unit, you should not fail to recall accepting the information that you want these purposes to use!

These purposes are only basic essentials. You will need some other purposes to make sure your plots look grand:

ax.stackplot()	Stack plot
ax.bar()	Vertical rectangles
Ax.axhline()	Horizontal line across axes
ax.barh()	Horizontal rectangles
ax.fill()	Filled polygons

ax,fill_between()	Fill between y-values and 0
ax.v0line()	Vertical line across axes

If you are still wondering about how you can use these purposes to plot your data, look at the following illustration. **Note** that the_x and_y adjustable have previously been loaded in for you:

Script.py	IPython Shell	Plot
1.#Bring in `pyplot` from `matplotlib` 2.Bring in matplotlib.pyplot as plt 3. 4.# Reset the plot 5.sha = plt.shape() 6.ax1 = 7.sha.add_belowchart(131) 7.ax2 = sha.add_belowchartt(132) 8.ax3 = sha.add_belowchart(133) 9. 10.# Plot the information 11.ax1.bar([1,2,3], [3,4,5]) 12.ax2.barh([0.5,1,2.5], [0,1,2]) 13.ax2.axhline(0.45) 14.ax1.axvline(0.65) 15.ax3.scatter(x,y) 16. 17.# Display the plot	In [1]:	

18.plt.show()		

Numerous functions talk for themselves meanwhile the titles are rather clear. But that doesn't mean that you need to give yourself limits. For instance, the fill_between() purpose is faultless for those who want to make rangeplots, but they can also be employed to make a weighted line chart. Just use the plotting purpose a few times to make sure that the ranges overlay andgive the delusion of being loaded.

Of course, just accepting the information is not quite adequate to make countless plots. Make sure you have manipulated your information in such a way that the imagining shows reason and can be comprehended. Don't be scared to do alterations to your array shape and combine arrays.

When you continue to move on and you begin to work with vector arenas or information supplies, you may want to check out the succeeding functions:

ax.violinplot()	Violinplot
ax.streamplot()	2D vector fields
ax.boxplot()	Boxplot
ax.quiver()	2D field of arrows
ax.hist()	Histogram
ax.arrow()	Arrow 2D vector fields

Now, of course, you possibly won't use all of the purposes that are logged in these charts. It truly rests on your information and the reason for using them. If you are completely new to information science, you may want to look at the arithmetical plotting measures first!

Equally, when you work with 2-D or n-D information, you may also find yourself in the necessity of some more liberal plotting measures, such as:

ax.clabel()	Labeled contour plot
ax.pcolor()	Pseudocolor plot
ax.contourf()	Filled contour plot
ax.pcolormesh()	Pseudocolor plot
ax.contour()	Contour plot

Note that sketch plots are employed to discover the possible association amongst 3 variables. Just like sketch plots, mock color plots can be employed for this motive, since they are an external plot as shown above. Of course, these are not all the functions that you can employ to plot your information.

If you are employing images or 2D data, for instance, you may also want to look at imshow() to display imageries in your subplots.

➢ **PyPlot Customization**

Inquiries about this database come from the fact that there are a lot of effects that you can do to make your plots personal and make sure that they are exceptional. Besides regulating the colors, you also have the choice to do modification indicators, linewidths, and line styles, legends, add text, and annotations, and swap the bounds and plan of your plots.

It is exactly the fact that there is an endless range of choices when it comes to these plots that make it problematic to set out some things that you need to know when you begin learning.

Always remember all of the codes illustrated all throughout this book for example and a guide. Likewise, remember that there are numerous responses for one problem and that you learn most of this stuff when you're getting your hands dirty with the database itself and when you run into dilemmas. You will see some of the most mutual inquiries and answers in this section.

➢ **Axes Deletion**

If you ever want to eliminate axes form your plot, you can employ <u>delaxes()</u> to eliminate and bring up-to-date the current axes:

Script.py	IPython shell	Plot
1.# bring in `pyplot` from `matplotlib` 2.bring in numpy as np 3.bring in matplotlib.pyplot as plt numpy as np 4. 5.# Reset the plot 6.sha = plt.shape() 7.ax2 = sha.add_subshape(131) 8.ax3= sha.add_subshape(132) 9.ax4 = sha.add_subshape(133) 10. 11.# Plot the information 12.ax1.bar([1,2,3],[3,4,5]) 13.ax2.barh([0.5,1,2.5], [0,1,2]) 14.ax2.axhline(0.45) 15.ax1.axvline(0.65) 16.ax3.scatter(np.rowgap(1, 2, 6), np.rowgap(1, 6, 6)) 17. 18.# Erase `ax3` 19.fig.delaxes(ax3) 20. 21.# Display the plot 22.plt.show()	In [1] :	

Note that you can reinstate an erased axis by totaling fig.add_axes(ax) after fig.delaxes(ax3).

➢ Removing the Legend from the Plot

There are several ways to answer this inquiry, but characteristically, it all comes back to the option that you can offer a legend():

- You can stipulate the loc or location option so that your legend doesn't fall in the Axes or subplot area.

- Otherwise, you can also add the bbox_to_anchor option to your purpose and accept a tuple with the direction in which you want to put the legend. In this case, the box is put in the upper right corner of the plotting area: ax. Legend(bbox_to_anchor=(1.1, 1.05)).

➢ Setting Plot Heading and Axes Labels

To modify your plot title and axes tags, you can follow one of the succeeding methods depending on which you want to make use of:

- The simplest way to set these things right is by employing ax.set(title="A title", xlabel="x", ylabel="y") or ax.set_xlim(), ax.set_ylim() or ax.set_title().

- If you want to work with the shape, you may likewise resort to fig.suptitle() to add a heading to your plot.

- If you are making use of the evasion settings that the database has to offer, you may want to employ plt.title(), plt.xlabel(), plt.ylabel().

- Describe your design sheet or switch the evasion matplotlibrc settings

➢ Fixing the Plot Layout

One thing you need to think about when you are employing subplots to shape up your plot is the tight-layout purpose, which will assist you to make sure that the plots fit together well in your shape. You preferably call it after you have plotted your information and modified your plot. That is before youcall plt.show() that you should employ plt.tight_layout().

Moreover, you may as well be fascinated to employ subplots_adjust(), which permits you to actually set the thickness and build for unqualified space amongst subplots, and likewise, fix the left and right sides and the top and bottom of the subplots.

➢ **Saving, Displaying and Finalizing Your Plot**

When you have completed all the essential customizations, you will want to display your plot because, as you have observed from working in the terminal, you just get to see that an item has been made, but you never see when the good plot changes every time when you make your changes. In the 1st illustration of this lesson, this was indirectly done.

Do you recall? It was this code:

Script.py	IPython Shell	Plot

#bring in the essential database and units
Bring in numpy
Bring in matplotlib.pyplot as plt
Bring in numpy as np
# Make information 	
x = np.rowgap(1,21, 211)
	In [1] :	

# Plot the information 	
plt.plot(x, x, label='linear')
 	
# Enhance a legend 	
plt.legend()
 	
# Show the plot 	
plt.show()		

The line plt.show() says that you want to view the plot. If you do this line, you will see a window popping up. And you will see if its appearances are what you had pictured in your head!

But hold on a second, this is where your questions start to come up. How can I save this and preserve this copy, and if it's not to your taste, can you empty the copy so that you can start a new? The next topic will go over these inquiries.

➢ **Saving An Image File**

For a png file, you make use of plt.savefig(). This can be done without trying to save an image file. With this, the only option you have to accept in this purpose is the file term, like in this illustration:

Save Figure

plt.savefig("foo.png")

Save Clear Figure

plt.savefig("foo.png", clear=True)

By just performing this line of the cryptogram, you will save the plot that you have completed to a copy file as another way of displaying it.

➢ Saving to a Pdf File

To reserve numerous Charts/plots to a pdf file, you need to use the pdf appendage, which you can just import:

```
# Import PdfPages

from matplotlib.appendages.appendages_pdf import PdfPages


# Reset the pdf file

pp = PdfPages('multipage.pdf')


# Save the character to the file

pp.savefig()


# Secure the file

pp.close()
```

➢ Cla(), Clf() or Close(): When should you use them?

When you are finally equipped with the review of your plot, it's time to move on with something else (conceivably with an additional plot!). When you are working with this information imagining collection for the 1st time, it might be bizarre at the beginning because you can, of course, close down the GUI damage that appears. However, that's naturally not the way you want to grip things, because it does not continuously work as well when you are working on numerous things at a time.

You must tell Matplotlib to shut down the plot that you have been working on so that you can move on. 3 functions will come in handy once you are at this point:

- plt.clf() to clear-out the whole figure,
- Employ plt.cla() to clear-out an axis, and
- plt.close() to close-out a pain that has popped up to show you your plot.

➢ ggplot2 Style

Matplotlib also gives you the selection to place the design of the plots to ggplot for your R fan. You can simply do this by putting in the following cryptogram:

```
# Import `pyplot`
import matplotlib.pyplot as plt

# Set the style to `ggplot`
plt.style.use("ggplot")
```

➢ RC

"RC" is typically for the preparation of files that typically end in RC. It originates from the drill of having configs as executables. They are reluctantly run and configure settings, for instance. Matplotlib has such an rc file to which you can make changes statically.

To actively make modifications to evasions in RC settings, you can use the rcParams variable:

Script.py	IPython Shell	Plot
1.# bring in the essential databases and units 2. bring in matplotlib as mpl	In [1] :	

```
3 bring in numpy as np.

4.bring int matplotlib.pyplot as plt
5.
6.# Uncomment subsequent line to
see the effect
7.#mpl.rcParams['lines.linewidth']   =
5
8.
9.# Make the information
10.x = np.rowgap(1, 21, 211)
11.
12.# chartt the information
13.plt.plot(x, x, label='linear')
14.
15.# Enhance a legend
16.plt.legend()
17.
18.# Display the plot
19.plt.show()
```

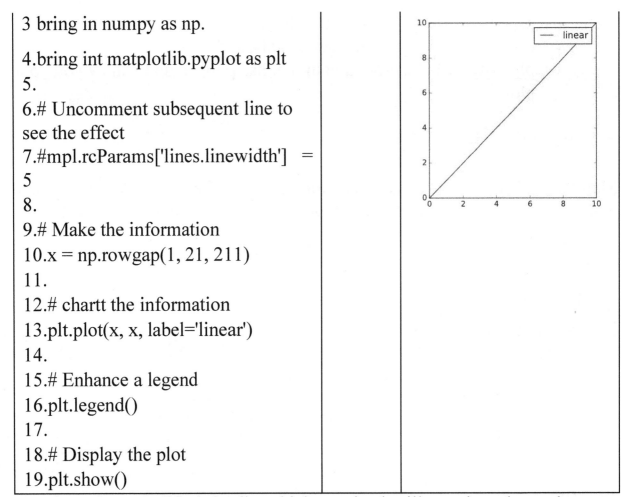

You have just modified the line thickness in the illustration above, but you can likewise do alterations to line thickness, figure size and dpi, axes, color and style, axis and grid properties, text and font properties, etc

If you want to work more slowly, you should know that you havea matplotlibrcconfiguration file, which you can employ to modify all sorts of assets (just like you did above with the line thickness parameter). If you want to search for this exact file, you can just run the following:

import matplotlib

matplotlib.matplotlib_fname()

Now, you can pull up the file and begin to play with the settings!

CHAPTER 6:

Jupyter & IPython

To completely comprehend what the Jupyter database is and how it varies from IPython, it may be stimulating to read a little bit more about how these fit into the past and the present of database usage.

➢ MATLAB, Mathematica & Maple: The Start of Database

MATLAB was unveiled by The MathWorks, and originated by Steve Bangert, Jack Little, and Cleve Moler, in the middle of the 1980s.

Thinking about the late 1980s, 1987 to be precise, this is when Theodore Gray began operating on what was to be the Mathematica database presentation layers. One year later, it was unleashed to the community. The Graphical User Interface permitted for the cooperative formation and editing of database forms that held printed database cryptogram, arranged manuscript, and a lot of different topographies such as charts text samples, arithmetic, tables, Graphical User Interface devices, and resonances. Standard word allowance abilities were there, such as actual bilingual spell inspection.

Thinking about how these databases were prearranged, you realize right away that they relied on a pyramiding of compartments that permitted for the silhouetting and dividing of forms, which you now also find in Jupyter databases.

Maple presented its first notebook-style GUI in the late 1980s. It was integrated with form 4.3 for the Macintosh. Forms of the fresh line for X11 and Windows shadowed in 1990. These initial databases stimulated and set the basics for others to grow and what would later be named "data science notebooks".

➢ Jupyter an IPython Notebook

There was an effort at structuring a database scheme with Wx, a gadget full of database tools and collections for making graphical user interfaces (GUIs) for cross-platform apps around 2005. Two Summer of Code pupils from Google operated on the example under two famous writers. Afterward, more effort was put forth on working with this major problem. It was less of a database scheme example than a clear out-of-the-core IPython cryptogram. It was also those clear-outs that aided to brand a clean notebook system.

The 2nd example for IPython was built in the summer of 2006 by Min Ragan-Kelley and counseled by Brian Granger. It was internet-based and hadan SQL database attachment, but work was stopped because the applicationof it eventually showed to be too complex with internet skills of the day.

The 3rd example of the IPython notebook created in October 2010 and was completed by a 3rd party on a couple-day hack. Lastly, as of 2011, Brian Granger was operating full time on the example of the internet notebook, originating on the work that he did in 2010 where he shaped the IPython kernel foundation and communication obligation with Fernando Pérez and PyZMQ with Min Ragan Kelley.

Project Jupyter began as a spinoff plan from IPython in 2014. The previous release of IPython before the split held a collaborative shell, the notebook server, the Qt console, and a solitary source. The plan was large, with instruments that were increasingly becoming more and more clear plans that occurred to narrate to a similar plan.

The scope of the plan was not the only goal why Project Jupyter was in progress. From 2011 to 2014, the IPython notebook began to work with other software idioms. The 1st one to come about was Julia, and then later the R. The fact that the IPython notebook, which was indirectly why the notebook was exclusively Python grounded, was likewise employed with kernels of other software idioms such as Julia and R.

➤ **Jupyter or IPython?**

The development of the plan and the resulting "Big Split" are the basics of comprehending the true modifications between them. But, as they are forever linked, you will irregularly find yourself skeptical about what is part of what.

Running the Jupyter Database

To use Jupyter, you need to download it because it is not included in Python. It is a separate database. The Python idiom can be downloaded in numerous ways. Two of them will emphasize just for the tenacities of downloading this Notebook. It is likewise hypothetical that you are employing the **Python 3 version**.

➢ **Installing**

pip is an accessible Python tool that suits you. To download this database, you can employ this:

$ pip install jupyter

The following is a widespread delivery of Python, and it's called Anaconda, which we have correspondingly covered earlier in this book. This Notebook has its individual downloader tool named **conda,** for short, which can be employed for downloading a 3rd contributor database. Nevertheless, this database comes with numerous practical collections pre-downloaded, including the Jupyter database, so you do not truly need to do anything else but download this one.

➢ **Starting**

Now that Jupyter is downloaded, let's begin to learn how to employ it. Employ something like your Doc file, to begin with, and generate an additional file and name it Sketchbook or something different that is simple to recollect.

After employing this, go to that place in your device and load the following command:

$ jupyter notebook

You should see the following:

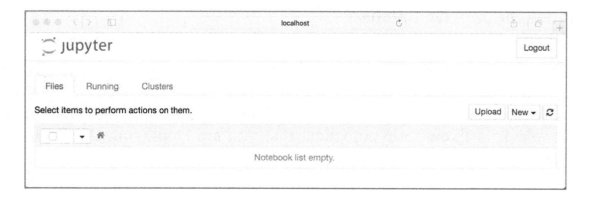

At this point, the command is not running; you are just using the server. Generating a Notebook comes next!

➤ **Generating**

Since you have covered this step, you would possibly want to learn how to generate a sketchbook file.

Assuming you selected Python 3, look on the higher right corner and click the refresh button. A list of selections will be shown then.

Your webpage should load like this:

➢ Identifying

With the Sketchbook open, look at the top of the sheet. You should see the word Untitled in bold. This is where you can change the heading. So, with it open, let's place our cursor over the heading and give it a left tap. Since this heading isn't expressing our project clearly, we will take some time to modify it.

After we have clicked the button, we will now see an in-browser exchange labeled Retitle or Rename Sketchbook. In here, we will call this Sketchbook/Notebook, Hello Jupyter.

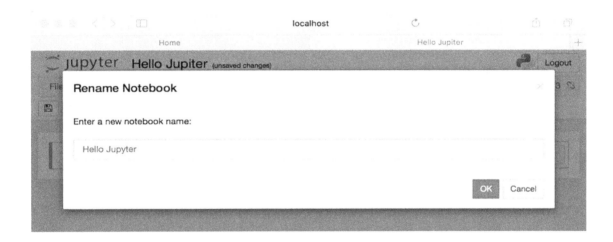

➢ Compartment Running

A sketchbook's compartment always opens to an employing cryptogramevery time you produce one. That compartment employs the core that you selected once you've begun your sketchbook.

Now that Python 3 is started as your core, you can begin to write a cryptogram in your cells. To run this cryptogram, you can use R, RStudio, or Shiny, for instance, to make it interactive.

Therefore, to check that things are going the way they should, some cryptograms can be added to the cells. You can also try to handle its features.

Let's now try to put into the cell the following cryptogram.

copy('Hello Jupyter!')

When you handle a compartment, it means that the substances of the compartment can be completed. Tap the run button once you have chosen a compartment. It's the one in the middle that resembles a play. If you find it easier, you can press Shift+Enter on your keyboard if you are using Windows and Command +Enter if you are using Mac.

Once the cryptogram is running, the output should look like this:

If you consume numerous compartments in your Sketchbook, and you use the compartments in chronological order, you can divide your variables and bring them in from the other compartments. This keeps it simple to isolate out your cryptogram into rational portions without requiring reimporting collections or reconstructing adjustable or purposes in each compartment.

When you are using a compartment, you will perceive that there are some 4-sided brackets near the term on the left adjacent to the compartment. The 4-sided brackets will automatically seal with a sum that tells the series that you have run the compartments. For instance, if you exposed a fresh Sketchbook and started the 1st compartment at the top of the Sketchbook, the 4-sided brackets will plug in the sum 1.

➢ **Set of choices**

The Jupyter has numerous choices at the top of the Sketchbook that can be employed to collaborate with your Sketchbook. Below is a short directory of the present choices:

- *Help*
- *File*
- *Cell*
- *Edit*
- *Widgets*
- *Kernel*
- *Insert*
- *View*

Now, let's go over these menus 1 by 1. This section will not go into full aspect for each option, but it will emphasis briefly on matters that are distinctive to the Sketchbook/Notebook app.

The first one is the Edit menu. You can copy, paste, and cut compartments. This choice is also where you would go if you are required a cell to merge, split, or delete. Rearranging compartments are also done here.

The Help menu, which does basically what the names say, does help. This is where you go to learn about the Sketchbook, control shortcuts, and lots of other important features and topics.

The File menu. It can generate new Sketchbook or open past programs. This is also where you would want to go to rename a Sketchbook. The most important set of items is the Save and Spot check choices. This permits youto generate a spot check that you can go back to if you needed.

The Cell menu permits you to modify a cell's category, although the toolbar is mostly used for that. Also, in the cell menu, you can move a cell up or down, or even run multiple cells.

The View menu is very valuable for changing the appearances of the heading and controls. You can also change the Line Numbers inside the cells to on or off. You can also mess around the toolbar of the cell.

The other useful characteristic in this set of choices is the ability to erase a compartment's production. Say you had plans to share your project with others, you would first want to get rid of the other productions you were working on, especially if some of it is private, in order for the cells to be run by others as well.

The Kernel cell is used to run the kernel that works in the back. You can rewire it, resume the kernel, closed it down, or even swap which kernel your Notebook is employing.

The Insert menu has a simple job, which is just inserting cells above or below the presently designated cell.

Widgets are essentially JS that can be added to the cells so that you can make lively content. The Widgets' set of choices is mainly for saving and clearing the widget state.

You will perhaps not be operating with the Kernel as much, but there will be periods when you are repairing a sketchbook that you will find you need to resume the Kernel. If that occurs, this is where you would go.

➤ Starting Terminals

Jupyter Notebook also permits you to begin more than just one Notebook. You can produce a folder, transcript file, or a Terminal in your browser.

The Terminal is possibly the greatest part of the group. It permits you to run any shell series that you may need to and run bash, Powershell, and more in your browser because it makes the operative schemes terminal to run continuously in the browser.

Running

Also situated on the home-based sheet of your server are two other important tags namely the Clusters and Running.

The Running tag lets you know the Sketchbook and Stations you are using. When you need to close out your server, this is very valuable, but be sure that you have kept all your information. Luckily, Sketchbook automatically-saves frequently. This aspect is great to be able to see what's running.

There is one more enjoyable thing about this tag. It's that you can browse your running apps and shut down what you don't need there.

➢ Rich Content

When it comes to content, Jupyter is good in helping you add to its cells rich content. In this segment, we will go over Code and Markdown and some of the effects you can apply to your cells.

Types of Cells

There are 4 cell categories in this Notebook. They are Code, Raw Nbconvert, Heading, and Markdown. Although in Python 3.6, there are only three. They are Code, Raw, and Markdown.

The Heading cell section is not reinforced anymore. In its place, the Markdown should be employed to your entire Headings.

When the Nbconvert tool is employed, you can formulate individually the cell group, Raw Nbconvert, for practices. Basically, when you change from a Sketchbook to another set-up, you can arrange this precisely in any way you prefer, because you are permitted to order a command using this tool.

The Markdown and the Code cell groups are the major functions that can be employed. You will use the Code when you want to configure sums, and the Markdown when you want to bring up images or charts of different sorts.

Text Styling

Markdown is supplied by Jupyter Sketchbook. It is a superset of Syntax and HTML. In this lesson, we will go over Markdown and some of the fundamentals of what you can finish with it.

Open a new cell and make sure you choose Markdown, otherwise, it will not work the same. Next, add the following code in the cell:

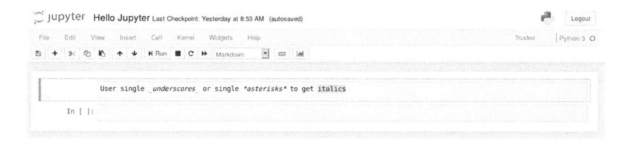

Once you have added your information and ran the cell, it should look like this in italics:

If bold is what you like for your typescripts, use a double asterisk or underscore.

Using Headings

Making headings in Markdown are easy to do. Just type in what you want it to say and employ pound symbol at the beginning. The more pound symbols you employ, the more small-scale the heading. Next, just hit run or shift + enter. Jupyter Sketchbook will result as shown below:

Then, when you run the cell, you will come up with a well-arranged heading:

Creating Lists

Generating a list (bullet points) is easy. You do this by adding additional splashes, asterisk, or signs. Check out this illustration:

Syntax and Code Highlighting

Markdown can be used in a cryptogram sample that you do not want your kernel to operate. You can use backticks to surround the cryptogram when it comes to inline cryptogram highlighting. The three-layered backticks and others can be employed if you prefer to place a cryptogram to stipulate the software idiom:

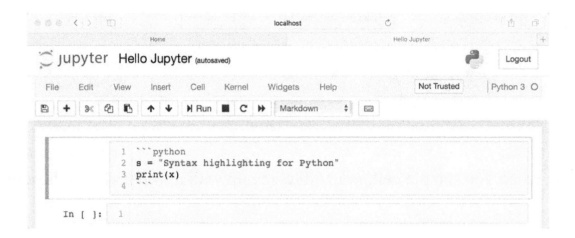

> **Sketchbook Spreading**

When using Jupyter Sketchbooks, you must remember that your outcomes will need to be shared with non-theoretical people, especially if you aretaking courses with the beginner programmers. In order for them to easily understand, you need to spread or change the Sketchbook to one of thefollowing set-ups by employing the Nbconvert tool originating from theJupyter Sketchbook.

- HTML
- LaTeX
- Reveal JS
- PDF
- Markdown
- Executable script
- ReStructured Text

The nbconvert tool employs Jinja designs to change your Sketchbook files (.ipynb), so they can be used by other set-ups.

Python has also completed a design machine called Jinja. Also, remember that Tex and Pandoc are where nbconvert rely upon so that it can spread to all the exceeding set-ups. Take note that the spread groups may not function if you do not have at least one of these.

nbconvert

The nbconvert demand doesn't use very many parameters, which makes studying how to employ it simpler. Expose a terminal and steer towards a file that holds the Notebook you demand to convert. This uncomplicated conversion demand can be shown as follows:

$ jupyter nbconvert <input

notebook> --to <output format>

Example Usage

Imagine that there is a Sketchbook called py_examples.ipynb and you must change it to a Portable Document Format. You can to that by employing this demand:

```
$ jupyter nbconvert py_examples.ipynb --to pdf
```

You ought to see some production that tells you approximately what the change processed. When you apply this demand, nbconvert will show caution and mistakes if there are any. Considering things go as planned, there is the file py_examples.pdf in your binder.

There is no difference in the procedures in the other folder groups. You just choose what group the nbconvert should be changed to (HTML, Markdown, PDF, and so on).

Use the Menu

Selecting the Download as a selection will help you to relocate your presently running Sketchbook by going to the File menu.

Doing this permits you to install all the set-ups that nbconvert bears. It is recommended that you learn to use nbconvert to transfer numerous Sketchbooks at once, which is roughly what the set of choices doesn't bear.

The advantage is that you don't have to learn it if you don't choose to.

Extensions for Notebook

Although Jupyter Notebooks consume loads of serviceability constructed within, you can always add new serviceability through additions. Jupyter supports 4 categories of additions:

- Kernel
- Sketchbook
- IPython kernel
- Sketchbook server

This section will thoughtfully emphasize on Sketchbook additions.

Allowances

A Sketchbook allowance (sballowance) is a JS component that you can pack into the many interpretations in the frontend of Sketchbook. Your allowance can also be inscribed if you have access to JS. An allowance can ingress the Jupyter JS API and the sheet's DOM.

Getting Allowances

You can employ Google or look around for Jupyter Sketchbook allowances. There are fairly a lot of them out there. The greatest widespread allowance groups are named **jupyter_contrib_sballowances.** This is an assortment of allowances that are produced and downloaded with pip.

Installing Them

Python's pip tool is used to download most Jupyter Notebook expansions, but sometimes, you will run into a problem. If your discovery is an expansion that cannot be downloaded with pip at that time, you will possibly have to employ the following demand:

$ jupyter nb expansion install EXPANSION_TITLE

This solely downloads the allowance but doesn't bring it to life. You must permit an allowance later when downloading it by running the following:

$ jupyter nb expansion enable EXPANSION_TITLE

In order for you to see the expansions, the Sketchbook kernel should be rebooted.

Jupyter SBExpansions Design Systems is a great meta expansion that is surely worth acquiring for handling other expansions. It permits you to allow and restrict your expansions from inside the Jupyter Sketchbook operator border and also demonstrate all the presently downloaded expansions.

Conclusion

Thank you for making it to the end of Machine Learning with Python: The Complete Beginner's Guide to Understand Machine Learning with Python from Beginner to Expert. I know that it seemed like there was no end, with all of the different types of Algorithms, Decision Trees, Pandas; Notations with its multiplication, exponents and square roots, logarithms, and so much more.

But hey! At least you found out that Decision Trees are not trees, and Pandas are not real-life Pandas!

Hopefully, this book was very informative to you and was able to provide you with all the step-by-step information that you need to play around with Machine Learning and Python. One good thing to know is that if you've enjoyed this book, it doesn't mean there is no more Python to learn. Venture out and expand your horizons. You can even buy another monitor so you can have a wider space to work on.

The next step in your process of learning Machine Learning with Python is for you to learn how to use a machine learning tool so that you can work out any problem with ease. You should also learn and practice datasets as much as possible. Then, it should be easy for you to transition into the details and theories of the Machine Learning Algorithms in this book. If you still find that you need a little help getting started, you can always join a class for beginners. Most beginner classes start with the basics of problem-solving and estimating probability distribution. So, if your good at problem-solving, and are more of a hands-on person, these classes will work great for you. Try out learning more on AI (Artificial Intelligence) while you're at it. This is a truly interesting topic to learn.

But, if after all of this you are still having problems learning machine learning, you do not have to worry. You can always re-read this book as long as you want until you have fully understood the topic. You can also keep on practicing and employing the techniques provided in this book until you get the hang of coding a program, especially in Python.

There is no need to rush. You can take all the time in the world. What's more important is that you truly understand what Machine Learning with Python is and you will eventually succeed in creating your own program.

Python for Data Analysis

The Guide to Learn How to Use Python for Data Analysis

Steve Blair

Introduction

Congratulations on purchasing *Python Analysis* and thank you for doing so.There are plenty of books on this subject on the market, thanks again for choosing this one! Every effort was made to ensure it is full of as much useful information as possible, please enjoy!

Python Development Frameworks

CWI: The Centrumvoor Wiskunde Informatica Amsterdam is the cradle of the Python language that is developing as a scripting language for the Amoeba project. As part of the CWI, the first official version of Python is published (0.9.0) in February 1991. Version 1.0 is also published in this structure.

NCRI: The Corporation for National Research Initiatives in Reston, Virginia is the second place in which the Python language developed, from 1995.

BeOpen: After the release of version 1.6 in 2000, the Python development team changed the base and created the PythonLabs team from BeOpen with Python version 2.0.

Python Software Foundation: This non-profit association was created in 2001. It hosted the development of the Python language from version 2.1. She is also at the origin of the license of use of the language; the Python Software Foundation Licence. In 2008, the Python development team decided to release version 3.0, which is not backward compatible with version 2.

The Python Software Foundation always hosts the source code of the language, many documentations, the package directory (PyPi) and managesthe license use.

It is clear as to what Python has sought during all the first years of development and that its focus on data processing has never been central inits development during these thirty years.

CHAPTER 1:

Python, Its Origins and Its Environment

1.1 The Origins and Evolution of Language

Since its inception, Python has been designed to make available to the largest number, a simple and intuitive development tool for creating scripts.

1.2 The Meeting between Python and Data Science

The emergence of data science is recent, and these new uses of data have often had difficulty finding suitable tools. Indeed, the data scientist must be a good developer while remaining a good data analyst. He has had to opt for a tool that would combine this demand with more and more strong development and automation (all the more so with the arrival of artificial intelligence and connected objects), with the need for a toolbox suitable for data applications.

Many avenues have been explored, in particular with the software R which continues to be a reference in data science but that could seem too oriented towards statistics for more developmentally oriented data scientists.

1.3 History, Origins and Evolution: From Birth To Version 3.717

Many other tools for setting up data science processes have been developed (most proprietors such as Matlab or SAS), but it turns out that Python (which combines powerful language and extremely simple) has managed to draw its pin.

The first real advance was the creation of NumPy (Numerical Python) package, which is still today the cornerstone of the Python ecosystem for datascience. On the other hand, setting up data-driven Python environments with Anaconda has also enabled a whole community to come together around Python and data. Finally, IPython and its notebooks (now Jupyter) have completed the ecosystem to provide data scientists with a very simple language but one which is extremely comprehensive for data science. This global environment resulted in the development of many packages and APIs, which today make Python the best tool to automate data science treatments.

The Current Evolution

In recent years, Python has taken an extremely important place in the world of data processing. While in the early 2010s, it seemed clear that in the world of open-source data processing tools, the software R was going to carve out the lion's share, a significant change has taken place since a few years. The emergence of Python as a language related to data science, machine learning, deep learning, and artificial intelligence is extremely fast.

Grace, an extremely active community under the PyData banner and frequent and numerous events (PyCon, PyData, JupyterCon, SciPyCon ...), language development took an unexpected turn. While we could hear in 2015 developers say that from the point of view of machine learning the development of Python was modeled on that of R with a few months late. Today, it is R who begins to model his developments in the field of machine learning, deep learning, and big data, on packages developed in Python. In 2018, KDnuggets, an influential blog in the world of data science, even surveyed thousands of data scientists around the world who, for the firsttime, and showed more users of Python than of R.

The Python adventure in data science is therefore recent but only because it is a language that adapts perfectly to the approach led by a data scientist, which would be: "better in programming than a statistician and better in statistics than a developer. "

1.4 The Future of Python

The near future of Python is above all the abandonment of version 2 and the general version 3. The other big current development concerns the use of interactive interfaces with Python as a communication language with more and more advanced APIs. We'll talk a little bit further about Jupyter's widgets that allow you to develop interactively and build interfaces in a few lines.

Python is increasingly used as a language to communicate with other environments. So Python can communicate with Apache Spark through PySpark medium, or with deep learning ecosystems such as TensorFlow. Calculations are no longer done in the Python engine but much more in engine devices using distributed infrastructures or GPU-based computations (Graphical Process Units). This trend is only beginning with the massification of data and requests for real-time treatments are ever more common.

Python can not answer these challenges alone but, combined with other tools, it allows the data scientist to manage the entire ecosystem of data processing, be it big, small, smart ...

1.5 Python Vs R Vs. The Rest of The World

If you read this book, you must have heard about other tools in data science. Today we find an extremely developed ecosystem in this domain with languages such as R and Python but also more software like Dataiku DSS, IBM-SPSS Modeler, Enterprise Miner SAS, Azure machine learning from Microsoft ... As a data scientist, you can be brought to cross some of these tools in your missions. It is therefore important to understand where everyone's strength lies.

We focus here on Python and its use by data scientists. So why is Python gaining ground on the competition?

In recent years, the global trend has shifted towards more code in the processing process and Python responds perfectly to this request. Thus, the data scientist tools are increasingly different from those of the BI analyst (business intelligence) which are more and more intuitive. In this context, two open-source tools take the lead: Python and R.

Regarding proprietary tools, a trend is becoming widespread. This is the use of languages such as Python or R inside these tools as soon as we need to perform complex operations. So Dataiku DSS, RapidMiner or KNIME integrate modules to develop in Python or R. Your skills in Python will, therefore, be valued as part of the use of these tools.

R

R and Python are today the indispensable bases of the data scientist. Furthermore, the rapid evolution of both languages leads to a form of healthy competition making them more and more complete for data processing. However, there are some notable differences that will guide your choices of the language decision to use for a project.

R is based on a language created for statisticians by statisticians, it is first and foremost on a descriptive and data modeling approach. The R outputs are outputs worthy of "classic" statistical software with many details. Python is not based on this approach, it's a language of programming to automate processes by just looking to calculate the bare minimum. As part of the current approaches to data application science, Python is more adapted to other needs than R.

On the other hand, Python is an extremely simple programming language based on a very readable syntax. Its understanding by many users is facilitated, which allows for better interaction between the different professions related to information systems (managers, developers, data scientists, data engineers ...).

To summarize, Python is the language of automation that integrates perfectly within a broader IT service framework and which adapts to the contexts of artificial intelligence (unstructured data, complex environments). It stays nevertheless lower than R for a statistician looking for statistical software.

R and Python are complementary today and will be very necessary for you frequently for your treatments.

Python's license is a "classic" free license, it allows you to reuse source code, modify it, market it, and to make all use without obligation to open your code. This is the type of license conventionally used for programming languages. All the Python ecosystem for data is based on this license. On the other hand, R is based on a more restrictive license, this is the GPL v3 license. This one gives responsibilities to the development community.

Indeed, if you use source code R and modify it to distribute it, you will be forced to make this code accessible to users (open source). Going again further, this license is "contaminating", that is, if you embed code licensed to your code, your code is licensed and must be open source. This point can frighten some developers who sometimes turn to Python. This difference between the two languages that are R and Python translates a difference of language development between the two communities. R developers are more in an idea to "force" advanced users to contribute to the project and Python developers are betting on a very wide use of the language that draws more contributions for language development.

1.6 Flow Processing Tools

The other tools of data science are for the most part facilitators, so the majority of these tools are based on Dataiku, RapidMiner's DSS flow creation(KNIME, IBM-SPSS Modeler ...) using your mouse. They simplify the life ofthe users and, depending on your needs, can save you time. However, everything these tools can do can be done directly with Python and they all incorporate ways to add Python code to streams.

These tools will allow you to create analyzes, from acquisition to analysis of data in a few clicks. For example, you can go for data in different formats at a first level, check and merge these data to the next level, transform the data, cut them out and apply and validate predictive models on these data. All this is included in a single stream.

Python will be very different from this visual treatment but will be able to reproduce this type of stream as a code. Moreover, as soon as bricks of your treatments become more complex, the use of Python inside each brick becomes necessary.

1.7 SAS

We will dwell here on a specific point because it concerns many users in the professional world. For some time now, many companies decided to migrate their infrastructures from SAS history to new languages (R and Python). It may be helpful to clarify a few points about this.

SAS is a proprietary software specialized in data processing. It accumulates nearly forty years of experience in this field and can not be replaced in a simple way. Companies have often relied on this tool for the processing of their data. Nevertheless, moving to a tool like Python can be justified for several reasons:

From an economic point of view: this is often the first reason given. In fact, SAS licenses are very expensive. But the change will also be expensive, it requires changing the ways of working and greater support for infrastructure than before.

From a technological point of view: this is the most important point. The transition to Python will provide access to much more powerful machine learning, deep learning, and unstructured data processing methods than with SAS.

It should be kept in mind that this change will lead to a number of advantages. Mainly the fact that Python is a language that will load the datain memory in your machine while SAS was using an intermediate system of tables stored on physical memory. You will need to change your study and gothrough more sophisticated queries to your databases. Then, the processing and analyzing process will be largely simplified.

Python will, therefore, provide you with significant flexibility but you will have to modify your approach to data management and code development with Python.

1.8 Other Languages

We compared Python to data science tools but another interestingcomparison can be being compared to other programming languages. Today many languages are available. We can cite so many from the data universe: Julia, MatLab, C / C ++, Scala. These languages all have their specificities, we can classify them into two categories:

Interpreted languages such as MatLab, Julia, and Scala are credible alternatives to Python in a data science-oriented framework.

1.9 How to Develop In Python?

Compiled languages such as C, C ++, Java that fall into another category and are aimed at more experienced developers. In some cases, they are more efficient than Python but they do not have a package and API environment as developed as Python.

1.10 How to Develop In Python?

This is a recurring question: "what software to use to code in Python? " The answer is not simple and we must first deconstruct some prejudices. Python is not a software, it's a programming language! So if you want to code in Python, just install it, launch a command terminal and type the word python. You can start coding. Of course, it is not

What you will do on a daily basis. The easiest way to get started with Python is to install Anaconda (Http: //www.anaconda.com). This is a multi-platform development environment form (Linux, Mac, Windows), integrating a Python interpreter but also have multiple features, including the IPython interpreter, Spyder IDE, Jupyter notebooks but also hundreds of packages to start quickly to code in Python. If you start your trip with Python, I can only advise you to leave with Anaconda. I will come back in detail about the installation procedures of these different components.

Another fundamental point: when we do Python, we develop computer programs. Be your goal the analysis of a small base of data or building a complex program of artificial intelligence, a number of questions related to the informatics development need to be ticked. These points are not specific to Python but are central to your working process as a data scientist.

Developing tools in Python is a simplified development process that allows real agility in the development but still requires some fundamental principles that will fit into the specific framework of data science.

The process of dealing with a problem in data science goes through a certain number of steps:

1. The definition of the business problem
2. The transformation of the business problem into a data science problem
3. Research and discovery of data sources
4. Data preparation and formatting
5. Model construction and fitting
6. Validation of the models
7. The answer to the question and the production of the models

All of these steps are central to the work process of the data scientist. The development will take place at different stages and Python will be a tool that will accompany, at best, during all these stages.

Your way of developing will depend mainly on points (1) and (7). Your process of development will depend on:

From the sponsor or the project leader: he is the one to answer. Depending on your role, your level of expertise, your expectations, you will not develop in the same way. Imagine that the problem raised by the CEO of your company, to answer this question, it will be necessary to provide tools that will be as less technical as possible, it could be a "classic" report or an interactive tool. If this question comes from a data scientist colleague, scripts or notebooks will often be sufficient to provide a satisfactory answer.

The expected deliverable: if it is a simple, one-off request for an analysis to be performed, simply develop a simple script and build a "frozen" report. On the other hand, if the expected (which is more and more the case) is an interactive tool or the production of an advanced machine learning algorithm, you will have to set up an extremely strict process of development.

To properly manage your data science project at the development level, you should keep in mind a number of points:

1. Determination of needs and objectives:

We will try to answer at this stage to a certain number of questions. What should the software do? What setting will it serve? Who will be typical users?

From the answers, the writing of specifications with the editor of the software is necessary.

2. Design and specifications:

We will then go into the details of user expectations. What are the features of the software? With which interface?

It is often at this stage that the appropriate programming language is chosen. It can be a combination of language (for the front, the back ...).

3. Programming:

This is the part that interests us in this book but it is not the most important part of the overall process. If the previous steps are poorly conducted, thenwe will not be able to achieve the expected results.

4. Tests:

Code always has bugs! Whether coding bugs or cases that we had not planned during the coding and therefore, we must test the code. The less technical the users are, the more you have to test your code.

5. Deployment:

We do not always have the need to deploy his code elsewhere than on his computer. But a lot of data science projects involve moving in production of developed algorithms. This part is critical and makes it necessary to have an extremely attentive system audit.

6. Maintenance:

This is a part often left aside by non-developers but it is absolutely central. Computer code is never perfect, so you have to maintain your code not only to correct problems but also to evolve the tool. The best-known versioning tool is called Git.

All of these steps must be kept in mind by the data scientist during the development of his tools in Python or in any language.

1.11 Tools for Encoding Python

When I hear about Python, one of the first questions I am asked is what environment I use every day. Unlike some languages (I think in the first place to R and RStudio), Python does not have an environment reference. So to answer the question, I use IPython as an interpreter, Anaconda to manage my environments and my packages, Spyder, PyCharm, Atom, Sublime, Jupyter Lab and the Jupyter notebooks to code.

To familiarize yourself with these environments, we will explore the main advantages.

Python and PyPi

Python is, of course, essential to code in Python. It is provided by Python

Software Foundation (PSF) as two versions: Python 2 and Python 3. We will come back in detail about the differences between these two versions in the following chapter. Python is installed by default on Macs and machines running on Linux (pay attention often in version 2). However, I advise you to install a version that will allow you to work directly in a data-oriented framework science. For this, the simplest solution is the use of Anaconda.

If you use your terminal (command terminal), to code in Python, you just have to enter the word python. This simplified command line allows you to submit scripts in the * .py format but also to code in a simple way. This approach is however neglected in favor of more advanced tools.

Python in its classic version is hosted by the site of the PSF on which you find all the information about the language and the executables to install it. In addition, you will find an impressive amount of documentation for perfecting yourself in Python at the following address:

https://www.Python.org/

This site is linked to the PyPi directory (https://pypi.org/) which brings together all the packages developed in Python. This extremely broad repertoire includes thousands of packages (more than 150,000 today) that are neither validated nor evaluated. They relate to all areas and not just data. This directory gives access to packages and usually refers to the GitHub site associated with the development of the project.

To install on your machine a package using the PyPi directory, you can download it but this approach is usually not suggested because you may not have all the necessary dependencies. We prefer to use the pip command from your command prompt (Linux terminal or Windows command prompt on Windows).

For example, to install NumPy, we will use:

pip install numpy

For this to work, you must have Python added to the path used by your machine. We often prefer the use of Anaconda to that of Python command and pip.

Anaconda

Anaconda is a free Python distribution that directly integrates a large number of packages (so it's no longer necessary to install them, but we can add more if necessary with the Conda package manager). Anaconda is also a company that offers solutions for the development of and setting up enterprise development environments. Anaconda is finally an environment system and a repertoire of packages geared towards data projects. Anaconda is multi-platform and allows you to work very quickly with adapted tools and the most important packages in data science.

You can download it here: https://www.anaconda.com/download/

Follow the instructions on the site and you can then launch the command prompt

Anaconda (Anaconda Prompt).

This window looks like a terminal but with a slight difference: the term (base) with the path to our repertoire. It's about the environment in which we work. The base being the root environment including all the packages that were originally installed with Anaconda as well and the ones you've beenable to add since.

Environments

An environment is a parameterization of the working ecosystem that can be exported to other machines in order to reproduce the treatments performed without having to install an environment that is too complex.

In Python, two environment management systems exist - virtual-env and Anaconda environments. We will focus on the environments of Anaconda, which proposes a simple solution to implement and, given the general use of Anaconda, which is most suitable for data science applications.

An environment in Anaconda is summarized in a .yml file that gathers all the information you need to run your programs:

- the version of Python

- packages and their dependencies

By default, when working in Anaconda, you use the environment root (base) where all available packages on your machine are accessible from yourcode. You will gradually add new packages in this environment which will make its reproducibility difficult to implement. I, therefore, advise you to set up for each project an environment in which you will only put the packages you need.

We start by checking the environments installed on the machine:

conda info --envs

Then we can create a new environment that we activate directly:

conda create --name my_env

#with Linux

source activate my_env

#under Windows

activate my_env

Once in your environment, you can add packages in the same way only in the root environment. The created environment is empty, but it can be interesting to clone an existing environment, rather than creating an empty environment. If we want to clone the environment mon_env in a mon_clone environment, we will use:

conda create --name my_clone --clone my_env

Replicate an environment

There are two approaches to replication:

You want to replicate an environment in terms of packages without specifying specific versions of operating systems, in which case we will use a .yml file that can be created using the command line:

export conda> environment.yml

Then we will load the created environment using:

conda env create -f environment.yml

You want to replicate your environment identically (a version of the packages on the same operating system). In this case, we will use a specification file that we will retrieve using:

conda list -e> spec-file.txt

In this second case, you can export this environment on a new machine, but it will have to have the same operating system:

conda create --name MyEnvironment --file spec-file.txt

You can then load scripts developed on your environment on the othermachine without any risk of compatibility issues. Anaconda today offers the best solution to manage your projects in Python.

IPython

IPython means interactive Python and simplifies the life of the developer. Indeed, IPython is presented as the Python command line but offers a lot of subtleties that will allow you to save valuable time. IPython is available in Anaconda.

The IPython Interpreter

To launch the IPython interpreter, just type the ipython command in your command line.

The main advantages of IPython are:

Automatic completion with tabulation

Access to help and source code functions through commands? and ?? after the name of the function "Magic keys" thanks to the % command

Access keys to the various calculation steps (In [], Out [])

IPython allows you to transform Python into an interactive language. Indeed, the IPython's quick command can simply retrieve commands and intermediate results.

The Specificities Of Ipython

The other specificities of IPython as an interpreter are many, to quote :

The input history.

The storage of outputs for a session with the possibility of references (Out).

Completion using tabulation for Python objects as well as for keywords and file names.

The ability to do specific actions with magic keys and actions on the operating system.

Simplified integration into other Python programs or into IDEs (development environments).

The advanced profiling system.

All these features make IPython an indispensable tool for your development. Often you will not even realize that you are using it because it is installed by default in most development IDEs, this is the case with Spyder too.

Spyder

We could talk here about PyCharm, Visual Studio or another IDE (Development environment). Your choice of IDE will depend on your habits and your preferences, try several and select the one that suits you best. We are talking about Spyder because it's a smart multi-platform solution for a user in data science. Spyder is a development environment (IDE) well suited to the development of scripts in Python for data processing.

It allows you to code and debugs your code quickly. It's based on the interpreter of IPython and displays a lot of useful information in the user interface. For R users, Spyder will remind you of Rstudio. You can launch Spyder, either from the shortcuts created or from the Anaconda prompt. Ifyou did not install Anaconda but only Python, you can install Spyder from the command prompt on your computer using the command

pip install spyder

Its interface is divided into several parts: the first part in which your Python scripts are open (left), the second part to access working directories and variables loaded into memory (top right) and the third part with an IPython interpreter in which the submitted code is interpreted (bottom right).

This simple interface will allow you to manage the majority of the developments needed in Python. In addition, Spyder offers an efficient debugger that allows you to test your code as well. The variable explorer will appeal to Rstudio regulars or Matlab to know all the variables loaded into memory.

The handling of Spyder is simple. Try to use it to familiarize yourself with its environment. The use of this IDE is well suited for users accustomed to working with Rstudio under R or having no usual IDE. If you use other IDEs frequently, it is likely that they are adapted to Python. Here are a few :

Atom

Microsoft Visual Studio

Sublime

PyCharm

Eclipse

VIM

For some time now, another new way of developing has emerged with the use of notebooks.

Jupyter Notebooks

Jupyter's notebooks appear as a new extreme solution, which is flexible and interesting to code in Python (but also in R, in Julia ...). These development environments are the ones we will focus on during this book for their capacity for sharing and learning.

What Is A Notebook?

It is a development system based on two tools:

A web browser in which you will see your code appear and in which you will develop and submit your code (prefer Firefox or Chrome to Internet Explorer).

A Python kernel that runs in a terminal on your machine. This one will submit the code you enter in the notebook.

The kernel part is not accessible but we must be careful to leave the terminal open as long as you work on a notebook in your browser. From a more technical point of view, the notebook is stored in the form of a JSON type file with a * .ipynb extension (from their old IPython notebook name). TheJupyter notebooks come from the separation in two of the IPython project: from a side with IPython and the other with Jupyter. The latter is today a very active notebook with many developments (his name comes from Julia, Python, and R).

The Jupyter notebook is a development interface that allows you to combine text (in markdown), formulas and code in the same document.

How To Install Jupyter Notebook?

Jupyter notebook is available in Anaconda, if you use it there, there is nothing to make. If you do not use Anaconda or work in an environment without Jupyter, just enter the command:

pip install jupyter

What Does A Notebook Look Like?

A Jupyter notebook looks like a simple web page in which we will be able to write:

code in Python (or another language if a kernel associated with this language is enabled)

text markdown (thanks to the markdown, we can integrate images, formulas ...)

In order to understand how they work, we will start with:

you launch Jupyter notebook from the created shortcut or from the command prompt with the command: jupyter notebook

A browser opens with the root directory. Note - By default, the selected root directory is the root directory of your user. If you want to launch yournotebook from another root directory (for example directly to the root of yourc: \ drive), you have two possibilities:

- launch a terminal or the command prompt Anaconda, place you in the directory in which you want to work and enter the command jupyter notebook.

- modify the launch parameter files of your notebook, under Windows, it is: \ .jupyter \ jupyter_notebook_con g

Once you have reached the directory in which you want to work, you just have to click on New and choose Python 3 as language. Here you will recognize the IPython command line. You then have all the IPython features directly in your browser.

The Jupyter notebook works as code cells, a cell can contain as much code as you want. Generally, we use a cell to do a series of actions resulting in the display of an intermediate result.

Attention, if you create functions or classes, their definition must be done in a cell by function/class (we cannot split the definition into several cells).

Make your notebooks even more interactive:

The Jupyter Widgets

Jupyter notebooks are equipped with new features. One of them, namely, widgets make a notebook much more interactive. There are two types of widgets, first, the ipywidgets that are related to IPython to render code interactive.

To install these ipywidgets, we use in the command prompt:

conda install -c conda-forge ipywidgets

Then, all that remains is to import into your code the widgets you need. This will allow you to build extremely interactive notebooks. You will find a full description of these widgets here:

http://ipywidgets.readthedocs.io/en/latest/index.html

The other widgets are much more advanced and will allow you to integrate more complex structures in your notebook. For example, to introduce interactive maps, we will use the ipyleaflet widget.

Just install it from Anaconda with the following code:

conda install -c conda-forge ipyleaflet

All of Jupyter's widgets are available here:

http://jupyter.org/widgets

Use Other Languages: Install New Kernels

Notebooks allow you to work in many other languages that are not Python. So, if you want to use notebooks to code in R, it's very simple. However, you can not combine the two languages in the same notebook. You will need to use two different notebooks.

So you will be able to add kernels for other languages. For R, you can just use for example R Essentials that install R and some basic packages:

conda install -cr-essentials

In this case, everything is installed in your base environment. For other languages, just get the right kernel.

Sharing and Working With Others on Notebooks

In what we've done so far, it was about launching our Python kernels in local notebooks. The interest of notebooks is to work remotely. It is very simple to create a Jupyter kernel on a remote server or in the cloud and access it directly from your machine. It is especially possible to do it directly on the cloud with Microsoft Azure or Amazon AWS. The creative process is extremely well documented and then you just need to connect to the notebook using an Internet address. Some of these services are even free provided you do not mobilize too much computing power.

When working on a remote server, the data you use must be using is accessible from this one. If you have local data, all you need to do is upload them in sftp or ftp, or make them available online (especially on GitHub).The kernels associated with Jupyter notebooks do not allow you to work at several servers based on the same data. When we have several users whoneed to connect to a server with multiple notebooks, the ideal project is the Open Source JupyterHub project.

You will be able to launch several instances of notebooks on a Linux server. This is the solution chosen by Binder to allow you to work on notebooks directly online. The installation of JupyterHub is simple and can be done quickly for a small structure. If your infrastructure is larger, access rights will have to be managed which can make setting up more complex.

Jupyterlab: The New Evolution Of Notebooks

The Jupyter project development team has been engaged for some time to set up a new working environment: the Jupyter Lab. This environment combines the power of notebooks and the ability to use multiple tools at the same time.

Like notebooks, the JupyterLab opens in your browser. It settles in submitting the order:

conda install -c conda-forge jupyterlab

And starts with the command:

jupyter lab

This interface allows you to not only launch notebooks for multiple languages but also to open consoles or any kind of files left in the browser.

In addition, creating views is a very interesting feature. If you have displayed data in your notebook, they appear in the form of output. In JupyterLab, go to the exit level and use the left mouse button to choose the option "Create a new view for Output". This output appears in a new window and remains available when you are elsewhere in your code. In addition, if you restart the display cell of this output with modifications, the view is updated.

JupyterLab is constantly evolving but today appears as a solution for open source development that is perfectly suited to the data scientist and his needs. The Jupyter project is a real step forward in the way of development.

1.12 Packages for Data Science

Python's development for data science is primarily based on reference packages to work on data while using the Python language. We will deepen these packages as we go along, but it is important to start by making a first overview. We will also detail the definition and creation of packages later.

Packages for Data Management And Numerical Computation

The two reference packages in this area are NumPy and Pandas. Without them, there is no data in Python. Even though today some packages are trying to overcome some of their faults, they remain central in the data processing. NumPy and its arrays3 allow having a well-optimized reference structure which is very easy to use. They are the basis of most other packages.

Pandas and its reference structures that are the Series and the DataFrame have allowed a real change of status for Python. From a programming language with thoughtful structures, it has moved to a language capable of competing with R and being accessible to data scientists. The methods and functions of Pandas and its structures allow users to store data having as many dimensions as necessary (a vector with a dimension, a matrix with two dimensions ...),the results that would be extremely difficult to obtain directly in Python in a single line of code.

Other packages appear today, especially with Numba or Dask which allow going to a higher level in terms of optimization with massively distributed calculation and a JIT (just in time) compilation system. Thanks to this,Python can compete with the Julia language in this niche.

Packages for Data Visualization

Visualization of data is an important step in the process of analysis for the data scientist. More or less advanced visualization tools have been developed by several members of the community. The main package is Matplotlib. It is extremely efficient in building any type of graph. We will see how much the personalization of graphics is possible with Matplotlib. In addition to this package that may seem complex to generate more advanced graphics, there are many other packages.

We will dwell on Seaborn which is itself based on Matplotlib but gives access to more "statistical" oriented and often more aesthetic graphics. Other packages are also available, especially for the visualization of interactive features. The two best-known packages for this are Bokeh and Dash.

In their most classic form, they allow building graphs using Javascript and an interactive web format. They also make it possible to build interactive data visualization applications, such as R.'s shiny package.

Packages for Machine Learning and Deep Learning

In the field of machine learning and deep learning, Python is really hitting the points. If machine learning has developed especially around a package, that package is Scikit-Learn. We will study it in detail in the rest of the book.

In recent years, a new field of high-speed data science is developing – deep learning. This deep learning uses algorithms based on deep neural networks that are complex and extremely cumbersome in computing power. TensorFlow is an environment that has developed to treat this type of model. It has a very powerful Python API. In addition, an additional silence package is often used in Python for deep learning. This is Keras whichconstitutes an extra layer in order to develop deep neural networks in a simpler way. In addition, Keras has the advantage of using the same code to develop models with different deep learning environments. All of these packages contributed greatly to making Python the language of reference for machine learning and deep learning.

Packages for Big Data

Big data is a big word that covers many elements. When we say big data, we are talking about distributed infrastructures that allow us to store and do massively parallel calculations on a cluster composed of many nodes (which are usually servers).

Python is a language well suited to communicate with these infrastructures. Indeed, it is very simple in Python to store or load data on a Hadoop cluster on the HDFS file system. We can easily make requests in the Hive.

What will bring a data scientist to make big data is Apache Spark. Gold, Python has a package named PySpark that allows direct communication with an Apache Spark environment. Plus, with the evolution of Apache Spark, on the one hand, DataFrame objects that look very much like those of Pandas and, on the other hand of predictive models with spark.ml that look like strongly to those of Scikit-Learn, the combined use of Spark and Pythontakes all its meaning for data processing. Moreover, Python is extremely interesting to communicate with other calculation systems including H2O.ai.

Other Packages for Data Science

The list of interesting packages in Python is extremely long. Especially, packages for web scrapping such as html5lib or Beautiful-Soup, scientific packages and statistical computing with SciPy and statsmodels and many others.

This is not a question of making an exhaustive list but of providing you the keys to handle and process data with Python.

To summarize, in this chapter, history, development approaches, tools and the Python reference packages for the data scientist have been presented. We will now look at the Python code more precisely.

CHAPTER 2:

Python from Scratch

This chapter will allow you to discover the Python language if you do not know already or if you need some reminders. We will get to some basic themes and some topics useful to the data scientist.

2. 1 Basic Principles

2.1.1 An Interpreted, High-Level, Object-Oriented Language

As we saw earlier, Python is above all a language of programming and it must be addressed taking into account this specificity. This language is simple and allows you to progress very quickly (hence its success with data scientists developers).

Python is a high-level interpreted language. Moreover, it is also an object-oriented language which means that it is based on classes that simplify its use. What does that mean?

An interpreted language: it is a programming language that is processed in a direct way (on this point it is close to R). An interpreted language as opposed to a compiled language, which requires a compilation of the code to make an executable program. The main advantage of an interpreted language is its debugging simplicity. Conversely, its main defect is its slowness. Unlike a compiled language, code blocks are not optimized to be extremely fast by the machine. In the case of Python, we treat the code line by line with the Python interpreter.

A high-level language: a high-level language is a language that is as close as possible to natural language, that is to say, which reads "as applies ". It is therefore extremely simple to implement but it's not veryoptimized. Conversely, a low-level language will come as close as possible tothe language of the machine to which it applies. The best-known low-level language is assembly language.

As a language, Python is based on a few principles:

It is based on indentation.

It is extremely flexible.

Its rules are set by the Python community.

We will dwell on all these points later. We will start by studying some important tool choices to code in Python.

2.1.2 Python 2 or Python 3

In 2008, the developers of Python within the Python Software Foundation decided to go from version 2 to version 3. But they also decided that big housework is needed in the language to clarify the code. That makes Python 3 not retro-compatible with Python 2. The millions of lines in Python 2 must be rewritten in order to be submitted in Python 3. After more than ten years of coexistence, Python 2 is disappearing. Indeed, more and more packages are announced that new features will not be developed in Python 2, whichwill inevitably speed up the process of switching to Python 3 (that's the case of NumPy for 2019). In addition, the completion of Python 2.7 maintenanceis officially announced for 2020.

The advice I give you is this: if you are working on a new project in Python, so start with Python 3 without hesitation! Python 2 can win if you get an important legacy and that by necessity you have to continue to code inPython. Even in this case, the option to port to Python 3 may impose itself.

To recognize a code in Python 2, just look at the displays using the command print in the code. Indeed, the print was a Python 2 command that became a function in Python 3.

PYTHON 2

>>> print 55 55

PYTHON 3

>>> print (55) 55

The differences between these two versions are widely documented by Python Software Foundation. Whatever happens, Python 3 remains the futureand a return to Python 2 is highly unlikely. As part of this book, we will always use Python 3.

2. 2 The Interpreters: Python And Ipython

The interpreter is the tool that translates your source code into action. IPython can be seen as an evolved version of the classic Python interpreter.

2.2.1 The Python Interpreter - An Advanced Calculator

The Python interpreter is a rich tool but also allows you to make simple calculations. So, once Python is launched from the command prompt, we can have :

4 + 6

10

You can use this line to submit code directly or to submit files in Python (in .py format)

x = 3

print (x)

3

To submit a file, we will use:

exec (open ("./ test.py"). read ())

The Python interpreter can be used as a simple calculator with classical mathematical operations:

2 + 5

7

2 * 5

10

2/5

0.4

2-5

-3

5 ** 2

25

5% 2

1

We see here that the power is noted ** (not to be confused with ^ which is a logical operator). The modulo% allows extracting the rest of the whole division and %2 lets us know if a number is even or odd.

As you can see in this example when dividing two integers, we get a decimal number (2/5 = 0.4). This was not the case with Python 2 but has been added to Python 3. You can of course code in the Python interpreter directly but we tend to prefer an improved interpreter: IPython.

2.2.2 The IPython Interpreter - An Opening Towards More Possibilities

As mentioned in the first chapter of this book, IPython offers new possibilities when you code in Python. Here, we will develop some of the advantages of IPython.

Auto-completion and help with IPython

This is a very important point and one of the strengths of IPython: it has very advanced completion tools. This completion is extremely powerful and will bring you help and your productivity is also constantly increased.

Access to help and code

You can very easily access the help functions and methods by using the combination (Shift + Tab).

In addition, using a question mark (?), You will have access to help (the docstring) and with two question marks (??), you will have access to the source code of the function studied.

The magic keys of IPython

IPython has many magic keys. These are specific commands, starting with% and that will simplify your coding. There are magic keys per line (cellmagics) that will apply to a single line of code. We use simple keys with a single sign% that applies to a line of code. There are also magic keys using %% which apply to the entire cell of a Jupyter notebook. If you want to get a list of all magic keys, just type %lsmagic.

A number of them are described:

%CD: Change of working directory

debug %: Enabling the interactive debugger

% macro: Ability to combine execution lines to repeat several actions (use macro macro_name input_number)

% notebook: Exporting IPython history in a Jupyter notebook whose name we provide

prun%: Profiling of a function

% PWD: Displaying the working directory

% run: Launching a Python file directly in a notebook

% save: Save as .py blocks of code

% time: Display of the execution time

timeit%: Display the execution time of order by repeating it several times

whos%: Display all objects and functions loaded in memory

All keys are available here:

http://iPython.readthedocs.io/en/stable/interactive/magics.html

In addition, IPython provides access to system commands using the exclamation point (!). For example, we can use:! ls that will display all files in the current directory as in the terminal.

Zoom: profiling and optimizing your code

In the list of magic keys, we can see that the functions% time and% timeit seem interesting. Their operation is simple: you have a code in Python using a function that seems inefficient. You will be able to use % timeit to test the launch of this function. % timeit, unlike % time, will launch this function many times to give you a more precise idea of his behavior:

In []:% timeit x = 5

Out []: 14.2 ns ± 0.0485 ns per loop (mean ± std dev of 7 runs, 100000000 loops each)

If you find that your function is a little slow, you still have to improve it. For this, other tools are solicited. For example,% prun breaks down all the steps followed by your code with an estimate of the time needed for each step. This key searches for bottlenecks in your code.

Zoom: Variables loaded in memory

Python is a language that loads all objects into memory. It may be interesting to know the state and number of objects loaded into memory. To obtain the list of these objects, we use% who. If we want more details on each object,we use% whos. We will have :

In []:% whos

Out []: Variable Type Data / Info

----

x int 5000

This will become more interesting for the arrays of the NumPy package. For other data structures, information is sometimes missing. For a DataFrame of Pandas, we can use the .memory_usage () method which gives us the size of each column in bytes. For a NumPy array, the property .nbytes is useful.

If you want to apply this to all the elements loaded into memory, you can use the getsizeof () function of the sys module.

Access to previous results

Another interesting feature of IPython is access to what you did previously. For this, we use different approaches:

To display the last output, use _

To recover the output Out [33] for example, we use _33

To get the last entry, we use _i

To recover the input In [33], we will use _i33

This simplification makes it possible to store input and output data in objects. An entry is automatically stored in a string.

Zoom: storing objects

Sometimes you have to process objects from one notebook to another or important calculations are needed to obtain a data structure. In this case, it is obviously not very efficient to restart the calculations at next launch or let your kernel run until the next scan. You can use the magic key% store which will allow you to store an object in a persistent and simple way. This is close to the pickle approach that we use in machine learning models but in a much simpler way.

In your notebook, you will do:

In []: list1 = [3,5,7]

% store list1

And in any other notebook or when your kernel will be reset, you can do:

In []:% store -r

print (list1)

[3,5,7]

If you want to see what is stored, just run% store all by yourself. If you want to erase everything that is stored, just enter% store -z. Many other options are available to you when using IPython. We will now return to the Python language to understand its use.

2. 3 The Basis For Starting To Code

2.3.1 The Principles

Python uses the = sign as allocation operator. When assigning a value to any Python5 structure, we use the operator =:

In []: var1 = 10

The variable var1 has the value 10. The type of this variable is automatically inferred by Python, which is a specificity of this language. Regulars of other languages like C may be confused by this. We never give the type of a variable, it is Python who takes care of the guess.

The different primitive types are:

int: integer

float: decimal number

str: string of characters

bool: boolean (True or False)

The type of a variable can be identified using type (). In [1]: var1 = 10

var2 = 3.5

var3 = "Python"

var4 = True

Type (var1)

Out [1]: int

In [2]: type (var2)

Out [2]: float

In [3]: type (var3)

Out [3]: str

In [4]: type (var4)

Out [4]: bool

Four variables of different types have been defined. If we change the value of a variable using the allocation (=) operator, we also change its type:

In [5]: var4 = 44

Type (var4)

Out [5]: int

Do not forget to use the tab key for auto-completion with IPython!

Note - Since Python 3.6, there are ways to force types when declaringvariables or in functions.

Note - In the scripts that appear so far, you see the Out terms [?]. This is an intermediate exit. If you want to show the result of a line of code, you will have to use the function print () and in this case, we will have:

In []: print (var4)

44

The other basic principle of Python is indentation. This means that the limits of the statements and blocks are defined by the layout and not by specific symbols. With Python, you must use indentation and passage the line to delimit your code. This allows you to not worry about other block delimiter symbols. By convention, we use a four-space indentation. For example, if we want to set up a simple condition:

In []: if var1 <var4: var1 = var4 * 2

It is, therefore, the indentation that allows us to say that the allocation var1 = var4 * 2 is in the condition. Later we will see in much more detail cases where indentation is central. In addition, this obligation to code using indentation makes it possible to obtain a more readable and cleaner code.

2.3.2 An All-Object Language

Python is an object-oriented language. This means that the structures used in Python are actually all objects. An object represents a structure that has properties (these are characteristics of the object) and methods (these are functions that apply to the object). It comes from a class that is defined in a simple way.

In Python, everything is an object. Thus variables, functions, and all structures are Python Object. This allows for great flexibility. For example, a string is an object of class str. Its properties and methods can be identified using the dot after the object name (using tabulation with IPython, all properties and methods of an object appear).

In []: string1 = "Python"

chaine1.upper ()

Out []: "PYTHON"

We see here that the .upper () method of the "string" object allows capitalizing the terms stored in the string.

2.3.3 Comments

As a data scientist using Python, you need to have a development that will allow any member of your team to understand the code that you develop. For this, there is only one solution: comment in your code.

Comments in Python are delimited by #. As soon as # is used in one line, the rest of the line is ignored by the interpreter and passed in the form of a comment. As far as possible, we try to avoid comments as a result of the line of code on the same line. We prefer to integrate comments on an independent line:

Definition of the variable x = 4

Call the print () function print (x)

Comments are essential and care must be taken to update them when you change your code.

2.3.4 Naming Conventions

Python is case-sensitive, so we need to put in place naming based on the use of upper and lower case. Naming different parts of your code is extremely important and is an integral part of Grante Python's philosophy.

Variables are always lowercase with separators of type _:

my_string = "Data"

mysample = Kmeans ()

MyData = pd.read_CSV ("donnees.CSV")

Functions are always lowercase with separators of type _:

print ("Data")

```
def my_function ():
```

```
pass
```

Classes are written without separators with a capital letter to the first letter of each word :

```
class MyClass:
```

...

```
mysample = LinearRegression ()
```

The packages are written in lowercase, if possible without separator:

```
import numpy
```

```
import mabib
```

These rules are of course only indicative and allow you to improve the workability of your code. If you are working on a project that did not follow these rules, the important thing is to stay consistent with this project to keep a readable code.

2.3.5 The Rules of Coding

When developing in Python, there are always many ways to code the same action. A number of rules are recommended by Python Software Foundation. They are gathered in the Python Enhancement Proposals (PEP) and especially in the PEP8: Style Guide for Python Code (https://www.Python.org/dev / peps / pep-0008 /).

We do not detail here all these rules, but we try to respect one maximum in the code that you will see in this book.

2.3.6 The Operators Logic

If we want to verify that an object is of the expected class, the most effective way is to use the is or is not operator:

```
In []: type (string1) is str
```

```
Out []: True
```

```
In []: type (string1) is type (integer1)
```

Out []: False

2.4 Structures (Tuples, Lists, Dictionaries)

Python is based on three reference structures: tuples, lists, and dictionaries. These structures are actually objects that may contain otherobjects. They have quite different utilities and allow you to store information of all types.

These structures have a number of common features:

To extract one or more objects from a structure, we always use the []

For numerically indexed structures (tuples and lists), the structures are indexed to 0 (the first position is position 0)

2.4.1 The Tuples

This is a structure that groups multiple objects in indexed order. Its form is not modifiable (immutable) once created and is defined using parentheses. It has only one dimension. Any type of object can be stored in a tuple. For example, if you want to create a tuple with different objects, we use:

tup1 = (1, True, 7.5.9)

You can also create a tuple by using the tuple () function. Access to the values of a tuple is done by the classical indexing of structures. Thus, if we want to access the third element of our tuple, we use:

In []: tup1 [2]

Out []: 7.5

Tuples can be interesting because they require little memory. Else, on the other hand, they are used as outputs of functions returning several values. Tuples as structures are objects. They have methods that are clean. These are few for a tuple:

In []: tup1.count (9)

Out []: 1

We often prefer lists that are more flexible.

2.4.2 Lists

The list is the reference structure in Python. It is modifiable and can contain any object.

Creating a list

We create a list using square brackets:

list1 = [3,5,6, True]

You can also use the list () function. The structure of a list is editable. It has many methods:

.append (): add value at the end of the list

.insert (i, val): insert value to the index i

.pop (i): retrieves the value of the index i

.reverse (): reverse the list

.extend (): extends the list with a list of values

Note - All of these methods modify the list, the equivalent in terms of classic code would be the following:

liste1.extend (list2)

equivalent to

list1 = list1 + list2

Lists have other methods including:

.index (val): returns the index of the value val

.count (val): returns the number of occurrences of val

.remove (val): remove the first occurrence of the value val from the list

Extract an Item from a List

As we have seen above, it is possible to extract an element using the brackets:

list1 [0]

We are often interested in the extraction of several elements. It is done by using the two points:

list1 [0: 2] or list1 [: 2]

In this example, we see that this system extracts two elements: the indexed element in 0 and the one indexed in position 1. So we have as a rule that i: j goes from the element I included in element j not included. Here are some other examples:

Extract the last element

list1 [-1]

Extract the last 3 elements list1 [-3: -1] or list1 [-3:]

A concrete example

Suppose we wanted to create a list of countries. These countries are ordered in the list according to their population. We will try to extract the first three and the last three.

In []: country_list = ["China", "India", "United States", "France", "Spain", "Swiss"]

In []: print (country_list [: 3])

['China', 'India', 'United States']

In []: print (country_list [-3:])

['France', 'Spain', 'Switzerland']

In []: country_list.reverse ()

print (liste_pays)

['Switzerland', 'Spain', 'France', 'United States', 'India', 'China']

There are other functions on the lists that will interest us later in this chapter.

The Comprehension Lists

These are lists built iteratively. They are often very useful because they are more efficient than using loops to build lists. Here is a simple example:

In []: list_init = [4,6,7,8]

list_comp = [val ** 2 for val in list_init if val% 2 == 0]

The list comp_list allows you to store the even elements of list_init set to the square.

We will have :

In []: print (list_comp)

[16,36,64]

This notion of comprehension list is very effective. It avoids useless code (loops on a list) and performs better than creating a list iteratively. It also exists in dictionaries but not on tuples that are unchangeable. We will be able to use comprehension lists in the framework of the manipulation of data tables.

2.4.3 Strings - Character Lists

Strings in Python are encoded by default (since Python 3) in Unicode. You can declare a string of characters in three ways:

string1 = "Python for the data scientist"

string2 = 'Python for the data scientist'

string3 = "" "Python for the data scientist" ""

The last one allows having strings on several lines. We will most often use the first. A string is actually a list of characters and we will be able to work on the elements of a string as on those of a list:

In []: print (string1 [: 6])

print (string1 [-14:])

print (string1 [3:20 p.m.])

Python for the Data Scientist

Data strings can be easily transformed into lists:

In []: # we separate the elements using space

list1 = chaine1.split ()

print (list1)

['Python', 'for', 'the', 'Data', 'Scientist']

In []: # we join the elements with space

string1bis = "" .join (list1)

print (chaine1bis)

2.4.4 Dictionaries

The dictionaries constitute a third central structure to develop in Python. They allow key-value storage. So far we have used items based on numerical indexing. So in a list, you access an element using its position list1[0]. In a dictionary, we will access an element using a key defined when creating the dictionary. We define a dictionary with braces:

dict1 = {"cle1": value1, "cle2": value2, "cle3": value3}

This structure does not require any homogeneity of type in the values. From this, we can have a list like value1, a boolean like value2 and an integer as value3.

To access an element of a dictionary, we use:

In []: dict1 ["cle2"]

Out []: value2

To display all the keys of a dictionary, we use:

In []: dict1.keys

Out []: ("cle1", "cle2", "cle3")

To display all the values of a dictionary, we use:

In []: dict1 .items ()

Out []: (value1, value2, value3)

One can easily modify or add a key to a dictionary:

In []: dict1 ["key4"] = value4

You can also delete a key (and the associated value) in a dictionary:

In []: del dict1 ["cle4"]

As soon as you are more experienced in Python, you will use more dictionaries. At first, we tend to favor lists dictionaries because they are oftenmore intuitive (with numerical indexing). However, more expert Pythonist will quickly realize the usefulness of dictionaries. In particular, we will be able to store the data as well as the parameters of a model in a very simple way. Plus, the flexibility of Python's for loop adapts very well to dictionaries and makes them very effective when they are well built.

2. 5 Programming (Conditions, Loops ...)

First of all, we must clarify an important point: Python is a very simple language to apprehend but it still has a defect: its slowness. The use of a Python loop is not an efficient process in terms of speed of calculation, it should only be used in cases where the number of iterations of the loop remains low. For example, if you have tens of thousands of documents toload for processing, you quickly realize how cumbersome a loop-based process is, and you often prefer other, more efficient tools for loading. groupsof data or to do it in a parallel way.

2.5.1 The Conditions

A condition in Python is very simple to implement, it is a keyword. As mentioned before, the Python language is based on the indentation of your code. We will use an offset for this indentation with four spaces. Fortunately, tools like Spyder or Jupyter notebooks will automatically generate this indentation.

Here is our first condition which means "if a is true then display" it is "true":

if a is True:

print ("it's true")

There is no exit from the condition, it is the indentation that will allow to manage it. Generally, we are also interested in the complement of this condition, we will use else for that:

if a is True:

print ("it's true")

else:

print ("it's not true")

We can have another case if our variable a is not necessarily a boolean, we use elif:

if a is True:

print ("it's true")

elif a is False:

print ("it's wrong")

else:

print ("it's not a boolean")

2.5.2 The Loops

Loops are central elements of most programming languages. Python does not break this rule. However, you must be very careful with an interpreted language such as Python. Indeed, the treatment of loops is slow in Python and we will use it in loops with few iterations. We avoid creating a loop repeating itself thousands of times on the lines of an array of data. However, we can use a loop on the columns of a data table to a few dozen columns.

The for loop

The Python loop has a somewhat specific format, it is a loop on the elements of a structure. We will write:

for elem in [1, 2]:

print (elem)

This piece of code will allow you to display 1 and 2. So the iterator of the loop (elem in our case) thus takes the values of the elements of the structure in the second position (after the in). These elements may be in different structures, but lists will generally be preferred.

Range, zip and enumerate functions

These three functions are very useful functions, they make it possible to create specific objects that may be useful in your code for your loops. The range () function is used to generate a sequence of numbers, starting from a given number or 0 by default and up to a number not included:

In []: print (list (range (5)))

[0, 1, 2, 3, 4]

In []: print (list (range (2,5)))

[2, 3, 4]

In []: print (list (range (2,15,2)))

[2, 4, 6, 8, 10, 12, 14]

We see here that the created range object can be easily transformed into a list with the list ().

In a loop, this gives:

for i in range (11):

print (i)

The zip and enumerate functions are also useful functions in loops and they use lists.

The enumerate () function returns the index and the element of a list. If we take our list of countries used earlier:

In []: for i, in enumerate (country_list):

print (i, a)

1 Swiss

2 Spain

3 France

4 United States

5 India

6 China

The zip function will allow linking many lists and simultaneously iterating elements of these lists.

If, for example, we want to simultaneously increment days and weather, we may use:

In []: for day, weather in zip (["Monday", "Tuesday"], ["beautiful", "bad"]):

print ("% s, it will make% s"% (day.capitalize (), weather))

Monday, it will be nice

Tuesday, it will be bad

In this code, we use zip () to take a pair of values at each iteration. The second part is a manipulation on the character strings. If one of the lists is longer than the other, the loop will stop as soon as it will arrive at the end of one of them.

We can link enumerate and zip in one code, for example:

In []: for i, (day, weather) in enumerate (zip (["Monday," "Tuesday"], ["good", "bad"])):

print ("% i:% s, it will make% s"% (i, day.capitalize (), meteo))

0: Monday, it will be nice

1: Tuesday, it will be bad

We see here that i is the position of the element i.

Note - Replace in a string

In the previous example, we saw the replacement in a string of characters. In fact, the% i and% s have been replaced by values given after the string characters with% (). This approach is simple and makes it easy to create strings with adaptable displays. So,% I means integer,% s wants say string and% f means oat. We can manage the display of numbers after the decimal point with% .2f to display two digits after the decimal point.

While loop

Python also allows you to use a while () loop that is less used and looks a lot like the while loop that we can cross in other languages. To exit this loop, we can use a station wagon with a condition. Warning, we must increment the index in the loop, at the risk of being in a case of an infinite loop.

We can have:

```
i = 1
while i <100:
i + = 1
if i> val_stop:
break
print (i)
```

This code adds one to i to each loop and stops when i reaches either val_stop, that is 100.

Note - The incrementation in Python can take several forms i = i + 1 or i + = 1.

Both approaches are equivalent in terms of performance, it's about choosing the one that suits you best.

2. 6 Functions

2.6.1 General

As soon as you start coding in Python, you will realize very quickly that one of the strengths of this language is its automation capability. The simplest use of this is creating functions. A function is an object that takes input arguments and that performs actions. In Python, a function is defined in a simple way: we use a keyword def and the name of the function. Then, allthat remains is to enter the arguments of the function and the two usualpoints.

```
def ma_fonc (a, b):
print (a + b)
```

This function displays the sum of both arguments a and b.

What do we notice in this example? There is no type definition associated with the arguments (typing). The content of the function is always based on indentation. This function displays the result but does not return anything. In general, a function returns a value. The return command is used for this purpose.

How to call a function?

ma_fonc (a = 4, b = 6)

ma_fonc (4.6)

ma_fonc (b = 6, a = 4)

You will notice that it is possible not to indicate the names of the arguments in the call of a function. In this situation, Python assigns values to arguments in the order that they were originally defined in the function.

2.6.2 The Arguments of A Function

Optional arguments

It is possible to have optional arguments in a function. For this purpose, we should give default values to optional arguments:

In []: def my_func (a, b = 6):

print (a + b)

In []: my_fonc (2,5)

7

In []: my_fonc (2)

8

It is clear that the only mandatory argument of our function is a. The second is optional and will not be required in the function call. When a function has many arguments, it avoids having to enter them all:

In []: def my_fonc2 (a, b = 6, c = 5, d = 10):

print (a + b + c + d)

In []: my_func (2, c = 3)

21

In []: my_fonc (2, d = 1)

14

All optional arguments must be placed after the required arguments.

Lists and dictionaries of arguments

Our function ma_fonc2 takes 4 input values of which 3 are optional. In the examples, we use individual values in the function call for each parameter. If we want to use either a list or a dictionary instead, there is a simple way: * and **.

In []: list_fonc = [3,5,6,8] my_fonc2 (* list_fonc)

22

In []: dico_fonc = {"a": 5, "b": 6, "c": 7, "d": 5} my_fonc2 (** dico_fonc)

23

Many applications of this approach will be possible to parameterize complex functions automatically.

Multiple arguments (args, kwargs)

Sometimes you want to handle more arguments in a function call than those defined directly. For that, we will add the parameters * args and ** kwargs. This is actually a tuple of mandatory parameters for args, the size of which is unknown, and a dictionary of parameters for kwargs, whose size is not known either. The function arguments are thus gathered in a tuple or in a dictionary.

def ma_fonc3 (mandatory_parameter, * args, ** kwargs):

print ("Required argument:", mandatory_parameter)

If we have arguments positioned after the mandatory arguments, we show them.

if args:

for val in args:

print ("Argument in args:", val)

If we have arguments of the type arg1 = ... located after the mandatory arguments, they are displayed

if kwargs:

for the key, val in kwargs.items ():

print ("Name of the argument and value in kwargs", key, val, sep = ":")

When we call this function, we get:

In []: my_fonc3 ("DATA", "Science", "Python", option = "my_option")

Compulsory argument: DATA

The argument in args: Science

The argument in args: Python

Parameter name and value in kwargs: option: my_option

In []: my_fonc3 ("DATA", other_option = "my_option")

Required parameter: DATA

Name of the argument and value in kwargs: other_option: my_option

In this code, we have combined the different options. This type is often used in arguments when nested functions are called so as to avoid having to name all the parameters of all the functions called. Of course, it's up to the user to properly name the parameters in the kwargs part.

2.6.3 The docstrings

This is a type of specific comment that applies to both a function to a class or a module and to explain the use of this one. A docstring is defined by "and will consist of one or more lines to explain the functionalities and parameters of a function. A number of rules on docstrings are defined by the Python Software Foundation in the PEP257 - Docstring conventions available here: https://www.Python.org/dev/ peps / pep-0257 /

Here is an example of a function with a docstring: def my_function (* args):

"This function calculates the sum of the parameters" "" if args:

return sum (args) else:

return None

A docstring can be displayed very easily without having to go into the code of the function:

In []: help (my_function)

Help on function my_function in module__main__:

my_function (* args)

This function calculates the sum of the parameters

my_function .__doc__

'This function calculates the sum of the parameters'

In []:? My_function

Signature: my_function (* args)

Docstring: This function calculates the sum of the parameters

File: c: \ users \ info \ <iPython-input-198-3e92fd468cd3>

Type: function

So we created a docstring on our function and we can call it using help () or .__doc__in Python and using? and the SHIFT + TAB keyboard shortcut in your Jupyter notebook.

2.6.4 Multiple Returns

When you want a function to return more than one object, just make a call return with multiple objects separated by commas. When we call this function, it returns multiple objects that can be allocated to multiple variablesor stored in a tuple.

def ma_fonc (a, b):

return a + b, ab

We will have :

In []: tu1 = my_func (2,5)

print (TU1)

(7, -3)

In []: val1, val2 = my_func (2,5)

print (val1, val2)

7, -3

This feature will be useful when you want to extract several parameters from a machine-learning model.

2.6.5 Lambda Functions

These are so-called anonymous functions. This means that one does not give any name to our function and we will create it on the fly. These functions can be very useful in the transformation of data into data science. To define a lambda function, we use the keyword lambda. A lambda function must be written in a single line and reflect a single action. For example, if you want a function that capitalizes words and separates them into a list, we can use:

In []: my_chaine = "Python for the data scientist"

In []: (lambda string: string.upper (). Split ()) (my_chaine)

Out []: ['PYTHON', 'FOR', 'THE', 'DATA', 'SCIENTIST']

So we apply the methods upper () and split () on the string.

We will use for example lambda functions on lists:

In []: my_list = [1, 6, 8, 3, 12]

new_list = list (filter (lambda x: (x> = 6), my_list))

print (nouvelle_liste)

[6, 8, 12]

Or structures for data processing:

frame_rs ['Budget_vs_moyen2'] = frame_rs ['Budget']. apply (lambda x: x / budget_moyen * 100)

In this case, a transformation is applied to a data column that divides the value of a variable by a mean value and then multiplies by 100. We willreturn to the lambda functions in the rest of this book.

2. 7 Classes and Objects

In an introductory book to Python for the data scientist, it may seem premature to talk about creating classes. Nevertheless, the understanding of Python passes by understanding classes and objects. It's not about building classes from your first use of Python but very quickly optimizing your code will ask you to go through there.

You will always be told that you can code in Python without ever using classes in your code. This is a reality but one has to wonder why most packages are based on classes, and Python itself bases all of its code on classes. This use comes from the fact that classes will simplify and secure your code. This will also allow you to factorize it.

2.7.1 What Is A Class?

This is what makes it possible to define an object. We could see that the objects are central to Python. To build an object of a given class, it is very simple:

object1 = Class1 (arg1)

We will see later in this book that machine learning models are based on classes

mysample = LinearRegression ()

A class allows you to create a specific object that fits your needs. So, this object will have characteristics and methods. For example, a boolean is an object of the bool class, it has properties and methods

BOOL1 = True

bool1.denominator

bool1.conjugate ()

2.7.2 How to Define A Class?

We use the keyword class. We use a constructor in Python, the class constructor is_init (expect double underscore). Then, we define all the attributes in the constructor by generally providing default values. Suppose we want to build an image object in which we can modify characteristics :

myImage class:

```
def __init__(self, resolution = 300, source = "./", size = 500):
    self.resolution = resolution
    self.source = source
    self.size = size
```

If we want to create an object from this class, we can use:

```
image_1 = MyImage (source = "./ docs / image1.jpg")
```

We will have :

```
In []: image_1.size
Out []: 500
```

So we see a first approach to simplify the creation of multiple objects. What interests us now is to associate methods with this class. For that, we just need to create functions whose first argument is self and which use the attributes of our class.

myImage class:

```
def __init__(self, resolution = 300, source = "./", size = 500):
    self.resolution = resolution
    self.source = source
    self.taille size =
def poster_caract (self):
    print ("Resolution:", self.resolution)
    print ("Size:", self.taille)
    print ("Source:", self.source)
def enlarge_image (self, factor):
    self.size * = factor
```

We can then have:

In []: image_1.agrandir_image (2)

In []: print (image.taille)

1000

We can see that the zoom_image method of the MyImage class has directly changed my object. Classes and objects include notions of inheritance and other standard functions.

2. 8 The Packages And The Module

2.8.1 A Bit Of Vocabulary

In Python, there are two types of structures for organizing your code: modules and packages. To put it simply, modules are .py files in which functions and classes are stored. Packages are structured directories in which many modules are stored.

2.8.2 Install a package

As we have seen earlier, Python relies on many packages, these can be based on your developments but often they have been developed by the community and shared on the PyPi (Python Repository). These packages are usually stored and shared in GitHub (www.github.com).

To recover a package, it must be downloaded and compiled if necessary. The process is as follows:

If you are using Anaconda, run the command prompt and, if the package is on the online Anaconda directory (some packages are hosted in the online Anaconda directory but are not included in the version you have installed on your machine), use:

conda install numpy

If you are not using Anaconda or if the package is not on the Anaconda directory, use the command:

pip install numpy

Just install a package once in an environment.

2.8.3 Loading a Package or Module Into Your Code

When you want to use the functions and classes of a package, you will need to load the link to the package in memory. This is done in a very simple way thanks to a Python import keyword. So, to load a package, we will use: import datetime

And we can use the elements of the datetime package, for example, to display the date of the day:

print (datetime.date.today ())

We prefer to use a shorter version of the package name for this:

import numpy as np

In this case, if we want to generate a random number from a function of the package NumPy, one must write:

print (np.random.random (1))

This is the version to focus on. There is also a way to import the elements of a package without having to use a prefix, we use in this case from pandas import *. This approach must be avoided, which involves many risks of overwriting when several packages are loaded. If we want to use a function or a class of a package without a prefix, we use this syntax:

from pandas import DataFrame

So just use the class DataFrame without prefix, but there is little chance of overwriting in this case.

2.8.4 Creating Your Own Module/Package

As soon as you start having a certain amount of code, you're going to account for the need to store it for reuse. For that, he will need a versioning system (public for open source or private) like Git by example. This is not anobligation but a good practice.

Create a module

Creating a module is extremely simple, just create a .py file in which you will store your functions and classes. You will then have to place your file in a directory that is in the PYTHONPATH. To identify this one, we will use the command:

import sys

sys.path

Once the file is in the right place, just use in your code:

import my_module

mon_module.ma_fonction ()

You can now use your classes and functions.

It can happen that your module starts to become too condensed or that you want to publish it in PyPi or on GitHub. We must then move on to the notion of a package. This is a structured set of .py files gathered in one directory. To define a package, you must add a file called_init_.py (with two underscores on each side).

This_init_.py file must be placed at the root of your directory. It allows initiating your package, this means that when you load your package into your code, Python launches the code that is in the file. We can very wellleave this empty file if you do not want to start upstream code. We can also add dependency checks on other packages or load a few classes. Once the initialization file has been created, we can structure its package with modules, subdirectories (if they are sub-modules, we will create a file initialization). If your_init_.py file is empty and your package is structured from this way :

mon_package

| -__init__.py

| - my_code.py

To run my_function which is in the my_code.py file, we use:

import my_package.mon_code

mon_package.mon_code.ma_fonction ()

This allows us to have a simple approach but it should be noted that the import is a little heavy in this case. You can add a pre-load of files that are in the directory directly in the__init__.py file. For that, you just need to add in the initialization file the following code:

from my_package.mon_code import *

Once this line is added, you will have in your code:

import my_package

mon_package.ma_fonction ()

If you are not comfortable with the import * code, you can do the imports separately for all functions and classes of your files. All you have to do is comment on your code, add docstrings from a quality, and publish your work to help improve the Python environment.

Note - The name of your package

If you want to share or use your package often, choose a name that is not already used on the PyPi (even if you do not have the intention to publish your package, it is necessary to avoid the risks of con it during the implementation of dependency dances). This name must be in lowercase.

2. 9 Go Further

2.9.1 Exception Handling

As we have seen in this chapter, Python is extremely flexible and can quickly lead to errors that are difficult to debug. To avoid the appearance of unwanted messages, we use Python's exception handling. This approach is very simple. If we define a function that calculates the ratio between two floats, it will return an error when the denominator is equal to 0 or when one of the two parameters will not be a number. To handle this, we will use:

def ratio (x, y):

try:

return x / y

except ZeroDivisionError:

print ("Division by zero")

return None

except TypeError:

print ("The entered type does not match")

return None

We can also use except alone, in this case, all the errors are directly supported without a given type. Many errors are spotted by Python's exception handling. If you want to prevent an action from being thrown in the exception, you can use the pass command.

Finally, there is a final command that goes to the end of the function and that will allow applying an action, whatever the case (error or not). It functions this way:

```
def ratio (x, y):

try:

result = x / y

except ZeroDivisionError:

print ("Division by zero")

else:

print ("The result is% .2f"% (result))

finally:

print ("The calculation is finished")
```

If we run:

In []: report (1,2)

The result is 0.50

The calculation is finished

If we run:

In []: report (1,0)

Division by zero

The calculation is finished

If we run:

In []: report ("&", 3)

The calculation is finished

TypeError Traceback (most recent call last)

You can also create your own types of errors by building specific classes.

Tip - If you have set up an error handling and want to debug your code without removing this management, you just need to add after your except, the word raise key.

2.9.2 Regular Expressions

Regular expressions are a very powerful and very fast system to search in strings. It's kind of a very push Search/Replace feature, which you will not be able to pass once you know how to use it. In Python, regular expressions are done with a package named re. When one wants to use regular expressions, we use:

import re

string = "info@stat4decision.com"

regexp = "(^ [a-z0-9 ._-] + @ [a-z0-9 ._-] + \. [(com | fr)] +)"

if re.match (regexp, string) is None:

print ("True")

else:

print ("False")

print (re.search (regexp, string) .groups ())

A regular expression is hard to read at first. The above expression verifies that the entered string is an email address. Let's detail the different parts of this expression:

^ [a-z0-9 ._-]: the accent takes the beginning of the character string, then wait for letters, numbers, dashes or dots

+ @ [a-z0-9 ._-]: we then wait for the sign @ and then letters, numbers, dashes or dots

+ \. [(com | fr)] +): finally, we wait for .com or .fr.

This first expression shows you the power of this type of approach. You can find all the details about regular expressions and the Python repackage here:

https://docs.Python.org/fr/3/library/re.html

2.9.3 The Decorators

Decorators are a specific type of function in Python that allows you to apply constraints to any function in Python. We have seen the functions above, their flexibility makes it possible to integrate functions in functions or to call a function from a function.

We have :

In []: def hello ():

return "Hello!"

In []: def hello_see (function):

print (function (), "Goodbye!", sep = "\ n")

In []: hello_good (hello)

Hello!

Goodbye!

These are classic functions; a decorator is a function a little different :

In []: def my_premier_decorator (function):

def hello ():

print ("Hello!")

function()

return hello

In []: def function_decoree ():

```
print ("Goodbye!")
```

In []: function_decoree = my_premier_décore (function_decoree)

In []: function_decoree ()

Hello!

Goodbye!

We see here that we build a decorator who takes a function as a parameter and that will automatically add "Hello! On the first line of the display. We will be able to call this decorator differently:

In []: @ my_first_corner

```
def function_decoree2 ():

print ("How are you?")
```

In []: function_decoree2 ()

Hello!

How are you?

If we take another example:

In []: # we define the decorator - verify username

```
def user_test (function):

def verif_user (* args):

if args [0] == "Emmanuel":

function (* args)

else:

print ("Bad user")

return verif_user
```

In []: # we define a bad user with the correct password

```
user = "Paul"
```

password_emmanuel = "Python"

In abstract

In []: # we define the function display_password which displays the word of pass only if the user is Emmanuel using the decorator @test_user

def display_password (user):

print ("My password is% s"% (password_emmanuel))

In []: # we call the decorated function

afficher_mot_de_passe (user)

Bad user

In []: # we change user

user = "Emmanuel"

In []: # we call the decorated function

afficher_mot_de_passe (user)

My password is Python

We see that when the user is the one defined in the decorator, the word password is displayed correctly. We can, of course, combine several decorators on the same function.

This chapter allowed us to lay the foundation necessary for the use of the Python language for a data scientist. We have studied the principles of language and more advanced applications, especially with classes or decorators. All these concepts are important to understand Python as a suitable programming language to data science.

CHAPTER 3:

Python And The Data

(NumPy and Pandas)

This chapter presents the main storage and processing structures of data in Python. These structures are based on two packages: NumPy and Pandas.

3.1 Data In The Era Of Data Science

Data science has many facets but its main characteristic remains the processing of the data. This data is the raw material on which the datascientist must work on. Knowing the data is essential.

A datum is a basic description of reality. This data, which we have the reflex to imagine in the form of a table, does not have a fixed format. An image, a video, a statement at time t, an annual average of production are all data. It's up to you to define the data and it's the first extremely important work. You have to be able to answer the question: how can I describe the reality around me? In this process, there is a lot of subjectivity involved. For example, when you decide to measure the number of visitors to a website, you will store data. These data are stored as lines.

Depending on what you have decided, a line can be associated with:

an individual who arrives on the site,

a number of individuals per hour,

a time of presence per individual on the site.

Depending on the data you have selected, you will be asked to answerdifferent questions. So why not store everything? Because for this it is necessary to completely define all the information related to a visitor, which in the case of a website is feasible but will become impossible for complex systems.

The data that you will have is the result of a selection process that must be as neutral as possible (if no purpose is predefined), or to answer a specific question. However, there are three types of data:

structured data,

semi-structured data,

unstructured data

3.1.1 The Type of Data

Structured data

This is the data in which it is customary to treat it as structured. They are usually organized as databases with columns and lines. They are composed of numerical values for quantitative data or textual values for qualitative data (expectation they should not be confused with textual data).

Most data processing algorithms are now based on structured data. One of the tasks of the data scientist is to transform unstructured data in structured data. This task is greatly simplified by Python. It is therefore expected to have one line per statistical individual and one column per variable in a statistical sense (not to be confused with variables in Python). An individual statistical variable can be a visitor to a website but also an activity during a given time (number of clicks per hour) or a transaction.

Unstructured data

These are data that do not have a standard structure, they are easily understandable for us but not by a machine. The most classic examples are:

textual data,

images,

videos, sounds ...

All these sources are central today in understanding the world around us and the work of the data scientist will be transforming them in order to process them automatically.

Semi-structured data

This data is halfway between the structured and non-structured data. This category includes data of the JSON type, pages, HTML, XML data. They are not organized in rows/columns but have beacon systems that can transform them quite simply into structured data

3.1.2 The Data Preparation Work

The preparation of the data is divided into many crucial stages like,

recovery,

structuring,

transformation.

Python will help you with these three steps. We will start with ourselves to tighten the structures that will allow us to store the data: the arrays of NumPy and the DataFrame of Pandas.

3.2 The Numpy Arrays

The development of Python-related data has mostly been done thanks to a package absolutely central for Python. This is NumPy (an abbreviation of Numerical Python). NumPy makes it possible to transform a very classical programming language in a numerical oriented language. It has been developed and improved for many years and now offers an extremely well-organized system of data management.

The central element of NumPy is the array that stores values in a structure supporting all types of advanced calculations. The strength of NumPy lies largely in the fact that it is not coded directly in Python but in C, which gives it an unequaled processing speed with the "classic" Python code. The goal of the NumPy developers is to provide a simple, fast and comprehensive tool to support the various developments in the field of digital processing. NumPy is often presented at the same time as SciPy, a package for scientific computing based on structure from NumPy.

NumPy is useful for both novice and seasoned developers seasoned. ndarray, which are n-dimensional structures, are used by all Python users to process the data. Moreover, the tools allowing to interface Python with other languages such as C or Fortran are not used only by more advanced developers.

3.2.1 The Numpy ndarray

An ndarray object is an n-dimensional structure that stores data. It has many interesting properties in relation to the three structures that we discussed in the previous chapter (the tuple, the list, and the dictionary)

Only one type of data is stored in a ndarray. We can have ndarray objects with as many dimensions as necessary (a dimension for a vector, two dimensions for a matrix ...).

Ndarray objects are a "minimal" format for storing data. Ndarray objects have specific optimized methods that allow you to do calculations extremely fast. It is possible to store ndarray in files to reduce the necessary resources. The ndarray has two important attributes: the type and the shape. When creating a ndarray, we can define the type and the shape or let Python infer these values.

To use NumPy, we always use the same method: import numpy as np. From now on, we use the term array to designate a ndarray object.

3.2.2 Building An Array

The simplest way to build an array is to use the function of

NumPy: np.array ()

We can create an array from a list with:

array_de_liste np.array = ([1,4,7,9])

This function takes other parameters including the type, that is to say, the typical elements of the array. The types are very varied in NumPy. Outside of classical types such as int, float, boolean or str, there are many types in NumPy. We will come back to this in the next paragraph.

We can create an array from a series of numbers with the function range () which works like the Python range () function.

In []: array_range = np.arange (10)

print (array_range)

[0123456789]

Apart from the arrange () function of NumPy, we can use the linspace ()

function which will return numbers in an interval with a constant distance from one to the other:

In []: array_linspace = np.linspace (0,9,10) print (array_linspace)

[0. 1. 2. 3. 4. 5. 6. 7. 8. 9.]

We see that 0 is the lower bound, 9 is the upper bound and we divide into 10 values. We can specify each time the dtype = in each function. From specific formats, there are functions to generate arrays.

3.2.3 The Type Of Data In The Arrays

The type of the array is inferred automatically but it can also be specified. So if we want to define an array filled with integers of type int, we will be able to do it with:

arr1 = np.array ([1,4,7,9], dtype = int)

In this case, the floats of my array are automatically transformed into integers. There are many types, here is a non-exhaustive list:

int: integers

float: decimal numbers

bool: booleans

complex: complex decimal numbers

bytes: bytes

str: strings

number: all types of numbers

The arrays, therefore, use the advantage of Python with automatic typing but also allow fixed typing, which can be useful in many cases.

3.2.4 The Properties Of An Array

We will use a NumPy function to generate arrays of random numbers, from a reduced normal centered distribution:

arr_norm np.random.randn = (100000)

If we want information on this array, we will use:

In []: print (arr_norm.shape, arr_norm.dtype, arr_norm.ndim, arr_norm. Size, arr_norm.itemsize, sep = "\ n")

(100000)

oat64

1

100000

8

We have thus displayed the shape of our array, the type of data stored and the number of dimensions. The shape is stored in a tuple, even for the case at a dimension. NumPy works like this so as not to differentiate the type of output. The shape attribute to the number of dimensions of the processed array.

3.2.5 Accessing Elements Of An Array

Access to elements of an array is very simple, exactly as in a list for a one-dimensional array:

mon_array [5:]

This gives access to the last elements of the array. We can nevertheless go a little further with this principle:

my_array [start: n: not]

Moreover, if you want to access elements that are not glued to each other, we can use lists of values:

In []: arr_mult = np.arange (100) .reshape (20.5)

arr_mult [: [0.4]] shape.

Out []: (20, 2)

In []: arr_mult [:, 0: 4] .shape

Out []: (20, 4)

We create here an array with integers between 0 and 99 that we transform into a matrix of 20 rows and 5 columns. The second line allows us to extract all rows from columns 0 and 4. On gets an array with 20 rows and 2 columns. In the second part of the code, columns are extracted from 0 to 3 using the two dots. If we want to extract lines, we can proceed in the same way:

In []: list_ind = [2,5,7,9,14,18]

arr_mult [list_ind,:] shape.

Out []: (6, 5)

Individuals whose indices are in the list_ind list are extracted. We display the size of the array obtained.

3.2.6 Handling Arrays With NumPy

Calculations on an array

One of the strengths of NumPy arrays is the ability to do calculations. For the difference of the lists, we can do calculations on the arrays:

Case lists: list1 + list2 will paste both lists

Case of the array: arr1 + arr2 will make a term addition to the term

It is generally assumed that the arrays have equivalent sizes. However, NumPy allows you to work on arrays of different sizes. This is what we call for broadcasting. Moreover, it must be kept in mind that all operations are done per element. For example, the * operator is a multiplication element by element. It is not a matrix product.

Broadcasting with NumPy

The notion of broadcasting is linked to the fact of managing vector computations on arrays of various sizes. NumPy allows you to do calculations on arrays with different sizes. The simplest rule is:

Two dimensions are compatible when they are equal or if one of the two is of dimension 1. Broadcasting is a way of extending large arrays to adapt them to operations on operators with larger dimensions.

Examples of broadcasting:

If you have two arrays built as follows:

In []: arr1 = np.array ([1,4,7,9])

arr2 = np.ones (3)

arr1 + arr2

Out []: ValueError: operands could not be broadcast together

shapes (4,) (3,)

In []: arr3 = np.ones ((3,4))

arr1 + OFF3

Out []: array ([[2,5,8,10],

[2,5,8,10]

[2,5,8,10]])

In the first case, the two arrays have a first dimension that does not have the same size, we get an error. In the second case, we see that the two arrays have a common dimension (4). Therefore, the addition of the arr1 values is done for each value of the arr3 array. If, for example, we want to apply a transformation to an image that has been preferably transformed into the array, the dimensions of the images will be: (1000, 2000, 3). You can refer to the following paragraph for details on the characteristics of an image. Let's apply a transformation vector of dimension 3, and we will have:

In []: image.shape

Out []: (1000, 2000, 3)

In []: transf = np.array ([100, 255, 34])

transf.shape

Out []: (3,)

In []: new_image = image / transf

new_image.shape

Out []: (1000, 2000, 3)

The vector transf is applied to all the pixels, even if the dimensions do not correspond to lay only partially. We divide the first color by 100, the second by 255 and the third by 34. We will come back later to the treatment of images with NumPy.

Manipulation of arrays

Most of the examples seen so far have one-dimensional arrays. The arrays often have more than one dimension. This is the case of an image that has three dimensions associated with the position of pixels and colors (RGB).

We will start by generating a structure that can look like an image:

In []: array_image = np.random.randint (1,255, (500,1000,3))

print (array_image.dtype, array_image.shape)

int32 (500, 1000, 3)

So we have a three-dimensional structure. If we want to extract elements, for example, the rectangle at the top right of size 100 by 200, we will use:

In []: array_image_rect = array_image [: 100, -200:]

array_image_rect.shape

Out []: (100, 200, 3)

Another approach may be to keep one pixel out of two; for that, you will need to use:

array_image_simple array_image = [:: 2 :: 2]

One of the most powerful methods for manipulating arrays is the reshape (). It is sufficient to provide the array with a new form (provided that theproduced dimensions are equal to the number of values in the initial array) for getting a suitable format array. Imagine that we have a size vector 1000 and we wanted to transform it into a matrix of size 100 by 10.

array_une_dim = np.random.randn (10000)

array_deux_dim = array_une_dim.reshape (100,10)

The .reshape () method has a specificity: it can take the value -1 for one dimension. In this case, it avoids having to calculate the size of this dimension. If we take the case of our image, we will often want to transform this array into three dimensions in a two-dimensional array (by stacking the pixels). For that, we could, of course, calculate the product of the number of vertical and horizontal pixels but we use:

In []: array_image_empile = array_image.reshape (-1,3)

array_image_empile.shape

Out []: (500000, 3)

It can be noted that from the point of view of memory when one changes the shape of an array, this does not change the data as it is written there. This changes only the shape attribute of the ndarray class. So we can just change this attribute to change the shape of an array:

In []: array_vec = np.arange (10)

array_vec.shape = (5,2)

array_vec

Out []: array ([[0, 1],

[2, 3],

[4, 5],

[6, 7],

[8, 9]])

Universal functions

Universal functions are functions of NumPy to calculate or to apply transformations in a very optimized way. Indeed, the operations in Python (especially the for loop) are not very optimized in terms of performances and speed. NumPy offers many features called universal allowing you to work on arrays which will accelerate your calculations. A simple example can be seen with the np.sum () function:

In []: %% timeit

sum = 0

```
for elem in arr_mult:
```

```
sum + = elem
```

Out []: 16.7 µs ± 132 ns per loop (mean ± std dev of 7 runs, 100000 loops each)

In []:% timeit sum (arr_mult)

Out []: 8.89 µs ± 104 ns per loop (mean ± std dev of 7 runs, 100000 loops each)

In []:% timeit np.sum (arr_mult)

Out []: 2 µs ± 19.3 ns per loop (mean ± std dev of 7 runs, 100000 loops each)

We see that using the sum () function of Python, we already divide the time by 2 compared to the loop. But using the universal function NumPy, np.sum (), the processing time is divided by 8.

Note - Many universal functions are available, both underform of NumPy functions, only as methods of the ndarray class. It is up to you to decide which approach you prefer to use.

Here is a list of interesting universal functions with their specificities:

Function Usage Example

Universal Tests of all elements

np.all ([[True, of an array are True True],

[True,False]], axis = 0)

array ([True, False],

dtype = bool)

Any Tests if at least one item

np.any ([[True,of an array is True False],

[False,False]], axis = 0)

array ([True, False],

dtype = bool)

Argmax- Returns the index of the value arr = np.arange (6).

Argmin- Maximum / minimum reshape (2,3); np.argmax (arr, axis = 0)

Argsort- Returns an array with arr = np.array ([3, 1, indices of initial data 2])

sorted np.argsort (arr); array ([1, 2, 0])

Average- Calculates the average (average arr = np.arange (6).

Mean- calculates the average reshape ((3,2))

np.average (arr, axis = 1,weights = [1./4,3./4]); array ([0.75, 2.75,4.75])

Clip- Reduces the range of arr = np.arange (5); data (data out of a np.clip (arr, 1, 3)

Interval- Become equal to terminals of the interval) array ([1, 1, 2, 3, 3])

Cov, corrcoef- Calculates the covariances and correlations associated with the array

Diff- Calculates the difference between arr = np.array ([1, 2, an element and the previous 4, 7, 0])

np.diff (arr); array ([1, 2, 3, -7])

Dot- Calculates the matrix product between two arrays

Floor- Calculates rounding for all a = np.array ([- 1.7, the floats -1.5, -0.2, 0.2, 1.5, 1.7, 2.0])

np. oor (a); array ([- 2., -2., -1., 0., 1., 1., 2.])

Round- Rounds the elements of an arraynp.round (a, to a number of decimals decimals = 2)

Fate Tri ascendant all np.sort (a, axis = 0) elements of the array. We will use the parameter axis to sort a larger array

Sum- Sum of the elements np.sum (b, axis = 1)

array ([1.22116361, 2.4267381])

Transpose- transpose an array (the lines b = np.random. become the columns) random ((2,3)) b.shape (2, 3)

np.transpose (b)

shape (3, 2)

Vdot- Calculates the vector product of two one-dimensional arrays where Vectorized function to test a condition on an array

Most of these functions are also methods related to the array object. We can often write b.transpose () or np.transpose (b). Attention, some methods directly modify the objects.

In the examples above, we often see the argument axis. This argument has a specific behavior. When not indicated, general work is on the flat array (all elements). When set to -1, we work on

the last axis (usually columns if we have two dimensions). When fixed at 0, we work on the first axis (usually the lines) and so on. All of these features have improved error handling and support broadband casting. Other universal functions are better suited to data, such as we will see it later.

The random number generation functions

NumPy has a set of functions to generate random numbers, these are gathered in the random module of NumPy. The main ones are:

randn () which makes it possible to generate numbers coming from a reduced normal centered law

random () which makes it possible to generate random numbers according to a uniform law between 0 and 1.

randint () that generates integers.

There are a number of generators derived from many laws of probability in this module.

Examples of use:

In []: # we generate a vector of random numbers from a reduced normal centered law np.random.randn (4)

Out []: array ([- 1.14297851, 2.13164776, 1.81700602, 0.93970348])

In []: # we generate a 2 x 2 matrix of random numbers from a uniform law between 0 and 1

np.random.random (size = (2,2))

Out []: array ([[0.9591498, 0.61275905], [0.70759482, 0.74929271]])

In []: # we generate a 2 x 2 matrix of integers between 0 and 4

np.random.randint (0.5, size = (2,2))

Out []: array ([[2, 0], [2, 0]])

Fix the seed for the generation of random numbers. It may happen that one wishes to generate several times the same random numbers. In this case, we will have to fix the seed to generate random numbers. NumPy offers two approaches to this: use np.random.seed () or create a np.RandomState () object.

The first approach will fix the seed of Python but may have impacts on calculations other than those of NumPy, we will prefer the second approach that is much cleaner.

We create an object of the class RandomState with a given seed that we can then use:

In []: # we create an object with a seed

rand_gen = np.random.RandomState (seed = 12345)

In []: # we create another object with a seed

rand_gen2 = np.random.RandomState (seed = 12345)

In []: rand_gen.randn (2)

Out []: array ([- 0.20470766, 0.47894334])

In []: rand_gen2.randn (2)

Out []: array ([- 0.20470766, 0.47894334])

This object can be used in other functions, especially in connection with Pandas and Scikit for machine learning. The other approach uses the np.random.seed () function. If you want to explore all the functions of NumPy, I advise you to start with the documentation available here: https://docs.scipy.org/doc/numpy/reference/index.html

3.2.7 Copies And Arrays Views

When we work on NumPy arrays, we often create new arrays. When you create an array from another array, copy is made. In concrete terms, this means:

In []: a = np.arange (10)

b = a

b [3] = 33

print (a [3])

33

In []: b.shape = (2,5)

a.shape

Out []: (2,5)

If we want to create an array that shares the same data as an existing array but which will not affect the shape of this array, we can create a view:

In []: a = np.arange (10)

b = a.view ()

b [3] = 33

print (a [3])

33

In []: b.shape = (2,5)

a.shape

Out []: (10,)

If we extract an array from another array, in this case we automatically create a view:

In []: a = np.arange (10)

b = a [: 4]

b [1] = 33

print (a [1])

33

In []: b.shape = (2,2)

a.shape

Out []: (10,)

Finally, you may want to make a complete copy of your array, in this case, we use copy, but pay attention to the necessary memory space if you have big arrays.

In []: a = np.arange (10)

b = a.copy ()

b [1] = 33

print (a [1])

1

In []: b.shape = (5.2)

a.shape

Out []: (10,)

3.2.8 Some Linear Algebra Operations

The interest of NumPy arrays is their matrix form. Classical calculation operations are terminated. We will, therefore, use functions for most matrix calculations. We bring together in the following table some useful linear algebra functions to the data scientist. We assume that we are working on 2 × 2 arrays called arr_alg (You can find examples in notebooks associated with this book).

There are many other functions in NumPy and this package is always evolving.

Universal function Usage

transpose- Get transpose of an array

inv- Get the inverse of a matrix

matrix_power- Calculate the power of a square matrix

dot- Make a matrix product

multi_dot- Combine multiple matrix products

trace- Calculate the trace of a matrix

eig- Extract the eigenvalues of a diagonalizable matrix

solve- Solve a system of equations

det- Calculate the determinant

matrix_rank -Calculate the rank of a matrix

3.2.9 Structured Arrays

The arrays we have used so far are arrays had only one type and no index other than the numerical index. Structural arrays are arrays in which several types can cohabit with names associated with these "columns". These arrays are not used much in practice but it is important to know their existence. We can create this type of arrays using:

In []: array_struct = np.array ([('Client A', 900, 'Paris'),

('Client B', 1200, 'Lyon')],

dtype = [('Clients', 'U10'),

('CA', 'int'), ('City', 'U10')])

In []: array_struct

Out []: array ([('Client A', 900, 'Paris'), ('Client B', 1200, 'Lyon')],

dtype = [('Clients', '<U10'), ('CA', '<i4'), ('City', '<U10')])

We see here that the array is created as a series of tuples with the values of a line. Here we have three columns in our array and two lines. The part of type is very important because it allows defining the name and the type of a column.

We use as types <U10 which is a type of NumPy for character strings of less than 10 characters. To get a column in our array, just do:

In []: array_struct ['Clients']

Out []: array (['Client A', 'Client B'],

dtype = '<U10')

To extract a value, we can use:

In []: array_struct ['CA'] [0]

Out []: 900

You can also create types or assign values directly to this type of array. These structured arrays seem interesting for data processing.

Nevertheless, this approach is not our preference. When we have data of different types with non-numerical indexes, we are interested in DataFrames and Pandas Series rather than structured arrays.

3.2.10 Exporting and Importing Arrays

It is not a question here of proposing a method of importing data but rather a method of storing arrays on your machine. NumPy allows you to store arrays either in text format or in binary format usually named .npy. It has functions to save or load arrays from files. Here is an example:

In []: array_grand = np.random.random ((1000000,100)) # we build an array

In []:% timeit np.save ("grand_array", array_grand)

Out []: 7.03 s ± 809 ms per loop (mean ± std dev of 7 runs, 1 loop each)

In []:% timeit np.savetxt ("grand_array.txt", array_grand) each)

Out []: 1min 20s ± 1.31 s per loop (mean ± std dev of 7 runs, 1 loop

In []: import os

os.stat ("grand_array.npy"). st_size

Out []: 800000080

In []: os.stat ("grand_array.txt"). St_size

Out []: 2500000000

In []:% timeit array_grand = np.load ("grand_array.npy")

Out []: 516 ms ± 15.2 ms per loop (mean ± std dev of 7 runs, 1 loop each)

In []:% timeit array_grand = np.loadtxt ("grand_array.txt")

Out []: 3min 28s ± 16.7 s per loop (mean ± std dev of 7 runs, 1 loop each)

It is clear that the use of savetxt () is clearly unprofitable. We use save () to store arrays and perform intermediate calculations.

We will come back many times to the NumPy arrays. These structures are central but can sometimes seem impractical for data scientists.

3.3 Series And Dataframes Of Pandas

It is to get closer to the classical structures of data analysis that Pandas was created by Wes McKinney. This package is based on structures of the type arrays but enriches them by creating DataFrames and Series.

For those who are used to using R, this notion of DataFrame should be familiar. The DataFrame is a tabular structure in which each column must- have elements of the same type. The DataFrame is a table with two dimensions, indexed by indexes for rows and columns for columns. The DataFrame is very useful for working on structured data tables.

3.3.1 The Pandas Series Objects

This is a list of values stored in a column near an array of NumPy. Its specificity is that the individuals in this list are indexed. A Series is an object halfway between a NumPy array (continuation of values of a given type accessible by numerical indexing) and a dictionary (list of values associated with keys).

Series Creation

We create a Series object using:

In []: from pandas import Series

In []: my_series = Series ([8,70,320, 1200],

index = ["Switzerland", "France", "USA", "China"])

ma_serie

Out []:

Switzerland 8

France 70

USA 320

China 1200

dtype: int64

A Series object can therefore be created from a list as above but also from a dictionary:

In []: from pandas import Series

In []: my_serie2 = Series ({"Switzerland": 8, "France": 70, "USA": 320, "China": 1200})

ma_serie2

Out []:

China 1200

France 70

Switzerland 8

USA 320

dtype: int64

Since we used a dictionary, dictionary elements are not ordered. So we see that in our Series object, the countries have been ordered in alphabetical order and not in order of appearance in the dictionary.

You can also build a Series object from a one-dimensional array of NumPy:

In []: from pandas import Series

In []: my_series3 = Series (np.random.randn (5), index = ["A", "B", "C", "D", "E"])

ma_serie3

Out []:

1.039354 B 0.022691 C -1.389261 D 0.188275 E 0.534456 dtype: oat64

We generated an array with random numbers from a normal distribution centered down and we get a Series object with the same type of data.

The indexes of the created Series objects can be extracted using the property index. Some information can be added to an object of the Series class, such as including the title of the Series and the title of the index.

Access items in a Series object

Elements can be easily extracted using two approaches:

In []: my_serie [: 3]

Out []:

Switzerland 8

France 70

USA 320

dtype: int64

In []: my_serie [["Switzerland", "France", "USA"]]

Out []:

Switzerland 8

France 70

USA 320

dtype: int64

We see here that we select several elements of the object. In this case, it is necessary to provide a list of elements (hence the presence of two brackets).

This Series object is extremely simple to handle. We can simply do queries on a Series object:

In []: my_serie [my_serie> 50]

Out []:

France 70

USA 250

China 1200

dtype: int64

In []: my_series [(my_serie> 500) | (my_serie <50)]

Out []:

Switzerland 8

China 1200

dtype: int64

For this second condition, we see that it is not about conventional operators of Python, we will use here & for and, | for gold and! for the not. Moreover, it is very important to use parentheses in this setting

Calculations on Series objects

Most of what we have seen with NumPy arrays is applicable to objects Series. Nevertheless, there is a very important difference: when you do an operation between two Series objects, the operation is done term-by-term but the terms are their index finger. For example, if you take a simple sum of two Series objects:

In []: from pandas import Series

In []: my_series3 = Series (np.random.randn (5),

index = ["A", "B", "C", "D", "E"])

ma_serie4 = Series (np.random.randn (4), index = ["A", "B", "C", "F"])

ma_serie3 + ma_serie4

Out []:

-0.641913 B 0.053809 C 1.177836 D NaN

E NaN F NaN dtype: oat64

We see here that the two Series have in common A, B and C. The sum gives a value that is the sum of the two Series objects. For D, E and F, we obtain a missing value because one of the two Series objects does not have a D, E, or F. So we have the sum of missing value and a present value that makes sense gives a missing value. If you want to take a nap assuming that the missing data are equivalent to 0, it is necessary to use:

In []: my_serie3.add (my_series4, ll_value = 0)

Out []:

A -0.641913

0.053809 C 1.177836 D -0.201225 E 1.107713 F -0.845924 dtype: oat64

We will work many times on Series and develop their properties in the rest of this chapter, especially with the notion of date.

3.3.2 DataFrame Objects From Pandas

The logical evolution of the Series object is the DataFrame. A Series object is a tool very handy for managing time series. But for data sets more than one column, the DataFrame will be the most suitable. A DataFrame can be defined as follows:

This is a columnar structure with as many columns as variables in your data and in which the data is accessed by column name or by line name.

Build a DataFrame

You can build a DataFrame from a list:

frame_list pd.DataFrame = ([[2,4,6,7], [3,5,5,9]])

This DataFrame has no specific column name or row name. The DataFrame created is composed of two rows and four columns, the indexes and the names of the columns, in this case, are automatically generated by Pandas.

We can also build a DataFrame from a dictionary:

dico1 = { "RS": ["Facebook", "Twitter", "Instagram", "Linkedin", "Snapchat"]

"Budget": [100,50,20,100,50]

"Audience": [1000,300,400,50,200]}

frame_dico = pd.DataFrame (dico1)

So we built a dictionary that associates values with each key; the first key concerns social networks, the second of budgets and the third hearings.

We see that the keys have taken the place of the name of the columns. The dictionary is an unordered structure, Pandas ordered the columns in alphanumeric order.

Building from an array:

frame_mult = pd.DataFrame (arr_mult [: 5,:], columns = ["A", "B", "C", "D", "E"],

index = ["Obs_" + str (i + 1) for i in range (1,6)])

Access and manipulate columns of a DataFrame

The elements of a DataFrame can be accessed directly by column using health: frame1.col1, but we usually prefer frame1 ["col1"]:

In []: frame_mult ["A"]

Out []:

Obs_1 0

Obs_2 5

Obs_3 10

Obs_4 15

Obs_5 20

Name: A, dtype: int32

So we extracted a single column. We notice that it has the format of an object Pandas Series.

If you want to create a new column in the DataFrame, just allocate values to a new column:

frame_mult ["F"] = frame_mult ["A"] * 2

If you want to delete this column, use the same method as for all objects in Python:

del frame_mult ["F"]

The columns are always added at the end of the DataFrame, we use the method .insert () to specify a position:

frame_mult.insert (0, "F", frame_mult ["A"] * 2)

This method modifies our DataFrame by adding in its first position a column of the name F with the values of column A multiplied by 2.

Access and manipulate rows and columns of a DataFrame

When working on a data table, you rarely want to work on a specific individual. Nevertheless, this can be useful for extracting a few lines. If we want to access one element per line, we will use .loc []:

In []: frame_mult.loc ["Obs_4"]

Out []:

15 B 16 C 17 D 18 E 99

Name: Obs_4, dtype: int32

If we prefer to access the elements using their numerical indexing, we use .iloc [] or directly the brackets:

In []: frame_mult.iloc [3]

Out []:

15 B 16 C 17 D 18 E 99

Name: Obs_4, dtype: int32

iloc and loc can take several dimensions, so if you want to extract the Obs_2 and Obs_3 elements for columns A and B, you can do it using:

In []: frame_mult.loc [["Obs_2", "Obs_3"], ["A", "B"]]

Out []:

B

Obs_2 0 1 Obs_3 5 6

With iloc, it would give:

In []: frame_mult.iloc [1: 3,: 2]

Out []:

B

Obs_2 0 1 Obs_3 5 6

Indexing DataFrames

You may need to modify the indexes of your data. For this, different options are available to you:

The .reindex () will allow to select columns and reorder the columns and lines.

In []: frame_vec = pd.DataFrame (array_vec, index = ["a", "b", "c", "d", "e"], columns = ["A", "B"])

In []: frame_vec.reindex (index = ["e", "c", "d"], columns = ["B", "A"])

Out []:

AT

e 9 8

c 5 4

d 7 6

If your goal is to rename variables, use the .rename () method:

In []: frame_vec2 = frame_vec.rename (map = lambda x: "Obs." + X.upper (), axis = 0)

frame_vec2 = frame_vec2.rename (map = lambda x: "Var." + x. upper (), axis = 1)

frame_vec2

Out {]:

Var. At Var. B

Obs. A 0 1

Obs. B 2 3

Obs. C 4 5

Obs. D 6 7

Obs. E 8 9

In this first version, we use a map, that is to say a modified function of trusting the indexes. In the first line, we use a lambda function to modify proud indexes of observations. In the second line, we use another function lambda to change the names of the columns. There is another way to rename indexes, which is done with dictionaries:

In []: frame_vec.rename (columns = {"A": "new_A"}, index = {"a": "new_a"})

Out []:

new_A B

new_a 0 1

2 3

4 5

6 7

8 9

We see here that we have renamed a column and a line of our DataFrame.

3.3.3 Copy And View Of Pandas Objects

Like NumPy's objects, it's important to understand how Series andDataFrame objects are allocated. When creating a DataFrame object or Seriesfrom another object, whether you are dealing with a copy or a reference depends on the original object. When working on an array, it's just about a reference to the values. Thus, we will have:

In []: arr1 = np.arange (6) .reshape (3,2) #on create an array

frame1 = pd.DataFrame (arr1) # we create a DataFrame from the array

frame1.iloc [1,1] = 22 # Modify a value of the DataFrame

In []: arr1

Out []:

array ([[0, 1],

[2, 22],

[4, 5]])

We see that the initial array is impacted by the modification of the DataFrame object. Yes you do the same thing with a list, Pandas creates a copy. Once you have created your DataFrame, if you allocate the same DataFrame to an object, it will refer to the first DataFrame. If you create a DataFrame from a part of your DataFrame, you get a view of your DataFrame. Finally, if you really want a copy, you will have to use the method .copy () but be attentive to the necessary space. You can create views as with NumPy using .view ().

Summarizing in this chapter we have seen the main structures for load and process data in Python. The arrays of NumPy allow manipulating data of one type with as many dimensions as necessary, especially with matrix calculus. The Series objects and DataFrames allow us to manipulate structures of structured data close to SQL tables.

#### CHAPTER 4:

Data Preparation and The First Statistics

This chapter allows you to discover a central stage in data science, that is, data preparation. We will use concrete examples to illustrate Python's tools for preparing data.

Data preparation accounts for at least 80% of the data scientist's work. This concept of preparation includes many stages: the acquisition and the charging of data in your Python environment, formatting data in order to extract information from it, the description of the data with the help of descriptive statistics, to arrive at the graphical representation of these data.

4. 1 Presentation Of Data

Throughout the chapters that follow, we will use different games of data. These datasets are, for the most part, from open1.Nousdata. We willnow briefly describe here the datasets that we will use recurrently in thework. If in the rest of this book, you realize that you are missing information on the analyzed data, I invite you to come back to this part. The data we use are made available by the producers of data. Many changes will be needed to process them.

4.1.1 Airbnb Rentals In Paris

Description

Data from Airbnb, which offers a market place to rent holiday homes, have been published. We are going to take an interest in those which are in the city of Paris.

Size and organization

These data are composed of three files that we will use. These files are quite large and are organized in the following way:

listing.CSV: 59,945 lines each representing a dwelling. We have 96 variables of various types, including all the descriptions of the website.

calendar.CSV.gz: 21,879,195 lines each representing the combination of each listing.CSV.gz and 365 days between 9/3/2017 and 9/3/2018. For each combination, we have the status and the price, if the accommodation isrented.

reviews.CSV.gz: 969581 lines representing customer comments, with the customer's name, the housing ID and finally the commentary in textual data. This table has 6 columns. There are many types of columns and we will detail some when we are processing this data.

Format

The data is in .CSV format.

Source

The data is available here:

http://insideairbnb.com/get-the-data.html

4.1.2 Employee Data for The City Of Boston

Description

This is nominative data on the employees of the city of Boston. It is open data available on the website of the city of Boston. We would have been able to choose another city in the United States, knowing that each city publishes this type of data (New York has 1.2 million lines).

Size and organization

This dataset has 22,245 rows and 10 columns. The columns are:

NAME: employee's name

DEPARTMENT NAME: department employing the employee

TITLE: title

REGULAR: salary

6 columns of premium details

TOTAL EARNINGS: total income

POSTAL: postal code

Format

The data is in .CSV format with comma separators. Amounts are coded with the apostrophe as a separator of thousands and one $ sign before the amount.

Source

Open data of the city of Boston:

htt ps: / / data. Boston. gov / dataset / employee - earnings - report / resource / 70129b87-bd4e-49bb-aa09-77644da73503

4.1.3 Data from Île-De-France Municipalities

Description

It is a dataset from the open data of the Île-de-France region. It bringstogether the municipalities of Île-de-France and, for each of them, 38 columns. These data come from INSEE data combined with data from the Ile-de-France region.

Size and organization

This dataset has 1,300 rows and 38 columns. The columns are of several types :

Digital for, for example, the population in 2014 (POP14), the median wage (MED14) ...

Strings for the LIBGEO column that gives the name of the commune.

Geolocated data for the geopoint2d column.

Format

The data is in .CSV format with semicolon separators.

Source

Open data of the Ile-de-France region:

https://data.iledefrance.fr/explore/dataset/base-comparateur-de-territoires/

4.1.4 Customer Data Of A Telecommunications Operator

Description

This is a dataset of customers of a telecommunications operator. These data are data from a real context but simulated. For each individual, the columns are filled with a mix of quantitative and qualitative data. The target variable is Churn? Which indicates if the customer has left his operator.

Size and organization

This dataset has 3,333 rows and 21 columns. The columns are:

Churn? : Target column with 2 modalities

15 numeric columns

5 columns representing qualitative variables (including 2 binaries)

Format

The data is in CSV format.

Source

This dataset is available in some packages. You can recover it directly to the site associated with the book.

4.1.5 SMS for The Classification Of Undesirable Messages

Description

This is an SMS data set in English with which, for each message, the spam/ham category is associated.

Size and organization

This dataset has 5574 lines and 2 columns. The columns are:

The label (Spam / Ham).

The message in text format.

Format

The data is in text format with tab separators.

Source

This dataset has been collected by Tiago Agostinho de Almeida and José Maria Gomez Hidalgo. It is on the UCI Machine Learning Repository:

https://archive.ics.uci.edu/ml/datasets/sms+spam+collection

4.1.6 The Fashion-MNIST Clothing Database

Description

This is a set of clothing photo data from 9 different categories in black and white. These images are stored as 28 × 28 pixel-sized images. For each image, the associated code is also available in the dataset. This dataset was created in order to have a credible alternative to the dataset MNIST of handwritten digits that is too simple to classify. They come from Fashion-MNIST: Novel Image Dataset for Benchmarking Machine Learning Algorithms. Han Xiao, Kashif Rasul, Roland Vollgraf. arXiv: 1708.07747

Size and organization

This dataset has 70,000 rows each with 784 columns (28 × 28 × 1).

Labels in the form of numbers between 0 and 9 are associated with it. The codes are the following: 0 - T-shirt/top, 1 - Pants, 2 - Sweater, 3 - Dress, 4 - Coat, 5 - Sandals, 6 - Shirt, 7 - Sneakers, 8 - Bag, 9 - Boots.

Format

Data is structured directly as arrays in Keras and TensorFlow packages. They are also available online.

Source

This database is available in several packages including Scikit-Learn and Keras. It is also available here:

https://github.com/zalandoresearch/fashion-mnist

4.1.7 The CAC40 index data for the year 2017

Description

This is a daily CAC40 index data set for the year 2017. For each date, different information on the daily price of the index is displayed.

Size and organization

This dataset has as many rows as open days of the stock market from Paris (255). It has 5 columns.

Format

The data is in .txt format with a semicolon separator.

Source

This is data from the Euronext website:

https://www.euronext.com/fr/products/indices/FR0003500008-XPAR

4.2 Tools For Loading Data

4.2.1 Import Structured Data

The majority of the data scientist's methods and treatments provide for the use of data in two forms:

Observation / Variable Data: A-line corresponds to an observation and a column to a variable, which can be either quantitative (numerical) or qualitative (non-numerical).

Distance matrices: these can be correlations, Euclidean distances, counting tables (confusion matrix) ...

These two data structures are often quite far from the raw data obtained before an analysis. It will, therefore, be necessary to think about the transformation of data.

4.2.2 The Processing Of External Data (CSV, SQL, xlsx, open data ...)

From this part, we will work on many datasets with very different types of data. Most of this data is available online either in open data or on specialized sites. The sources are stored in a GitHub directory in which the codes of the whole of this book are available.

One of the Pandas' strengths is the import and export of data. This package has a very broad set of functions to load data into memory and export them in various formats. We will develop many examples.

The formats supported by Pandas

Pandas dedicate an entire subdirectory of the package to import and export data formats that can be used with other tools. We can mention CSV, txt, Excel®, SAS®, SQL, HDF5 formats ... Depending on the format, the tools will be different but the principles remain the same. So, to import a dataset, we will create an object of the type DataFrame from Pandas, for a file CSV, we will use:

frame_CSV = pd.read_CSV ("mon_CSV.CSV")

If we want to create a file from a DataFrame, we can use:

frame_CSV.to_CSV ("mon_CSV.CSV")

Many options are available for these functions.

Upload a CSV file

The CSV format (comma separated values) is the most developed format. However, CSV is problematic on French machines. Indeed, the French CSV is composed of point separator-commas and not comma separators.

The read_CSV () function of Pandas is a function with a number of impressive parameters, we only focus here on a few which are important. In the case of a classic CSV file, only one parameter is needed. It's about the path to the file. Your file can be directly on your machine but it can also online. In this case, you just need to enter a web address. Other parameters which may be useful when processing CSV:

delimiter: to give the format of separators between values in the file. Useful in the case of a CSV with semi-colon separators,

decimal: to specify the decimal separator. Useful in the case of a CSV with decimal separators using a comma,

index_col: to specify the position of the column serving as an index in the created DataFrame (note the columns are always indexed to 0),

header: to tell if the title of the column is in the first line. If this is not the case, we can use the names parameter to provide a list with the name of the columns for the DataFrame,

dtypes: in the case of large datasets, it may be interesting to provide a list of column types or a dictionary in order to avoid Python having to guess them (which will avoid some warnings),

chunk size: in order to load a base in pieces and thus avoid overloading the memory (see box for this case),

and many other parameters, including the processing of missing data, the transformation of dates, the encoding of strings ...

In the case of Airbnb, the data is in CSV format with an index column in the first position.

listing = pd.read_CSV ("../ data / listing.CSV", index_col = 0)

Import a very large CSV file

Python and Pandas are not suitable for processing very large data. Nevertheless, we can find alternatives when the data is too bulky to be loaded into memory. Big data is a solution for this type of data but it requires more substantial infrastructure and is not necessarily easily accessible.

If you still want to use Pandas and Python, the easiest way is to import your file in chunks using the chunk size option. Here are the steps that we can follow if one wants to work on the Sirene base of French companies, which is 8 GB and is too heavy to be loaded into memory on a personal computer.

First stage :

Get a visualization of the base and its first lines: frame_sirene_10 = pd.read_CSV ("sirene.CSV", nrows = 10)

Second step:

Select the variables of interest to minimize the size of the database load.

Third step :

Load the database into memory. We can have different approaches. You can use Pandas and vary the chunk size so as not to overload the

import memory:

chunksize = 100000

chunks = []

```
for chunk in pd.read_CSV ('sirene.CSV', chunksize = chunksize,

low_memory = False)

chunks.append (chunk)

frame_sirene = pd.concat (chunks, axis = 0)
```

Make sure to use a well-adapted chunk size (not too big to avoid overloading and not too small to avoid a too long calculation time). If that is not enough, other tools will have to be used. In particular the Dask package, which is a distributed computing package, which will allow you to load DataFrame close to those of Pandas and more efficient in terms of memory used.

However, the use of Dask will limit your possibilities in terms of treatment compared to Pandas. Here are some lines to do this:

```
import dask.dataframe as dd

frame_dd = dd.read_CSV ('sirene.CSV')
```

Once you've worked on a bulky base, you often come to such large outings. It will then store these results on physical memory. For this, two formats are preferred today:

The HDF5 format, favored by users of Pandas (.to_hdf ()).

The parquet format, which is a very simple column storage format to use and which adapts very well to environments such as Apache Spark or the Dask package (.to_parquet ()).

The Dask package is a package in full development, especially by teams of Anaconda, we'll talk about it at the end of the chapter.

Import an Excel file

Microsoft Excel remains one of the basic tools for processing data. In most of the data science projects, you will have to cross an Excel file, which will be used either to store data or to store references or information annexes.

Pandas have tools to import data into Excel without having to go through a CSV transformation (often tedious if you have workbooks with many leaves). Pandas rely on three packages to import data

Excel: xlrd / xlwt, openpyxl. These packages are not mandatory dependencies of Pandas so they will not be installed if you only install Pandas (They are in the Anaconda distribution). If you have an error message, you will have to install them directly from your terminal (command prompt).

There are two approaches to import Excel data. We use here bank credit data spread across several sheets of an Excel workbook.

The approach pd.read_excel ()

This approach resembles CSV import. To recover the Excel file, it must know the name or the position of the sheet which interests us:

frame_credit = pd.read_excel ("../ data / credit.xlsx", sheetname = 0)

We can see that to retrieve several sheets with specific names, we need to loop on this function which can be heavy in terms of calculation (reloading the workbook). However, you can load all the leaves in on single object usinga list of sheet names or the term none for the sheetname parameter.

frame_credit = pd.read_excel ("../ data / credit.xlsx", sheetname = "data")

In addition, this function has many options, particularly for the drawing of tables included in Excel sheets. In order to extract only the columns A to F of one of our sheets, we will use:

frame_credit_af = pd.read_excel ("../ data / credit.xlsx", sheetname = "data", usecols = "A: E"

The ExceFile approach ()

It's about using a Pandas class to create an object of the type ExcelFile. This object has many methods and offers the possibility of extracting leaves faster and automatically, so we can have:

objet_excel = pd.ExcelFile ("../ data / credit.xlsx")

dico_frame = {}

for sheet in object_excel.sheet_names:

if leaf. na ("_ data")> 0:

dico_frame [sheet] = objet_excel.parse (sheet)

In this case, we store in a DataFrame dictionary the associated data sheets with the suffix _data in their name.

The .parse () method allows you to apply many parameters inherited from the read_excel () function. Both approaches are equivalent. The choice will be made according to the context.

Retrieve cells in an Excel sheet

To recover cells in an Excel sheet, we will be able to use:

frame = pd.read_excel ("../ data / credit.xlsx", sheetname = 0, parse_cols = "C",

skiprows = 5, nrows = 10, header = None)

Import a table from a SQL database

SQL is a central language of data science. The majority of relational databases can be queried using the SQL language. It is nowadays one of the three languages most used by data scientists (after Python and R). SQL will allow you to extract data tables that can then be loaded into memory in DataFrames.

To go from the SQL database to Python, you need a connector that allows you to connect to the database and make queries directly on it. A central package to Python is very useful for this purpose: it is SQLalchemy which has today replaced the many specific packages that could exist in SQL databases based on the basic type: MySQL, PostgreSQL, SQLite ... SQLalchemy has the advantage of providing a single approach.

So we will create a connector that will connect to the base and then we can launch queries directly with Pandas. To start, you need to import the necessary SQLalchemy tools. Generally, we import create_engine:

from sqlalchemy import create_engine

Depending on the type of base used, the parameters of this connection may vary. Here are three simple examples:

An SQLite database: it is an easy-to-use portable database. This type of base often has neither username nor password. Suppose we use an SQLite database, hosted directly in the working directory:

ma_con = create_engine ("sqlite: ///ma_base.sqlite")

A MySQL database: in this case, we will have a link to this database with a user name and password:

ma_con create_engine = ('mysql: // user: passwd @ adresse_base ")

An Oracle database: we will use the same type of connection for this basic type as before:

ma_con = create_engine ("oracle: // user: passwd @ adresse_base")

Once your connection to the base has been created, you can use the methods of the instantiated object to check the properties of the SQL database and the tables from which it is composed. For example, we can use the code:

ma_con.table_names ()

Moreover, this connection will allow us to make queries in SQL on a base and create a DataFrame containing the recovered data. For this, Pandas has three distinct functions: read_sql, read_sql_table, read_sql_query.

We prefer the read_sql_query function which is often more efficient and allows advanced queries in SQL. The SQL language is a language in its own right and we will not detail his grammar in this work. To load an entire table into a DataFrame, we will use:

frame_sql = pd.read_sql_query ("SELECT * FROM table1", my_con)

This is the simplest version, but there are more complex queries. By default, Pandas opens a connection and closes it with each import of data (we will not need to close the connection later). For example, we are going to work on textual data stored in a SQL database as multiple tables. We want to recover the elements of a table by applying a filter to a column. To apply this code, you only need to recover the SQLlite data:

we connect to the sqlite database

ma_con = create_engine ("mysql: ///../data/ma_base.sqlite")

check its contents

ma_con.table_names ()

we build a SQL query

my_request = "" "SELECT var1 = 1 FROM table1" ""

we build our DataFrame frame1 = pd.read_sql_query (my_request, my_con) frame1.head ()

Tip - It can happen that in SQL queries or character strings, you have both "and", which will cause you problems.

For a string of characters, we will use:

frame = pd.read_sql_query ("" "SELECT * FROM table WHERE "var1" == 'mod1' "" ", con)

Overall, once you have long strings, the triple quotation marks become helpful.

If you want to run SQL queries from Python without necessarily loading data in a DataFrame, we can do it with:

from sqlalchemy import create_engine

eng = create_engine ('postgresql: /// db')

con = eng.connect ()

query = "" "..." ""

con.execute (query)

con.close ()

Import data from the web

The web is a domain rich in data sources, you have necessarily heard talk about web scrapping to retrieve data from the web. The data scientist may need to retrieve data from the Internet without wanting to do web development. In this part, two approaches will be examined. The classic approach of scrapping and the approach with Pandas. Regardless of the approach, Beautiful-Soup is a central package.

It will allow you to recover any HTML content from a web page and extract information from this website. If for example, we want to scrap a site, we will have to start by inspecting the HTML code linked to this site. If you want to retrieve all the package names of an article on Python packages for data science, we will have to identify the tag linked to these names and then we can start working in Python.

By inspecting the html code, we find this code:

<div class = "x-agreement-heading"> <a id = "tab-5b02e7bbbe1a3" class = "x-

accordion-toggle collapsed "role =" tab "data-x-toggle =" collapse-b "

data-x-toggle = "5b02e7bbbe1a3" data-x-toggle-group = "5b02e7bbbe08d"

aria-selected = "false" aria-expanded = "false" aria-controls = "panel-

5b02e7bbbe1a3 "> Jupyter Notebook, a more intuitive interface </a> </

div>

It seems that the division div tag of what we are looking for is named x-accordion-heading. We will use Python to retrieve the contents of the page :

In []: from requests import get

In []: url = 'https://www.stat4decision.com/en/packages-python-data- science /'

answer = get (url)

print (answer.text [: 50])

<! DOCTYPE html> <html class = "no-js" lang = "en-US" pr

The response object that we created is requests.models.response object. We will then extract from this page the div tags of the type searched:

we import BeautifulSoup from bs4 import BeautifulSoup

we create an object by using the Python parser

html_soup = BeautifulSoup (reply.text, 'html.parser')

we are looking for the div we are interested in

package_name = html_soup. nd_all ('div', class _ = 'x-agreement-heading')

In package_names, we have everything in the title of each div. We will now extract from this element the names of the packages that are found at the beginning of each title:

In []: # we loop the elements of the created object

for div_name in package_names:

we print with a capital letter in first letter

first words before a comma print (div_name.text.split (",") [0] .capitalize ())

Jupyter notebook

numpy

Scipy

pandas

Statsmodels

Scikit-learn

matplotlib

bokeh

Seaborn

Keras

So we automatically retrieved the textual values that we were interested in. It is not a question here of developing more notions related to the HTML language but if you want to go further on this side, you will need some basics. If your goal is to directly load tables into DataFrame objects, things are simplified. Pandas, combined with Beautiful-Soup, makes a lot of the work for you.

Imagine that we want to retrieve sports data, for example, tennis. We will use Wikipedia's tennis data and try to store the information on grand slam tournaments

ma_page = pd.read_html ("https://fr.wikipedia.org/wiki/Grand_Chelem_de_tennis", header = "infer")

#The table of male records is in 14th position on the page

```
tables_records = my_page [13]

tableaux_records.head ()
```

We thus recovered the table of the record players in terms of victories in the tournament of the grand slam in a list of DataFrame objects.

The operation of this tool is simple: we get all the tables of the HTML language found on the page in a list. This list has as many elements as tables, each array is then stored in a DataFrame. We will be able to extract the DataFrame from the list to analyze it.

Data adapted to big data

Pandas mainly offer three data formats related to big data:

HDF5 data, parquet data or gbq data.

Other types of data

Pandas can recover many data formats by always using the functions of the type pd.read _... We thus find formats like SAS or Stata native in Pandas. If you want to use other formats, you have two possibilities:

Transform the format in the data creation tool into a more traditional format.

Retrieve a Python package that will allow you to do the transformation.

Import data from R

In data science, we sometimes have to work with R in addition to Python. In this case, one can, of course, extract a file in CSV since R then load it in Python as mentioned above. Sometimes we store in R data using. Rdata format or other R formats.

We will first have to check that we have installed the rpy2 package. For that, in your device, enter the command:

install rpy2 or pip install rpy2

Once this package is installed, it will be necessary to use rpy2 which makes it possible to make language R in Python and combine it with Pandas. Our goal is to transform a. Rdata file in Python DataFrame. This requires some manipulation. It's simpler to create a function that does this for us:

```python
import pandas as pd

from rpy2.robjects import r

import rpy2.robjects.pandas2ri as pandas2ri

def load_ chier_rdata (le_name):

r_data = r ['get'] (r ['load'] (le_name))

df = pandas2ri.ri2py (r_data)

return df

frame = load_ chier_rdata ("./ data / my_read.rData")
```

This code, therefore, uses the R objects of rpy2 to load the file into R objects and the functions of pandas2ri to load the R object into a DataFrame.

4.2.3 Loading And Transforming Unstructured Data

(images, sounds, json, XML ...)

One of Python's strengths in data processing is its ability to transform unstructured or semi-structured data into structured data. By the treatment of some examples, let's look at how you can work on data that you were not used to dealing with other tools. We will use four examples:

images,

sound data,

textual data stored as JSON,

XML data.

Work on images

The import of images is usually done using the format in an array. Indeed, any image can be stored in a compound three-dimensional array of integers between 0 and 255. This array is composed of two dimensions allowing us to locate the position of each pixel in the image and a dimension composed of three columns giving the color (R: red, V: green, B: blue). To recover an image in an array, we use:

```python
import imageio
```

```
arr_image = imageio.imread ("chier.jpg")
```

We can then work on this structure. If we want to transform this image into a two-dimensional structure, we can use the .reshape () method of the created array.

```
arr_image arr_image.reshape = (-1.3)
```

This gives a two-dimensional array in which the pixels are stacked. In this case, the proximities between the points are not preserved. We can not study more shapes or proximities in an image. If we want to work on an image, we will have two possibilities:

Use a package of the Scikit-Image type that will make it possible to transform an image.

Use deep learning methods that will take input images directly from the algorithms.

With the following code, you will be able to generate an image from simulated data:

```
array_image np.random.randint = (0.255, (1000,1000,3)). astype ( "uint8")
import matplotlib.pyplot as plt
plt.imshow (array_image)
plt.save g ("my_image.jpg")
```

We generate integers between 0 and 255 and we build an image of 1000 x 1000 pixels. We will pass this type uint8 to be able to display it with the function imshow of Matplotlib.

If we want to recover many images, we can do it iteratively using for example Scikit-Image:

```
from skimage.io import imread_collection
# your way
image_dir = '../data/train/*.jpg'
```

we create a structured gathering all the images of the directory im_dir = imread_collection (image_dir)

```
print ("Name of the le:", im_dir. the [0])
```

```
# display of the image
```

```
plt.imshow (im_dir [0])
```

The work on the images will be included in the chapter on machine learning.

Work on sounds

If you have a .wav file and want to transform it into data, you can use the tools available in SciPy. You may have a file in mp3 and want to turn it into adata structure. As a first step, the Jupyter environment allows you to listen to sound files directly into your notebook. We can do it with this code:

```
import IPython.display as ipd
```

```
ipd.Audio (./ data_sound / train / 2022.wav ')
```

To load sound data, we will use a specific package named Librosa which will help us recover sound data:

```
In []: import librosa
```

```
In []:% matplotlib inline
```

```
import matplotlib.pyplot as plt
```

```
import librosa.display
```

```
In []: data, sampling_rate = librosa.load ('./data/2022.wav')
```

```
print (sampling_rate)
```

```
22050
```

```
In []: plt. gure (gsize = (12, 4))
```

```
librosa.display.waveplot (data, sr = sampling_rate)
```

This code is used to extract data from a sound extract. We can store sounds in objects and then use them in learning processes. In addition, the Librosa package offers many transformations in order to obtain smoothed and usable data.

Work On JSON Files

A JSON file is a very classic file for semi-structured data storage. You will often come across datasets stored in JSON but also web pages using JSON as the storage format (this is the format of data storage of a Jupyter notebook). Importing a JSON is extremely simple with Pandas, we will use pd.read_json ():

issues_pandas = pd.read_json ('https://api.github.com/repos/pydata/pandas/issues?per_page = 10 ')

issues_pandas [['state', 'title', 'updated_at']]. head ()

We thus recovered the last ten issues related to Pandas using the API of Official GitHub and we display the DataFrame obtained by selecting thethree columns to display.

Work on semi-structured XML files

For XML files, we will use a package named XML that will allow us to decrypt the XML file. Pandas do not have direct tools for transforming XML into DataFrame because the semi-structured aspect of XML forces us to kill afew steps before filling a DataFrame.

We will start by recovering an XML file, such as this catchall CD log in XML format:

import requests

user_agent_url = 'https://www.w3schools.com/XML/cd_catalog.XML'

XML_data = requests.get (user_agent_url) .content

The following code is a bit more complex. A class is created to to switch from an XML file to a DataFrame:

import XML.etree.ElementTree as AND

class XML2DataFrame:

def__init___(self, XML_data):

"" "Builder of the class" ""

self.root = ET.XML (XML_data)

def parse_root (self, root):

```python
"" "Returns a list of dictionaries that use children in the XML. "" "

return [self.parse_element (child) for child in iter (root)]

parse_element def (self, element, parsed = None):

if parsed is None:

parsed = dict ()

for key in element.keys ():

parsed [key] = element.attrib.get (key)

for child in list (element):

self.parse_element (child, parsed)

return parsed

def process_data (self):

structure_data = self.parse_root (self.root)

return pd.DataFrame (structure_data)
```

Once you've created this class, you can instantiate an object of that class and display the resulting DataFrame:

```python
object_XML2df = XML2DataFrame (XML_data)

XML_dataframe = XML2df.process_data ()

XML_dataframe.head ()
```

This sub-part allowed us to see how comfortable Python is for transforming unstructured or semi-structured data into structured data. But once these structured data are obtained, there are still some key steps in the preparation of these data.

4.3 Describe and Transform Columns

4.3.1 Describe the Structure Of Your Data

Whatever type of structure you use; the arrays, the Series or DataFrame, we usually use a property of these objects: the property .shape. It always returns a tuple, which will have as many elements as dimensions in your data. We will have for example:

In []: array_image.shape

Out []: (1000, 1000, 3)

In []: series_bourse.shape

Out []: (100000,)

In []: listing.shape

Out []: (59945, 96)

This information is important but is not very detailed. When working on a DataFrame, we will look for a lot more details. For that, we will use the .info () method. If we take the dataset of the occupations of the Airbnb housing, we will have:

In []: calendar.info ()

Out []:

<class 'pandas.core.frame.DataFrame'>

RangeIndex: 21879195 entries, 0 to 21879194

Data columns (total of 4 columns):

listing_id int64

date object

available object

price object

dtypes: int64 (1), object (3)

memory usage: 667.7+ MB

This simple output is extremely informative, we have:

The size of our DataFrame with the number of "entries" (this is the number of rows) and the number of columns.

For each column, the data type is displayed. We are here in the case of a very large data set. If the data set was smaller, we would also have missing data.

A summary of the dtypes (a column of integers and four columns of the object). The types of columns in a DataFrame may be numeric types or objecttypes that represent all other types).

The memory used by the DataFrame.

This description is therefore very important to understand our data. Another important step is the study of the aspect of our DataFrame, we can, for example, display the first lines of the dataset.

calendar.head ()

If we change the parameter of this method, we can change the number of lines.

Tip - tail () will look for the last five lines.

Tip - The number of columns to be displayed is often quite large.

Jupyter notebook will very often show you the symbol ... in the web display. To modify this and display all or more columns, you just need to modify the associated options, we will use:

pd.options.display.max_rows = 500

pd.options.display.max_columns = 100

Another important property of Pandas DataFrame is .columns. Indeed, it has two uses:

display the column names of your DataFrame,

create a structure to have a list of columns that we can use for automation.

In []: calendar.columns

Out []: Index (['listing_id', 'date', 'available', 'price'], dtype = 'object')

In []: # we can loop the columns of our DataFrame for col in calendar.columns:

print (col, calendar [col] .dtype, sep = ":")

listing_id: int64

date: object

available: object

price: object

4.3.2 Which Transformations for the Columns Of Your Data?

The data you have loaded so far have three forms that we have already studied: 9 arrays of NumPy, Pandas Series, DataFrame of Pandas. Your goal as a data scientist is to extract as much information as possible out of these data. For this, we will have to shape them in an intelligent way. Let's study different transformations needed to work on data: type changes joins, the discretization, the processing of temporal data, digital transformations, column processing with qualitative data, the processing of missing data, the construction of cross tables.

4.3.3 Changes in Types

Typing the columns of a DataFrame or array is very important for everyone for the treatments in data science. Here we focus on Pandas DataFrame structures. Pandas are going to automatically infer types if you have not specified a type for the import the data or create the DataFrame. By default, Pandas will use three main types:

int int 32 or 64 bit,

float decimal numbers in 32 or 64 bits,

Object objects that gather most other types. There are also booleans and all types defined by NumPy. The listing database of AirBnB is obtained by web scrapping and some information can not be processed directly. Indeed, when information about the columns, we see that the column price is typed in Object then that they are decimal values.

Out []:

<class 'pandas.core.frame.DataFrame'>

RangeIndex: 59945 entries, 0 to 59944

Data columns (total 96 columns):

id 59945 non-null int64

...

price 59945 non-null object

...

dtypes: oat64 (21), int64 (13), object (62)

memory usage: 43.9+ MB

We will first try to understand the reason for this bad typing.

In []: listing ["price"]. Head ()

Out []:

$ 59.00

$ 93.00

$ 2 110.00

$ 3

$ 371.00

It is clear here that the coding of this column includes the sign $ in front of each number. By the way, we do not see it here but a thousand separators are the comma, which was not taken into account.

As we are working on a Pandas structure, we will avoid treating the lines by one but we will instead apply a transformation to all lines simultaneously. To get rid of the $ in the first position, we have three possibilities:

In []: # eliminate the first element

% timeit listing ["price"]. str [1:]

Out []: 13.5 ms ± 159 µs per loop (mean ± std dev of 7 runs, 100 loops each)

In []: # replaces all $

% timeit listing ["price"]. str.replace ("$", "")

Out []: 23.7 ms ± 432 µs per loop (mean ± std dev of 7 runs, 10 loops each)

In []: # eliminates the first element when it's a $

% timeit listing ["price"]. str.strip ("$")

Out []: 19.6 ms ± 146 µs per loop (mean ± std dev of 7 runs, 100 loops each)

We see that these three approaches are quite different, the first is the most efficient in terms of computing time but it is also the most dangerous in case of an error in our data.

We could also use regular expressions to perform these steps. There are two steps left: eliminate the commas and transform the variable into numerical variable:

In []: listing ["price"] = pd.to_numeric (listing ["price"]. Str.strip ("$") \
.str.replace ("," , ""))

In []: listing ["price"]. Dtype

Out []: dtype ('oat64')

So we managed to change our column. If we want to automate this treatment, just create a loop on the columns. We use the following code:

for col in listing.columns:

if listing [col] .dtype == object:

listing [col] = pd.to_numeric (listing [col] .str.strip ("$") \ .str.replace (",", ""), errors = "ignore")

We used the errors parameter of the to_numeric function. This one serves to manage errors. For example, when Pandas can not make the transformation to digital, it returns a default error. In our case, it is obvious that some variables are objects that can not be transformed into digital variables. For these cases, we use errors = "ignore", which allows us not to do the transformation while continuing the execution.

The most classic change of type is, therefore, the passage from object to digital. Nevertheless, other changes are sometimes necessary. If we study the "instant_bookable" column, we want to be able to take into account this column to pass it in Boolean:

In []: # approach with NumPy

%% timeit

```
listing ["instant_bookable"] = np.where (listing [" instant_bookable"] == "f",
False, True)
```

Out []: 4.4 ms ± 66.7 µs per loop (mean ± std dev of 7 runs, 100 loops each)

In []: # approach with a dictionary and Pandas

%% timeit

```
listing ["instant_bookable"] = listing ["instant_bookable"]. replace ({"f":
False, "t": True})
```

Out []: 6.82 ms ± 44.4 µs per loop (mean ± std dev of 7 runs, 100 loops each)

We see in this code that when you want to replace two values, the use of the NumPy's np.where function can be a solution, but you need to be alert to the risks related to incorrect coding of the variable. As soon as we have more than two values or when we have doubts about the values of the column, the combination of .replace () and a dictionary is effective. We will, therefore, tend to favor this second approach.

There are many cases of data cleansing based on errors in typing. What we will see throughout this chapter can help you answer your specific issues.

4.3.4 Joins and Concatenations

The joins between DataFrame

The joins between DataFrame are a powerful Pandas tool that looks like the tools available in SQL. A join is to build from two DataFrame, a DataFrame using what's called a joining key that will be an identifier of the lines present in the two initial DataFrames.

The join function of Pandas is the pd.merge () function. It takes two DataFrame objects as parameters and then, as optional parameters:

on: choice of the join key (s).

how: choice of join method. You have to choose between left, right, inner and outer.

left_on (and right_on): If the join keys do not have the same name from one table to another.

index_left (and index_right): here we will give a boolean if the index of the DataFrame is used as a key.

On Airbnb data, we will use an inner join to associate the reviews of the accommodation:

In (): global_airbnb = pd.merge (listing, reviews, left_on = "id", right_on = "listing_id", how = "inner")

global_airbnb.shape

Out []: (969581, 104)

We see here that we have collected the columns of the two DataFrames. In this case, the DataFrame reviews are much larger than listing, the DataFrame obtained collects the keys common to both DataFrames but when there are several repetitions of a key, the combination is repeated.

The concatenation of arrays and DataFrames

The concatenation is slightly different from the join. It's just sticking right or below a data structure at the current structure. So there is no notion of join key but only a dimension to specify. If we want to concatenate two arrays, we will use the function np.concatenate (). This function also applies to DataFrames, but there is another function pd.concat () for DataFrames that can be used. These two functions are very different. The function of NumPy sees any structure as an unindexed matrix. So, if in your two structures concatenated, the order of the columns is not the same, so the concatenation will result in combinations of different columns. It is for this reason that, if you work on a DataFrame, we will prefer pd.concat ().

If we want to add lines to a DataFrame, we will use:

listing_concat_1 = pd.concat ([listing_s_1, listing_s_2], ignore_index = True)

The ignore_index parameter does not take into account the index and renumber the observations in the resulting DataFrame. In this case, if acolumn is missing for one of the two DataFrames, the observations in this column will be coded with missing data.

If we want to add columns, we will use:

listing_concat_2 = pd.concat ([listing_s_1, listing_s_2], axis = 1)

We will use axis = 1 to work on the columns. If an individual is not present in one of the two DataFrames, then it will be allocated missing values. This approach is close to a join in the indexes. If you wish to just paste two DataFrames, one next to the other without using the indexes, we will use:

array_concat = np.concatenate ([listing_s_1, listing_s_2], axis = 1)

In this case, we obtain an unindexed array for which the concatenation was made depending on the position of the lines and not their index. Attention, it is necessary that two DataFrames have exactly the same number of rows.

4.3.5 Management of Line Duplications

It often happens in data that lines are duplicated by mistake or that you want to check the duplication of some lines. Pandas have two tools to handle this type of data: duplicated () and drop_duplicates ().

If we want to check if lines are duplicated in the DataFrame on the employees of the city of Boston, we just need to do:

In []: boston.duplicated (). Sum ()

Out []: 0

It turns out that there is no duplication. We could have focused only on the name, department, and title of the employees:

In []: boston.duplicated (['NAME', 'DEPARTMENT NAME', 'TITLE']). Sum ()

Out []: 4

So we have four duplicate elements, we can now see them:

boston [boston.duplicated (['NAME', 'DEPARTMENT NAME', 'TITLE'], keep = False)]

We use keep = False to display duplications as well as the duplicated element. We can now get rid of duplications, we will use for this:

boston_no_dup = boston.drop_duplicates (['NAME', 'DEPARTMENT NAME', 'TITLE'], keep = "first")

In this case, we keep the first one. We can ask to keep the last (last) and we will use sorts to order the results to get rid of irrelevant duplications.

4.3.5 The Discretization

Discretization makes it possible to transform a quantitative variable (the age of individuals) in a qualitative variable (one age class for each individual). For this, we use two functions of Pandas: pd.cut () and pd.qcut ().

Constant Intervals

If we want to create a class variable based on constant size intervals from minimum to maximum, we use :

In []: listing ["price_disc1"] = pd.cut (listing ["price"], bins = 5)

list ["price_disc1"]. head ()

Out []:

1 (-9.379, 1875.8)

2 (-9.379, 1875.8)

3 (-9.379, 1875.8)

4 (-9.379, 1875.8)

5 (-9.379, 1875.8)

Name: price_disc1, dtype: category

Categories (5, range [oat64]): [(-9.379, 1875.8] <(1875.8, 3751.6] <(3751.6, 5627.4] <(5627.4, 7503.2] <(7503.2, 9379.0]]

Pandas automatically created intervals from -9,379 to 93,79.

The value of -9.379 is calculated by Pandas as the minimum at which 0.01% of the range is subtracted (the maximum minus the minimum). Pandas use this method because, by default, the lower bounds of each interval are excluded. We see here that the new variable has as values the intervals. If you want to check the interval distribution, just use the .value_counts () method:

In []: listing ["price_disc1"]. Value_counts ()

Out []:

(-9.379, 1875.8] 59926

(1875.8, 3751.6] 14

(7503.2, 9379.0 3

(3751.6, 5627.4] 2

(5627.4, 7503.2] 0

Name: price_disc1, dtype: int64

Also, if you want to give names to intervals, you can do it using the labels = parameter of the cut () function:

listing ["price_disc1"] = pd.cut (listing ["price"], bins = 5, labels = range (5))

The "constant intervals" approach is the classic approach to building a histogram on your columns. These results that we have just seen push us to orient ourselves towards another approach.

User-defined intervals

If you want to create customized intervals, you just have to give the terminals of these intervals. We use :

In []: listing ["price_disc2"] = pd.cut (listing ["price"],

bins = [listing ["price"]. min (), 50,100,500,

list ["price"]. max ()],

include_lowest = True)

list ["price_disc2"]. value_counts ()

Out []:

(50.0, 100.0) 30076

(100.0, 500.0) 15555

(-0.001, 50.0] 13802

(500.0, 9379.0] 512

Name: price_disc2, dtype: int64

We, therefore, replace the number of intervals by a list of values (here we take the minimum and the maximum of the data). In order to include the minimum, we add include_lowest = True.

Constant frequency intervals

It is often interesting to build intervals with a number of individual constants due from one class to another. For that, we will use another function of Pandas named pd.qcut (). It takes the same type of parameters as the previous function but it will create classes of similar size (in the number of individuals):

In []: listing ["price_disc3"] = pd.qcut (listing ["price"], q = 5)

list ["price_disc3"]. value_counts ()

Out []:

(-0.001, 50.0] 13802

(85.0, 120.0) 12215

(67.0, 85.0) 11904

(120.0, 9379.0] 11708

(50.0, 67.0) 10316

Name: price_disc3, dtype: int64

Pandas did their best to properly distribute the data in the intervals. Since there are a lot of equal prices, he could not get intervals with perfectly equal frequencies.

4.3.6 Sorting

Sorting is an important tool in data science. It happens to you very frequently that you want to sort data. Each package has sorting tools, we will study two: that of NumPy and that of Pandas.

Sorting NumPy

If we stay on a NumPy array in its most classic sense, this one contains a .sort () method that applies very well on a single-dimension array, we can have:

array1 = np.random.randn (5000)

array1.sort ()

This method modifies the array1 and sorts more and more. If you want to make a descending sort, we can use:

array1 [:: - 1] .Sort ()

As you can see, this method is not very effective for complex sorting. We will use another method named .argsort ():

table = np.random.rand (5000, 10)

table [table [:, 1] .argsort ()]

So we sort on the second column of our array. We can then return the result of this sorting. Sorting on .argsort () is extremely efficient but applies primarily to an array.

Pandas Sorting

Pandas have an extremely efficient DataFrame sort function that is very similar to an SQL approach of sorting. It has many parameters and allows sorting on several keys in different directions. If we take our data on Airbnb housing, we want to sort the data in ascending order of number of rooms, then by decreasing price health level. For this, only one line of code is needed:

listing.sort_values (["bedrooms", "price"], ascending = [True, False])

So we have a powerful tool based on key lists. As in the case of joins with Pandas, when you have multiple variables or sort parameters, you can place them in a list. By default, sorting Pandas sorts by column with the axis parameter = 1. If you want to sort by line, you can change this setting.

Pandas also allow you to sort the indexes using .sort_index (). The Pandas sorting tool is less efficient in terms of speed of execution than that of the .argsort () of NumPy. Nevertheless, the greater possibilities and the fact of working on a more complex structure, such as the DataFrame, confirms in the use of Pandas sorting for our analysis.

4.3.7 Temporal Data Processing

Python has many tools for working on dates, including the datetime package natively present in Python. This one is structured around the datetime format based on a POSIX time. This format uses time units coded in codes in the following table.

Year / Month / Week / Day

Y / M / W / D

Hour / Minute / Second

h / m / s

Ms / microsecond / nanosecond

ms / us / ns

The standard date format in Python is: "2018-10-28 11:32:45"

Many functions can be used for data processing with Python, but we will be interested in the processing of dates for the tools of the data science that are NumPy and Pandas. NumPy recently has launched a datetime type that allows you to work on dates in the arrays. Pandas have always been very adept with dates, it is indeed in a time series processing perspective, that Pandas was developed and in this context, dates and times are paramount.

Dates with NumPy

Recently, it is possible to work with dates inside an array of NumPy (since NumPy 1.7). Thus the function np.datetime64 allows to create dates, and the datetime type can be used to create arrays. One can for example use arrange () to generate a series of weeks from January 2017 to January 2018:

np.arange ("2017-01-01", "2018-01-01", dtype = "datetime64 [W]")

There are many functions for working on dates with the differences based on the timedelta () function. We can also work on the days worked. This part of NumPy is constantly evolving. NumPy's documentation is the best tool to follow progress.

Dates with Pandas

It is clearly Pandas who have the ascendancy over the treatment of dates in data science. With efficient and easy-to-use functions, working on dates is now extremely simplified. Pandas have serious advantages in taking into account dates in particular with the integration of data formats in data import. However, if your data has not been imported correctly, it is very simple to transform sea strings in a DataFrame or Series in dates. For this, we use:

In []: pd.to_datetime (['11/12/2017', '05 -01-2018 '], day rst = True)

Out []: DatetimeIndex (['2017-12-11', '2018-01-05'], dtype = 'datetime64 [ns]', freq = None)

This creates a DatetimeIndex that can be used in a Series or in a DataFrame. We can also give a date format using the parameter = Format.

It is often interesting to deal with many dates. We very often want to automatically generate date sequences. Let's imagine we have daily quotation data of a stock market index, and that we want to transform these data into a series indexed to the working days during which the bank is open. Data for the year is stored in an array.

index_ouverture = pd.bdate_range ('2017-01-01', '2017-12-31')

pd.Series (data, index = index_opening) .plot ()

So we used bdate () to use the working days.

You can also use date_range () with different parameters. If for example, we want to generate an index with readings every 2 hours between February 1, 2018, at 8:00 am and March 31, 2018, at 8:00 am, we will use:

In []: time_index = pd.date_range ('2018-02-01 08:00:00', '2018-03-31 08:00:00', freq = '2h')

print (index_time.shape, index_time.dtype)

Out []: (693,) datetime64 [ns]

Many possibilities are available for the processing of dates and hours. So, rather than dates and times, you prefer to use periods (this amounts to using a month rather than the first day of the month as value of your index), you can do this with the function period_range ().

In []: pd.period_range ("01-01-2017", "01-01-2018", freq = "M")

Out []: PeriodIndex (['2017-01', '2017-02', '2017-03', '2017-04', '2017-05', '2017-06', '2017-07', '2017-08', '2017-09', '2017-10', '2017-11', '2017-12', '2018-01'], dtype = 'period [M]', freq = 'M')

We have generated a series of months. This can be done over weeks (W), quarters (Q), years ...

If we want to generate periods, we can do it thanks to pd.period ():

In []: pd.period_range (pd.Period ("2017-01", freq = "M"), pd.Period ("2019-01", freq = "M"), freq = "Q")

Out []: PeriodIndex (['2017Q1', '2017Q2', '2017Q3', '2017Q4', '2018Q1', '2018Q2', '2018Q3', '2018Q4', '2019Q1'], dtype = 'period [Q-DEC]', freq = 'Q-DEC')

In addition, you can process time zones in a simplified way with Pandas using the .tz property. By default, a date is not associated with any timezone:

In []: index_time.tz is None

Out []: True

To set a time zone, you usually do it in the function date_range (), which has a parameter tz =. Time zones can be defined, with a string including a combination zone / city ("Europe / Paris"), you can get an exhaustive list by importing:

from pytz, import common_timezones, all_timezones

all_timezones

If you have already defined your dates and want to add them a time zone, you will use the tz_localize () method. Let's imagine that we generate data every two hours in Paris, we want to transform this index by passing Noumea time zone in New Caledonia, here is the code:

In []: index_hours = pd.date_range ("2018-01-01 09:00:00", "2018-01-01 18:00:00", freq = "2h")

index_hours_paris = index_hours.tz_localize ("Europe / Paris")

index_heures_paris

Out []: DatetimeIndex (['2018-01-01 09: 00: 00 + 01: 00', '2018-01-01 11: 00: 00 + 01: 00 ', '2018-01-01 13: 00: 00 + 01: 00', '2018-01-01 15: 00: 00 + 01: 00 ', '2018-01-01 17: 00: 00 + 01: 00'], dtype = 'datetime64 [ns, Europe / Paris]', freq = '2H')

In []: index_hours_noumea = index_hours_paris.tz_convert ("Paci c / Noumea ")

index_heures_noumea

Out []: DatetimeIndex (['2018-01-01 19: 00: 00 + 11: 00', '2018-01-01 21: 00: 00 + 11: 00 ', '2018-01-01 23: 00: 00 + 11: 00', '2018-01-02 01: 00: 00 + 11: 00 ', '2018-01-02 03: 00: 00 + 11: 00'],

dtype = 'datetime64 [ns, Paci c / Noumea]', freq = '2H')

When dealing with time series, we can use the rolling tool:

pd.Series (data, index = index_opening) .plot ()

pd.Series (data, index = index_opening) .rolling (window = 10) .mean (). plot ()

The second line displays the average taken on 10 adjacent points.

4.3.8 Treatment of Missing Data

Missing data is a field of data science in its own right. Their treatment requires thinking well beyond a few lines of code. In all your data science projects, you will be confronted with missing data, they are divided into threemain types:

Missing data "completely randomly": in this case, the absence of data is the result of a random process. This type of data is not very common in reality.

The missing data randomly: the hypotheses are here a little looser compared to the previous case. It is assumed that the fact that a datum is missing does not depend on the value of this datum, but may depend on external variables.

Missing Data Not Randomly: This is missing data in a process that can be identified. For example, missing data about individuals who are not involved in a question.

Depending on the type of missing data, the treatments will be very different.

Thus, for the first two cases, we can think of methods of imputation while for the third it will not be possible to do that.

Missing data in Python

NumPy has a standard code to handle missing data, this is of NaN. An element of an array can be defined as missing data in using:

In []: table = np.random.rand (5000, 10)

table [0,1] = np.nan

table [0,1]

Out []: nan

The advantage of using this coding lies in the fact that the nan does not alter the type of your array and they are not taken into account in statistics calculations. Descriptive with the adapted functions:

In []: vec = np.ones (10)

vec [3] = np.nan

np.nansum (vec)

Out []: 9.0

When you import data with Pandas, this one will automatically replace the missing data with nan codes.

Deletion Of Missing Data

The simplest approach to dealing with missing data is to delete observations with missing data. Pandas has many methods for this. If we take the salary data for employees of the city of Boston, we can use:

In []: #on recovers the data

boston = pd.read_CSV ("../ data / employee-earnings-report-2017.CSV")

the global table boston.shape

Out []: (22245, 12)

In []: # the table when removing rows with missing data

boston.dropna (). shape

Out []: (123, 12)

In []: # the table when removing the columns with data quantes

boston.dropna (axis = 1) .shape

Out []: (22245, 4)

Completion By Mean, Mode Or Median

Before completing our data, we will have to transform our data Boston from way to have digital data. Taking inspiration from the code seen above for AirBnB data, we can do that with:

```
for col in boston.columns:

if boston [col] .dtype == object:

boston [col] = pd.to_numeric (boston [col] .str.replace (r " \ (. * \)", "")
\ .str.replace ( "", ""). str.strip ( "$") errors = 'ignore')
```

In this code, we first delete the parentheses using an expression, then remove the commas and remove the acronym $ when it is at the beginning of the chain.

We now have eight columns in the float with salaries. We can now work on the missing data. There are two ways to complete by the average or the median.

A first using Pandas:

```
# for the average

for col in boston.columns:

if boston [col] .dtype == np.number:

boston [col] = boston [col]. LLNA (Boston [col] .mean ())

# for the median

for col in boston.columns:

if boston [col] .dtype == np.number:
```

boston [col] = boston [col]. LLNA (Boston [col] .median ())

for the mode, we use a condition inside the loop call

which is equivalent to what we were doing above

the mode calculation returns a Series object and not a value like the loop

methods, hence the [0]

for col in boston.select_dtypes (object) .columns:

boston [col] = boston [col]. LLNA (Boston [col] .mode () [0])

It is also possible to complete the average with the boston command =Boston. llna (boston.mean ()), but this command has some extremely bad performance.

The Scikit-Learn package also allows for average replacements or the median:

we import the class from the module preprocessing from sklearn.preprocessing import Imputer

we create an object of this class with the imputation strategy as parameter

imputer = Imputer (strategy = "mean")

we build a new dataset by applying the # method. t_transform ()

boston_imputee = impute. t_transform (boston.select_dtypes (np.number)) This approach may seem more complex but it has two strengths:

It stores the imputed values: In []: imputer.statistics_

Out []: array ([61455.76428393, 2722.55503378, 3875.57645036, 15761.12561486, 22166.98263445, 19292.67593892, 16133.73926073, 71517.44743088])

It allows this approach to be applied to new data. Imagine that we are trying to predict data with an algorithm, in these new data, there are missing data. We can use the impute object to complete these data using our initial data:

boston_new__imputee = imputer.transform (boston_new.select_dtypes (np.number))

Conclusion

Thank you for making it through to the end of *Python Analysis*, let's hope it was informative and able to provide you with all of the tools you need to achieve your goals whatever they may be.

Python is a simple language that should allow you to focus on the implementation of automated processes in data science. Nevertheless, it is necessary to master the environment. This first part will allow you to, first of all, understand the specificities of the Python language in a broad sense, its subtleties, and its bases. It will also allow you to set up an environment of work-oriented data science in order to master all aspects of Python as a language to process data and automate processes.

These simple approaches allow you to quickly process missingdata. Nevertheless, it must be borne in mind that completion by value is dangerous. It does not change the position of the sample (average or median) but it modifies the variability of the sample (the variance, the standard deviation).

However, the majority of the methods of analysis use this variability to build models.

The Addition Of A New Modality

For qualitative variables, and when non-random data are missing, we will store all the missing data in a new modality. For this, we will create a new modality with the method. LLNA ().

Advanced Methods

Much more advanced methods based on machine learning algorithms will help predict the value of missing data. Sometimes, we use multiple imputation methods or closer neighbors. With Scikit-Learn, we can do it but we prefer to use a specialized package such as fancy imputes which offers many algorithms. We will not develop this aspect here because these packages are still experimental and are beyond the scope of this book.

Finally, if you found this book useful in any way, a review on Amazon is always appreciated!

Python Data Science

The Ultimate Guide on What You Need to Know to Work with Data Using Python

Steve Blair

Introduction

Congratulations on purchasing Data Science Python and thank you for doing so. The following chapters will discuss all the steps that we need to use to start our Data Science project and finally get some insights and good information out of all that data we have been collecting. Even better, we are going to take a look at how we can complete this project with the help of

the Python programming language! To start this guidebook, we are going to take a look at some of the basics that come with the Python language, and how it can work so well with the processof Data Science. We will also add in some information about what Data Science is all about, and how Python and Data Science can come together to provide us with amazing results in the process. We can then spend somemore time on the Python language and what comes with it before moving on to more about getting started with Data Science.

Next on the list is a look at some of the best libraries that we can use to help handle our Data Science project. We will start out with a look at the NumPy library, and the Pandas library, since these are the two most commonly used programming libraries to help with the different parts of a Data Science project. We can later expand out to some of the other options, like Jupyterand TensorFlow as needed.

With this information under our belt and some of the Python libraries set up and ready to go, it is time to take a look at some of the different parts of the puzzle we can explore in the Data Science project. We will look at the basics of collecting and preparing the data, working with data cleaning and preparation, what is data wrangling, how to take all of our information and plot it to make a visual, how to work with data aggregation and groupoperations, and a look at what the time series is and how it relates back to ourwork in Data Science.

To end this guidebook, we are going to take a look at a few other topics as well, ones that will ensure that we get a full understanding of Data Science and the steps that we need to take to make this process work. We will take an in-depth look at Machine learning and how it fits in with Data Science, and even explore some of the practical examples of Python Data Science at work so we can finally see the results that we want.

There is so much that we are able to do with the help of Data Science, and when we put it to work, with the help of the Python Programming Language, we can really dive deep into our data and learn some interesting insights that never were available to us in the past. When you are ready to learn somemore about Python Data Science, make sure to check out this book to get started.

There are plenty of books on this subject on the market, thanks again for choosing this one! Every effort was made to ensure it is full of as much useful information as possible; please enjoy it!

CHAPTER 1:

Why Python Works So Great for Data Science

The first topics that we need to take a look at here are Python, and how it can work with Data Science. There is so much that we can learn about the Python language, and because of all the extensions and libraries that come with this coding language, we can put it to work with helping out with the process of Data Science. There are a lot of parts that come together for each of these topics, so let's dive right in and see how they both works, separately, and together.

The Basics of Python

The first topic that we need to spend a little bit of time on is the Python Coding Language. As we go through some of the different processes that come with Data Science and other similar topics, it is likely that you willneed to create a model. These models are useful because they can be trained to take on data and provide the results that you need in the process. Andwhile there are some choices that you can make when it comes to working with these models, Python is one of the best options out there.

Python is simple and easy to use coding language. It was designed to be fun and to open the world of programming and coding up to novices and beginners. Just because it is easier than some of the other coding languages to learn, though, doesn't mean that you aren't getting a strong and powerful option from the start. Thanks to some of the power that does come from the Python language, we are able to work on complicated tasks and codes, including Machine learning and Data Science.

With this in mind, we need to take a look at some of the benefits of Python, along with some of the basics that come with this coding language over some of the others. The first benefit is that this coding language is easy to learn. The whole design of this coding language was to make sure that even beginners would be able to jump on board with coding and see some great results in the process. Whether you just want to add in a new coding language to your arsenal, or you have never done any coding in the past, the Python language is the right choice for you.

Even with all of the ease of use, Python has a lot of power behind it. Many people are worried that getting started with this language because they think it will be too easy, and it won't be able to handle some of the difficult tasks that are needed with Machine learning and Data Science. But when we add in the right functionalities and the right libraries, along with the Python language, we are able to make this all work well for our needs, and Python will have all the power for programming anything.

There are a number of libraries that come with the Python language that make it stronger and helps you to accomplish all of the tasks that you want. The traditional library that comes with the download of Python is going to have a lot of neat classes and functions to it as well, and many of the codes and programs that you want to write out will work just fine with this.

However, there may be times when the library just doesn't have the functionality that you are looking for. The traditional Python library is not good at handling some things like scientific work and mathematics. This doesn't mean that you are out of luck though. It simply means that we need to find another Python library that we can add to the Python language and get these types of projects done. There are a lot of options here, so you just need to find the one that will help you to finish up your own project.

Another benefit that comes with the Python language is that it is considered an Object, Oriented Program, or OOP. This means that the language is going to rely mainly on classes and objects to keep things organized and to ensure that all of the parts are able to stick together and stay in the locations where you want them. This makes the language and all of the codings that you do with it easier to work with overall and will ensure that you see some great results in the coding that you do even as a beginner.

The Python language has a large community that you can rely on when things get tough to code. Sometimes, a new programmer is going to work hard on their code, and it is just not turning out the way that they want. Or maybe there is something brand new that they want to learn, and they are not sure how to make this happen. The fact that Python has a large community is a big benefit for these very reasons.

Because of all the benefits that come with Python, and because so many programmers throughout the world are working with this coding language, it has developed a large community over the years. This is great for those who get stuck on a project, who have questions, or those who just want to learn something new along the way.

This coding language also does a great job of helping out on more complex coding projects including Data Science and Machine learning. Even with all of the other choices out there, Python is still the number one choice to handle Data Science and Machine learning tasks. We are able to bring out Python to provide us with all of the models that are needed for Data Science, and since many of these models are created with Machine Learning in mind, it makes sense that we would be able to use this coding language to help with these kinds of projects as well. No matter what data you need to get through, or what you are hoping to find while creating your model, the Python coding language is going to help us to get it all done.

There is just so much to love when it comes to working with the Python language, and that is why it is often the thing that is brought up any time that we need to create a model with Machine learning. Regardless of the questions that you need to be answered, or the business problem that you want to solve, Python is one of the easiest ways to get it all done.

What Is Data Science All About?

Now that we know a bit about the Python language, it is time to explore how it can be used with the process of Data Science. And the best way to explore this a little bit is to see what Data Science is going to be all about. This can give us a better understanding of how these two topics are going to work with one another, and why a business would want to work with Data Science in the first place to help them succeed.

When we look at Data Science, we will see that as time goes on, it continues to evolve as one of the most promising and in-demand career paths for those who are skilled professionals. This says a lot about how companies all over are working with this process when they are working with all the data they have collected. And today, those data professionals who are successful understand that they have to be able to go past some of the traditional skillsof analyzing large amounts of data, programming skills, and data mining.

In order to uncover some of the useful intelligence for their organizations, data scientists need to master the full spectrum of the Data Science life cycle, and it needs to possess a level of understanding and flexibility to maximize returns for each of the phases of this process.

As the world has entered into a time of big data, the need for a lot of storage has grown as well. This is actually one of the machine challenges and concerns for many industries until about 2010. The main focus of this was to build up a framework and some solutions to storing all of this data that weren't hard to use or too expensive. Luckily, there are now a few different frameworks out there that can handle this kind of process, which makes it easier to focus more on how to process all of that data, rather than on whereto store it.

Data Science is basically the process that we need to follow in order to gather, clean, wrangle, analyze, and visualize our data. The hope of doing this one is to learn some of the best predictions and insights that are found in all of that data. This can help a company to keep ahead of the competition, figure out which products to release, how to find a new niche, how toincrease customer satisfaction and so much more.

Now, it is time to take a look at some of the reasons that we need Data Science. Traditionally, the data that we worked with would be smaller in size,and it would be structured. This allowed us to use some simple tools from business intelligence to help us analyze all of this information. Unlike thedata that is found with some of those traditional systems, which is mostly unstructured, most of the data that companies are able to get ahold today is going to be semi-structured or unstructured. And there are often large amounts of data that we need to focus on as well.

This is going to complicate things quite a bit. When the data is so large, and we are not able to get it all in a structured form, this is going to make it harder to read through the data and get any insights out of it. But with the help of Data Science and a good data analysis in the process, you will find that we can still get through this data, but we need to use different methods.

The data that we work with to gather predictions and insights will come from a lot of different sources, and the sources that you work with will often depend on what kind of question you would like to answer or what business problem you would like to solve. Simple tools of BI are not going to be able to process the huge volume and variety of data. And this is why we need to make sure that we pick out some analytical tools that are more advanced and complex. This ensures that we are able to process, analyze, and draw insights out of the data we have.

Of course, this is not going to be the only reason why so many companies are starting to take a look at Data Science. Nor is it the only reason that this Data Science has become so popular. Some of the reasons that companies are going to rely on this Data Science, and all of the tools and techniques that come with it will include:

Being able to learn the precise requirements that your customers have with your business. This is possible if you just use the existing data you hold onto, such as the customer's age, income, browsing and purchasing history and learn from this. This is all data that you have been collecting for some time now. But with Data Science, we are able to take all of that data and use it to train our own Machine Learning models more effectively. Over time, and with the right kind of data, it is easier to use the model to effectively recommend new products to customers, with the precision that you need to make the sale.

That is just one example of what we are able to do when working with Data Science. We can look at the idea of the smart car that is developed by Google right now. These kinds of cars have to collect a ton of data, from many sources, in order to learn how to behave on the road. A self-driving car is going to collect live data from things like lasers, radars, and cameras to create a good map of its surroundings.

Based on the data that the self-driving car is able to read from, the car will then learn when to make different decisions. It will learn when to go faster or slower when to overtake other cars, were to make a turn, and more. And all of this is done with the help of your big data, and some great Machine Learning algorithms.

Data Science is also a big part of a process that is known as predictive analysis. A good example of how this one works is with weather forecasting. Data that comes from a variety of sources, such as ships, radars, aircraft, and satellites, can be collected and then analyzed before building up some weather models. These models, once they have gone through some of the proper training, will not only be able to forecast the weather for us, but they will be great at predicting the occurrence of a natural calamity and the likelihood that this calamity is going to happen. If it is used in the proper manner, and it is trained to show some accuracy, it could help us to take the right measures ahead of time to save many lives.

We have spent a lot of time talking about Data Science so far in this section, but we need to go a bit further into some of the basics of this process, and not just how we can benefit from this process. Many companies are increasingly using the term of Data Science, but it is hard to know exactly what this term means? What are the skills that are required to become a data scientist? And is there a difference between Data Science and business intelligence? And how are we meant to work on the decisions and predictions within thisprocess?

These are just a few of the questions that can be raised when it comes to working with Data Science. But first, Data Science is going to be a blend of principles of Machine learning, algorithms, and other tools that all have the goal of discovering some of the hidden patterns that can show up in the data. The difference that comes between the process of Data Science and what statisticians have been doing for years is found between explaining and predicting.

Data Analysis is going to spend their time explaining what is going on by processing the data and learning the history that comes with it as well. But a data scientist is not only going to do what is called an exploratory analysis to learn the insights in the data, but it will also use a variety of algorithms from Machine learning to identify the occurrence of a particular event in the future. This means that a data scientist is going to be able to look at the data from a lot of angles to see what is there, and sometimes these angles are brand new.

So, to keep it simple here, Data Science is primarily going to something that we use to make good decisions and predictions. And this is all done with the help of several different tools and techniques including Machine learning, prescriptive analytics, and predictive causal analytics. Let's take a look at each of these and see how they will help us through the process.

The first type that we are going to take a look at is known as Predictive Causal Analytics. If you are working with a model and you want it to predict the possibility that an event is going to happen in the future, then we need to apply the Predictive Causal Analytics to it. A good example of this is when a bank provides money on credit. They would use this model to help them figure out the probability of the customer making their credit payments on time. If they are highly likely to pay the amount each month, and on time, then they are more likely to get the loan.

With Predictive Causal Analytics, we can build up a model that will perform the process of predictive analytics. But these analytics are going to be done on the payment history of the customer, allowing the bank or the financial institutions to predict of the payments on this debt will be paid out on time or not. It may not be 100 percent accurate because people are hard to predict all of the time. By analyzing some of the past behavior of that particular person, though, we are able to get a better idea of how they are going to behave in the future.

Then we have prescriptive analytics. If you are working on a project and you want to create a model that has the intelligence of taking its own decisions and the ability to modify it with some dynamic parameters, then it is time to pull out the prescriptive analytics to get it done. This is a new field that comes with Data Science, and it is all about providing advice based on the data that you have.

This model is not only going to predict for us, but it is going to help suggest a range of prescribed actions and shows the associated outcomes that we can get with it. The best example that we can look at for this one is the self- driving car from Google. The data that the vehicle is able to gather is going tohelp it to learn how to drive on its own. You are capable of running some algorithms on this data to ensure there is some intelligence brought into it. This enables the car to take some decisions, like when to turn, which path to take, and when to speed up or slow down.

Another option here is Machine learning. Machine Learning can come in at several points of the process, but first, we are going to look at how Machine Learning can be used to make some good predictions. If you are working with a lot of transactions, such as what we see with a financial company, and we want to build up a new model that can determine a future trend, then the algorithms that come with Machine learning are some of the best to make all of this happen.

These Machine Learning Algorithms are going to fall under the category of supervised Machine learning, basically, because we already have the data that we want to base our models on, and that we can use to train all of our machines. For example, a model that detects fraud is going to be trainedusing some of the historical records that are available for purchases that turned out fraudulent in the past.

Another way that we can use Machine learning is with pattern discovery. If you are working on a model or a project, but you don't have any parameters based on which you can make some predictions, then it is time to do some work. We need to still go through our set of data and find some of the hidden patterns that are inside. These patterns are going to be used to help us make some meaningful predictions overall.

This is a good example of what we are allowed to do with an unsupervised Machine learning Model as there aren't going to be any predefined labels for the grouping when we get started. There are a lot of algorithms and techniques that we can use for this one, but one of the most common to help with pattern discovery will be Clustering.

Let's say that your job is to work with a telephone company and you want to be able to expand out your network. Your goal is to put towers in a new region and you must make sure that the towers are placed in the right areas and locations in order to reach the maximum number of customers at thesame time. The Clustering Machine learning Algorithm is going to be the perfect technique that we can use to find these tower locations while ensuringthat all of the customers receive an optimal amount of signal strength.

We are going to go through some of these steps a little bit later in this guidebook, but it is important to know the steps that come with completing our own Data Science process. Some of the main steps that are found in data analysis, and in the process of Data Science, will include:

5. **Discovery:** This Is the time where we look for the data that we want to use, often from a variety of sources.

6. **Data preparation:** Since the data comes to us from many different sources, we use this stage to prepare it and organize everything so it works with the model later on.

7. **Model planning:** This is where we are going to determine the best techniques and methods that we can use on the data, helping us to draw up the best relationships between the variables.

8. **Model building:** With this phase, we are going to develop the sets that we need for training and the ones that we need for testing. This ensures that our model is going to be accurate and work the way that we want.

9. **Operationalize:** With this phase, we will be able to deliver some of the final reports, briefings, code, and technical documents, and more.

10. **Communicate the results:** At the end of it all, we need to be able to come out and communicate what we were able to find within the data. Often this is done with some visualizations, such as a graph or a chart, to get the work done.

Data Science can easily pair together with the Python Coding Language in order to get things done. Python is adept at handling the large amounts of data that are needed for a Data Science project. This language will help us to clean and organize the data, plan out our model, and even build up the model so that we can get the best results and really learn what insights are out there for us within all of this data.

There are many companies that are going to rely on the basics of Data Science and all that comes with it. There are a lot of processes that come with Data Science, and it isn't just about gathering up the data. This is a good place to start, but we also need to spend some time exploring how to clean and organize the data, how to wrangle the data, working with Machinelearning and various algorithms within it to create models to look at the data and provide you with insights and predictions as needed. We also have a step that will take some time working with data and making it appear in a graph orchart, ensuring that it is easier to understand complex types of data in just a few minutes.

There are a few other coding languages that can do the same kind of thing. But none of them are going to combine the ease of use, and the power, thatwe can find with the Python Coding Language. When we can add all of these together, it becomes so much easier to really get through that data in a quick and efficient manner and to ensure that we will see the results that we want.

#### CHAPTER 2

The Basics of Python That Everyone Needs to Know

B efore we dive into some of the other things that we need to know to get started with Data Science and how Python is able to handle some of the complexities that come with Data Science, it is now time for us to take a look at some of the basics that come with the Python coding language. There are a lot of simple parts that are in this library, and being able to learn about them, and understanding when they will show up in some of the codings that you do, can make you more efficient as time goes on as well. With that said, let's dive in and learn some of the basics of the Python code to make it easier to get started.

The Statements

Statements are pretty simple in Python. These are just the strings of code that you write out and that you want the compiler to list out on the string. When you tell the compiler the instructions that you want it to work on, you will find that those are the statements of your code. As long as you write them out properly, the compiler will read them and show up the message that you want on your screen. The statements can be as short or as long as you would like, depending on the code that you are working on.

The Comments

As you are writing out the code, you may find that there are times you want to include a little note or a little explanation of what you are writing inside the code. These are little notes that you and other programmers are able to read through in the code and can help explain out what you are doing with that part of the code. Any comment that you write out in Python will need to use the # symbol ahead of it. This tells the compiler that you are writing out a comment and that it should move on to the next block of code.

You can add in as many of these comments as you need to explain the code that you are writing and to help it make sense. You could have one very another line if you would like, but you should try not to add in too many or you may make a mess of the code that you have. But as long as the # symbol is in front of the statement, you can write out as many of these comments as you would like and your compiler will just skip out of them.

What are Classes?

There are a lot of different things that we can talk about when it comes to the Python Language. But one of the most important topics that we are going to take a look at is the classes in Python. These classes, to keep things as simple as possible, are going to be containers that can hold onto the objects and other parts of the code. You have to take some time to name all of the classes in the proper manner and put them in the right spots of the code to help get them to work the right way, and of course, we are going to take each of these classes with the right objects to get the code to work.

It is possible to store pretty much anything that you would like inside a new class that is designed. But the major rule with this one is that you have to make sure that the objects you choose for one class are pretty similar in one way the items don't have to be identical to one another, but when someone looks inside one of these created classes and understand why you put all of those objects together in that class.

For example, you don't have to just put cars into the same class, but you could have different vehicles that show up in the same class. You could have some items that are seen as food in one class. You can even have items that are all going to be the same color. As the programmer, you are able to get some freedom when creating the class and storing objects into these classes, but when another programmer looks at the code, they should understand how all of these items or objects go with each other.

Classes are going to be very important when it is going to come time to write out the code. These are going to hold onto the various objects that you want to write into the code and will ensure that each of the parts will be stored properly. They will also make it easier to call out these objects, and other parts of the code when it is time to use these during the execution of thecode.

The Operators

Another thing that we can work on with some of our codings are the operators. These are often ignored or forgotten because we assume that they are not that important or that they play too small of a role in the work that we are trying to do. But while the operators are simple to use, this does not mean that we should ignore them and not get the full benefits from them as well.

There are several different types of operators that we can work with on a regular basis. We can work with the arithmetic operators to help us add together, or subtract, or do another mathematical equation on our code. There are the logical operators, the comparison operations, and more, that can help us make sure that we will get the results that we want.

Assigning a Value to a Variable

One thing that we can work with while writing some codes is assigning a value to a variable. A variable is basically going to be a piece of storage on the computer. We can leave it blank, but at some point, to make sure that our code is going to work the way that we would like. This means that we need to be able to take some kind of value and assign it back to the variable, or that space in the memory, so we can use it later on.

The process of adding value to the variable is pretty easy. You just need to use the equal sign between the two. So, pick out the value that you want to assign over to a specific variable, and then make sure that the equal sign shows up between the two. You can technically add in as many values to the same variable if you would like, as long as we make sure that the equal sign is there.

The Control Flow

The idea of the control flow in the work you do with coding is not meant to be too difficult to work with. It is just going to tell us how to read through the codes we write, to ensure that the compiler is going to be able to handle the different parts. To keep with the ease that we talked about earlier with Python, we have to remember that this language is going to write out the codes from left to right. We will look at some of the examples of how this code will look later on, but you will find that the codes are written out in the same manner that we see the words on a page in a book or on a website.

The Python Functions

Another topic that we need to take a look at when it comes to working on our codes in Python is known as the functions. These functions are basically a set of expressions that can be like statements as well. These are going to be some of the very first-class objects that we are going to work within the code, which is a great thing because we will not have to add in a lot of restrictions in order to use these as we go. You will be able to work with the functions in a similar manner that we can with some other values, like strings and numbers, and they are going to have attributes that we are capable to bringout with the prefix of dir.

Now, these functions are very diversified and there are many attributes that you can use when you try to create and bring up those functions. Some of the choices that you have with these functions include:

- **__doc__:** This is going to return the docstring of the function that you are requesting.

- **Func_default:** This one is going to return a tuple of the values of your default argument.

- **Func_globals:** This one will return a reference that points to the dictionary holding the global variables for that function.

- **Func_dict:** This one is responsible for returning the namespace that will support the attributes for all your arbitrary functions.

- **Func_closure:** This will return to you a tuple of all the cells that hold the bindings for the free variables inside of the function.

There are different things that you can do with your functions, such aspassing it as an argument over to one of your other functions if you need it. Any function that is able to take on a new one as the argument will be considered the higher-order function in the code. These are good to learn because they are important to your code as you move. These are just a few of the different topics and options that you can work with when it comes to writing out codes in the Python language. Learning how all of these can workand how we can use them to write our own codes. With this in mind, let's move on to some of the other things that we need to work with when it comesto creating our own models of Data Science.

CHAPTER 3:

The NumPy Library and
How It Can Help with Data Science

The library that we are going to start our journey with Data Science is the NumPy Library. This is going to be an open-source package of Python. It can be used for scientific and numerical computing. In many cases, though, it is a library that is used for more efficient computation on arrays when it is needed. This library is going to be based, as well as written, on two main programming languages, including Python and C, and the programmer can decide which of these two languages they would like to use at any time.

While NumPy can be used with the C Coding Language, it is considered a Python package, and the name of this library stands for Numerical Python. There are a variety of things that you are able to do with this kind of library, but it is going to be used in many cases to help us process multidimensional arrays that are homogeneous. It is going to be one of the core libraries to help out with some of the scientific computations.

Hence, we can see how this library is going to be powerful when it comes to multidimensional array objects and integrating tools that can be useful any time that we want to work with these arrays. It is important in almost all ofthe scientific programming that we can do with Python, whether this includesa project in bioinformatics, statistics, and Machine learning.

The NumPy Library is also going to provide programmers with some good functionality that is written out well and will run in an efficient manner. It is mostly focused on helping us to perform some operations that are mathematical on a contiguous array, much like what we see in lower-level languages that handle arrays as well, such as C. To make this easier, it is going to be used to handle the manipulation of numerical data.

Thanks to this language, there are a lot of times when we can add in this language to our coding, and get more work done. This is a very good computational library to work with and specifically works with arrays and projects that are more scientific. With this in mind though, Python can also be used as an alternative to MATLAB with the help of the NumPy Language.

One thing that we will notice when it comes to using the NumPy language is that it is really going to be one of the most used. This is due to the fact that Data Science techniques need all of that work done on matrices and large-size arrays. And some of the heavy numerical computation needs to be done as well to extract out the predictions and the insights we are looking for. There may be a few methods that we can use to make this happen, but all of the mathematical functions that are needed for it fall under the NumPy library, so why not just use that to make things easier?

Some programmers worry that the NumPy Library is too basic and won't be able to meet all of their needs with Data Science. Yes, this library is one of the most basic of the Python statistical and scientific libraries, but it is still considered one of the most important when it comes to working with Python and scientific computing.

We can also add to this that there are a lot of other libraries that work with Data Science, Machine learning, and other tasks, that will depend on the arrays from NumPy as their basic inputs and outputs. This means that if we ignore all that the NumPy Library is able to accomplish, then we are missing out on a lot of other neat things that we can do with this library as well.

To add to all of this, the NumPy Library is going to provide us with some neat functions that will allow a developer to perform basic and sometimes more advanced functions of statistics and mathematics on multi-dimensional arrays and matrices with fewer lines of code to get it all done. You will find that the n-dimensional array, which is going to be seen by the name of Ndarray, is the main functionality that comes with NumPy. These are going to be homogeneous arrays and all of the elements that come inside that array will need to be of the same type for this to work.

Now, if you have worked with Python in the past, you may see the array from NumPy, and think that it is simply the same thing as a Python list. And there are some similarities that come with the two of these. One thing to note with it though is that the arrays of NumPy are going to be much faster than what we can find with a Python list. However, the Python list is going to be more flexible than the arrays because you can only store the same type of data in each column. You have to decide which one is the best for your projects or your models and work from there.

There are a lot of different features that come with the NumPy Library as well, and many of these are going to assist Python in providing some Data Science help as well. Some of the top features that come with this particular Python Library will include:

3. It can help us reshape our arrays. Because it is so good at doing this, it often allows Python to become a more efficient, and easier to use, alternative to MATLAB.

4. It provides us with a variety of functions for arrays.

5. It includes some homogeneous arrays that are multidimensional. The Ndarray is going to be a part of this as well, which is just going to be a n-dimensional array.

6. It is able to combine the Python and C languages together, which can add in some more flexibility and power to the coding that you do.

The next question that comes with this library is why we should consider using this language for some of our scientific computing, or our codingneeds. There are a few options here but remember that the array from NumPy is sometimes considered the same thing as a list from Python. The good newsis there are three main reasons why we would choose to work with the array rather than the list, and that includes that there is less use of the memory, the array can perform faster, and they are more convenient to work with.

The first reason with this one though is that the array is not going to take up as much space in the memory as we see with the Python list. Then, it is going to also be pretty fast when it is time to execute the codes and models that you want to use. And finally, the arrays are often a lot easier and more convenient to work with compared to some other options, including Python lists, so adding these into your toolbelt can be important.

There are many advantages that will show up when we choose to work with the NumPy library with Python, rather than some of the other options. Keep in mind though that there are a ton of different coding libraries out there that also work with Python, so it is all going to depend on what works the best for you, and what kind of process of coding you would like to work on the most. With this in mind, some of the advantages that we can enjoy when it comes to working with the NumPy library includes:

The NumPy array is going to take up less space than we see with some of the other options, including the Python list. The arrays that come with this library are going to be smaller than the Python list. To start, the Python list has the ability to take up at least 20 MB of space on the memory, based on how big the list is to start with. And then the array will take up much less at just 4 MB. The arrays are often going to be a lot easier to access when it is time to read them or write them out.

And the second benefit that comes with this library is that the performance of speed is great. The NumPy array is able to perform computations at a much faster rate than what we will see with the Python list. Because this library is open-sourced, it is not going to cost anything to use it, and it is going to rely on Python to get things done. And since we can combine the C code, especially existing codes from this language from before, it is easier than everto get some important projects done.

Now, as we can see from this chapter, NumPy is going to be a really strong library when we look at all of the high-quality functions that this library holds onto. Anyone is able to perform large computations or calculations, and thanks to this library, it can all be done with just a few lines of code. This is one of the things that makes the NumPy library perfect for those who want to work on numerical computations. If you are going to do some work with Python and Data Science, then it is worth your time to download the NumPy Library and get familiar with some of the features and functions that come with it.

CHAPTER 4:

Manipulating Data with the Pandas Library

T he next library that we are going to take a look at is known as the Pandas Library. This library is one of the best when it comes to Machine learning and Data Science, and will stand for Python Data Analysis Library. According to many sources on this library, Pandas is going to be the name because it is derived from the term of panel data. This is basically an econometrics term that handles data sets that are multidimensional in structure.

Pandas are going to be seen as a bit game changer when it is time to analyze the data that you have used the Python Language, and it is often going to be the number one Python Library to use when it is time to handle data munging and wrangling. It can also handle all of the other aspects of Data Science that you want as well, making it an all in one library for your needs. Pandas are also going to be open-sourced, free for any programmer to use, and is one of the best Data Science libraries to focus on.

There are a lot of cool things that come with the Pandas Library, so taking some time to look it over and figure out what it all entails will help you with a lot of Data Science projects. One thing that is cool with Pandas is that it is able to take almost any kind of data and will then create an object in Python with rows and columns. These are going to be called the data frame and it is going to look pretty much like what we see with Excel. If you have worked with the R Programming Language before, then you will see some similarities here as well.

However, compared to working with the dictionaries or lists that come with Python, or through loops or list comprehensions, the Pandas Library is going to be so much easier overall. The different functions that come with Pandas can make it a much easier library to work with, especially when it comes to some of the complexities of working with Data Science.

Installing the Pandas Library

The next thing that we need to take a look at here is how to actually install the Pandas Library and get it all set up. To install this library, we need to have a Python version that is at least 2.7 or higher. The Pandas Library is not designed to work with any of the older versions of Python, so if you have one of the older versions, it may be time to upgrade. At this time, you need to make sure that some other deep learning libraries are in place. Pandas are going to be dependent on a few other libraries, based on what you would like to accomplish. It really needs to have at least NumPy associated with it, andif you want to do something like plotting with your information, then you need to work with Matplotlib. Because you need a few extras that go withthis library, we may want to consider installing a package to make sure thatall the extras are there when you need them. The Anaconda distribution is a good option to work with and it can work on all of the major operating systems including Linux, OS X, and Windows systems. Pandas is able to work with the Python IDE, including options like Spyder or the Jupyter Notebook. But to get these to work, the Pandas library has to be installed and ready to go. The Anaconda extension will come with both of the IDE or Integrated Development Environment, so that can make things easier to handle.

Importing one of these libraries means that you need to first load it into your memory, and once the installation is all done, you will be able to open up the needed files and work with them at any time. to make sure that you can import Pandas in the right manner, all that you need to do is run the following code below:

- *Import pandas as pd*
- *Import numpy as np*

If you would like to make some of the codings that you do a bit easier, you would add in the second part (as pd) because it allows you to access Pandas with just the pd.command, rather than having to go through the process of writing out pandas.command each time that you wish to use it. As we can see with the code above as well, you need to import NumPy at this time. NumPy is a useful library to work with any scientific computing in Python, and often the Pandas library will need to pull out functions and other parts from this to get things done. At this point, Pandas is up and running and ready for us to use.

The Benefits of Using Pandas

With that work done, it is time to take a look at some of the many different benefits that come with using the Pandas library. There are a lot of benefits to this one, and it is one of the most popular options that come with this kind of Data Science work. With this in mind, let's take a look at some of the benefits that we are able to see with the Pandas library.

The first benefit that comes with the Pandas library is the data representation. Pandas are going to provide programmers with a streamlined form of data representation. This is going to be important as you analyze and work to understand the data that you hold onto a bit better. When you can simplify some of the data representation that you have, it is going to facilitate better results for some of your projects in Data Science.

The second benefit of this library is that it provides us with a way to get more work done, without having to do as much writing. This is actually one of the biggest advantages that we are able to see with this library. With the traditional form of Python, we may have taken many lines of code to get the work done, without any support libraries, but with Pandas, we can get that same work done in just one or two lines of code. This means that by using Pandas, we can shorten up the procedure of handling the data that we have. When we can save all of that time, we are allowed to focus more on the algorithms that we need for the data analysis. An extensive set of useful features is next on the list of Pandas benefits. Pandas are going to be seen as really powerful in the coding world. They are able to provide us with a big set of commands and features that are important, and which can be used to easily look through the data and analyze it. We can use Pandas in order to perform various tasks including filtering out the data based on conditions that we set, or segregating and segmenting the data according to the preferences that we would like to meet. The next benefit that comes with working with Pandas is that this library is able to handle a large amount of data in an efficient manner. When the Pandas Library was originally created, its goal was to handle large sets of data in an efficient manner. Pandas can really helpus to save a lot of time and hassle because it can import large amounts of dataquickly and efficiently.

The Pandas Library is also able to make data customizable and flexible. There is a huge set of features in Pandas that can be applied to the data that you have. This can be great for beginners because it helps us to customize, edit, and pivot that data according to what we want to see happen. This is going to ensure that we can get the most out of our data each time. And finally, the last benefit that we will see with the Pandas library is that it is made for Python. Python is one of the biggest and most sought-after programming languages in the whole world, and it has an extensive amountof features that we can enjoy. And with just the amount of productivity that isoffered, it is no wonder that many people want to learn how to code in this language. Because of this, and all of the great features that come with Python,the fact that we are able to code with the help of Python in Pandas is going to be a great thing. It allows the programmer to tap into the power of many libraries and features that work with Python, which adds in some of the strength and power that we need with our coding.

Now, there are a few disadvantages that come with this library compared to some of the others, but often there are ways to work around these. Some of the disadvantages that can come with the Pandas library that programmers need to be aware of include:

1. **The learning curve is steeper:** Pandas was thought to have mild learning slow in the beginning. But the more that you explore the library, the steeper the learning curve is going to become. Sometimes the functionality of this library is going to get confusing, and for beginners, this is going to bring on some challenges.

2. **The syntax can be hard:** While Pandas is going to work with the Python language, sometimes it is going to add in some challenges when it comes to the syntax that has to be used. Switching back and forth between Python and Pandas codes can cause some problems.

3. **It doesn't work well with 3D matrices:** If this is something that you want to work with, it can be a drawback of this library. If you are planning on just creating a 2D matrix, then this will not be a problem at all.

4. **Bad documentation:** Without a good amount of documentation to go along with the project, it can be difficult to learn a new library. The documentation that comes in Pandas isn't going to do much to help us get the harder functions of the library done. This is going to slow down our learning procedure and can make coding difficult.

Viewing and Inspecting the Data

One thing that Pandas is able to do to help with our Data Science project is to work with viewing and inspecting the data. In reality, Pandas is able to help with all of the various processes that you may want to do with Data Science, but right now, we are just going to focus on this part. You can use a variety of the functions that come with Pandas in order to take a look at what is in the data, figure out if there are any missing or duplicate values, and then make the changes as needed to work on your data analysis.

With this in mind, it is also possible for us to get some statistics on the entire series, or an entire data frame. Some of the codes that you would need to use to make this happen includes:

3. **Df.mean():** This one is going to help us return the mean of all our presented columns.

4. **Df.corr():** This one is going to return the correlation between the columns that are in your frame of data.

5. **Df.std():** This one is going to help us see what the standard deviation ends up being between each of the columns.

6. **Df.median():** This one is going to help us see what the median of each column is like.

7. **Df.min():** This one is going to help us see the lowest value that is present in each of our columns.

8. **Df.max():** This one is going to help us see the highest value in each of our columns.

9. **Df.count():** This one is going to help us by returning the number of all of the non-null values that show up in each column of the data frame we are using.

There is just so much that we are able to do with the help of the Pandas Library, and learning how to make all of this come together and work foryour needs can make a difference in how well the Data Science project worksfor you. Depending on the kind of data that you want to sort through, and what your end goal is with the data, you may choose to go with another library to help out with the various parts. But if you want to just go through the whole process of Data Science on your own, without having to switch back and forth between the libraries and the processes that you are using,then the Pandas library is the right one for your needs.

#### CHAPTER 5:

Collecting and Manipulating Data

When we are working on the process of Data Science, there are a few steps that need to happen in order to actually see the insights and predictions that will offer you some sound business decisions. The first step out of this process is going to be collecting and manipulating the data. You can't go through and complete analysis if you don't first have some data to look through. And that is where this chapter is going to come in and help. Collecting the data that we need to help train and test our models for use can be so important. Having it set up to find the right information, the information that will help us solve a business problem, or answer some questions, can ensure that the model we choose is going to complete the job. With that in mind, let's take a look at some of the best topics that we need to consider when it is time to collect the high-quality and pertinent information needed in Data Science.

Where Should I Collect Data From?

The first question that we need to take a look at when it is time to work on this step is where a company should collect its data from. This is often going to depend on what your company is hoping to achieve when they work with the data. Are you looking to gather information on what would make your customers happy? Then you may want to go straight to the customer and ask them some survey questions. If you want to learn more about what the competition is doing, then you may want to look for another source to help you with this.

There are a lot of different ways that a company is able to collect data, and many sources that they are able to work with as well. Some of the more popular options that are available for collecting data include industry papers, surveys, research, social media, transactional information, recommendation sites, and anywhere else that would hold onto the data and information that you think will answer your biggest business challenges.

Unstructured vs. Structured Data

While you are searching for the data that you want to use during this process, you are going to run across the idea of unstructured and structured data. Understanding how these two types of data are similar, and how they are different will make it easier to know which kind you want to collect as you work with this process.

Structured data is usually the kind that is thought of as a more traditional form of data. It is going to consist mainly of many types of text files, and the information is going to be well-organized in the process. Structured data is going to be stored inside a warehouse for data, and it can be pulled out for analysis at any time that we need it. Before we add in the era of big data and all of the new sources of data that we can use, structured data was the only kind available and would help organizations make many of their important business decisions.

Structured data is nice because it is easy for us to digest and really organized. This means that analytics would be possible through the use of legacy solutions in data mining. To be more specific, structured data is going to be made up for things like customer data, including addresses, the names, and contact information of your customers. In addition, businesses can also collect up some of the transactional data they need as their structured data source, which can consist of things like financial information. But this financial information needs to be stored up appropriately to meet compliance standards.

Most companies would prefer to work with this kind of data. It is neat and organized and can be really easy to build a model around and get some good results in the process. Unfortunately, it is not always possible to collect structured data. It takes a long time and can get expensive. Many companies, if they can, will get some structured data, and then combine it together with unstructured data to meet their needs.

The second type of data that we can explore is Unstructured Data. This is a big type of data that is growing more and more, and it is being used by companies in order to leverage new and emerging data sources. These new sources of data can come from a lot of different sources, including mobile applications, the Internet of Things, social media, and more.

Since there is so much diversity that shows up with the sources of unstructured data, it can cause businesses more trouble to manage it than they would have with structured data. Because of this, companies are facing some challenges with their data in manners that they just weren't before, with a lot of creativity coming into the mix to pull out the needed insights and data to analyze. The growth of data, and the maturation of data lakes, and other platforms are all a direct result of companies gathering more unstructured data than ever before. The traditional environments for data warehouses are not able to keep up with the new types of data that companies want to take some time to analyze. Because of this, there are now more storage places than ever to hold onto all of that unstructured data and make it work for you.

While the unstructured data is often harder to organize and read through, it can still provide us with some unique opportunities to get ahead. There is more information that we can gather when we talk about unstructured data. It is often less expensive to collect and store. And often, this information is going to bring out a lot of new predictions and insights that can keep us ahead of the game.

Collecting the Data

When we are the best planning on how we should collect the needed data, it is important that we are aware of many best practices and practical considerations for addressing any of the logistical challenges that a company can face when they reach this part of the process. Implementing a plan that helps you to collect data requires attention on a lot of matters, including:

4. Making sure that you can get the senior leadership, as well as some of the key stakeholders, to agree to this process. This group can include a lot of different people including customers, tenants, employees, union representatives, management committees, and the boards of directors for the company.

5. Establishing what will be the steering committee, or selecting someone to be accountable and consulted for all of the big decisions about this process. This may include some things like the design, communication management, logistics, finances, and coordination of all the parts.

6. Determining who is going to be responsible for collecting the data. This could be employees who are trained for the job, or some experts to handle this.

7. Identifying the technology, people, resources, and logistics that are needed to develop and implement initiatives for data collecting.

8. Anticipating and addressing concerns of key stakeholders and any of the questions that come about with the project.

9. Designing a strategy for consultation and communication that is going to explain the initiative of data collecting and encourages the highest possible participation rate.

10. Protecting the personal information and privacy of those who you collect the data from, and using carefully controlled procedures when it comes to collecting, storing, and then accessing the data. All the confidentiality and dignity of the other person needs to be respected at all times.

11. Minimizing the impact and even the inconvenience for those who are affected in the workplace or the service environment. This can go even as far as choosing the best time to collect the data.

12. Aiming to have as much flexibility as needed to allow for some changes without a ton of expenses or inconvenience for anyone.

13. Consider working with a pilot phase or a test period that will allow you to improve and even modify some of your methods of data collecting, any time that these changes are needed.

How Long Should I Collect Data For?

One question that a lot of data scientists are going to have is how long they should collect the data. They want to make sure that they are collecting the data for long enough to gather enough and learn some valuable insights from that information. But they don't want to drag it on for too long, wasting time and money and not learning anything in the process.

The amount of time you will spend collecting the data is going to vary based on what your goals are, and what your business problem is all about. You want to collect the data for as long as needed. When you feel like you have gathered the amount of information that is needed to answer your business question or the challenge your business is facing, then it is time to stop working with this data collecting altogether.

The first step that we need to follow when it is time to work on the process of Data Science is working with collecting and then manipulating our data. This process does take some time, as most businesses want to make sure that they can gather a lot of information in a short amount of time. But this is the data we will use to create our models and organize things as much as possible. With high-quality data and lots of it, we can create the models that we need toreally find the predictions and the insights that our business needs.

CHAPTER 6:

Data Cleaning and Preparation

The next topic that we need to take a look at in our process of Data Science is known as data cleaning and preparation. During the course of doing our own data analysis and modeling, a lot of time is going to be spent on preparing the data before it even enters into the model that we want to use. The process of data preparation is going to include a lot of different tasks, including loading, cleaning, transforming, and rearranging the data. These tasks are so important and take up so much of our time, an analyst it is likely going to spend at least 80 percent of their time on this.

Sometimes the way that we see the data stored in a database or a file is not going to provide us with the right format when we work with a particular task. Many researchers find that it is easier to do ad hoc processing of the data, taking it from one form to another working with some programming language. The most common programming languages to use to make this happen include Perl, R, Python, or Java.

The good news here though is that the Pandas library that we talked about before, along with the features it gets from Python, can provide us with everything that we need. It has the right tools that are fast, flexible, and high-level that will enable us to get the data manipulated into the form that is most needed at that time. There are a few steps that we are able to work with, in order to clean the data and get it all prepared, and these include:

What Is Data Preparation?

Let's suppose that you are going through some of the log files of a website and analyzing these, hoping to find out which IP out of all the options the spammers are coming from. Or you can use this to figure out which demographic on the website is leading to more sales. To answer these questions or more, an analysis has to be performed on the data with two important columns. These are going to include the number of hits that have been made to the website, and the IP address of the hit.

As we can imagine here, the log files that you are analyzing are not going to be structured, and they could contain a lot of textual information that is unstructured. To keep this simple, preparing the log file to extract the data in the format that you require in order to analyze it can be the process known as data preparation.

Data preparation is a big part of the whole Data Science process. According to CrowdFlower, which is a provider of data enrichment platforms that data scientists can work with, it is seen that out of 80 data scientists, they will spend their day in the following:

a)   60 percent of their time is spent on organizing and then cleaning the data they have collected.

b) 19 percent is spent on collecting the sets of data that they want to use.

c) 9 percent is used to mine the data that they have collected and prepared in order to draw the necessary patterns.

d) 3 percent of their time will be spent doing any of the necessary training for the sets of data.

e) 4 percent of the time is going to be spent trying to refine the algorithms that were created and working on getting them better at their jobs.

f) 5 percent of the time is spent on some of the other tasks that are needed for this job.

As we can see from the statistics of the survey above, it helps us to see that most of the time for that data scientist is spent in preparing the data, which means they have to spend a good deal of time organizing, cleaning, and collecting, before they are even able to start on the process of analyzing the data. There are a few valuable tasks of Data Science like data visualization and data exploration, but the least enjoyable process of Data Science is going to be the data preparation.

The amount of time that you actually will spend on preparing the data for a specific problem with the analysis is going to depend on the health of the data directly. If there are a lot of errors, missing parts, and duplicate values, then this is a process that will take a lot longer. But if the data is well-organized and doesn't need a lot of fixing, then the data preparation process is not going to take that long at all.

Why Do I Need Data Preparation?

One question that a lot of people have when it is time to work on the process of data preparation is why they need to do it in the first place. It may seem to someone who is just getting started in this field that collecting the data and getting it all as organized as possible would be the best steps to take, and then they can go on to making their own model. But there are a few different reasons why data preparation will be so important to this process and theywill include the following:

3. The set of data that you are working with could contain a few discrepancies in the codes or the names that you are using.

4. The set of data that you are working with could contain a lot of outliers or some errors that mess with the results.

5. The set of data that you are working with will lack your attributes of interest to help with the analysis.

6. The set of data that you want to explore is not going to be qualitative, but it is going to be quantitative. These are not thesame things, and often having more quality is going to be the most important.

Each of these things has the potential to really mess up the model that you are working on and could get you results or predictions that are not as accurate as you would like. Taking the time to prepare your data and get it clean and ready to go can solve this issue, and will ensure that your data is going to be more than ready to use in no time.

What Are the Steps for Data Preparation?

At this point, we need to take some time to look at some of the steps that are needed to handle the data preparation for data mining. The first step is to clean the data. This is one of the first and most important steps to handlingthe data and getting it prepared. We need to go through and correct any of thedata that is inconsistent by filling out some of the values that are missing and then smoothing out the outliers and any data that is making a lot of noise and influencing the analysis in a negative manner.

There is the possibility that we end up with many rows in our set of data that do not have a value for the attributes of interest, or they could be inconsistent data that is there as well. In some cases, there are records that have been duplicated or some other random error that shows up. We need to tackle all of these issues with the data quality as quickly as possible in order to get a model at the end that provides us with an honest and reliable prediction.

There are a few methods that we can use to handle some of the missing values. The method that is chosen is going to be dependent on the requirement either by ignoring the tuple or filling in some of the missing values with the mean value of the attribute. This can be done with the help of the global constant or with some of the other Python Machine Learning techniques including the Bayesian formulae or a decision tree.

We can also take some time to tackle the noisy data when needed. It is possible to handle this in a manual manner. Or there are several techniques of clustering or regression that can help us to handle this as well. You have to choose the one that is needed based on the data that you have.

The second step that we need to focus on here is going to be known as data integration. This step is going to involve a few things like integrating the schema, resolving some of the conflicts of the data if any shows up, and even handling any of the redundancies that show up in the data that you are using.

Next on the list is going to be the idea of data transformation. This step is going to be important because it will take the time to handle some of the noise that is found in your data. This step is going to help us to take out that noise from the data so it will not cause the analysis you have to go wrong. We can also see the steps of normalization, aggregation, and generalization showing up in this step as well.

We can then move on to the fourth step, which is going to be all about reducing the data. The data warehouse that you are using might be able to contain petabytes of data, and running an analysis on this complete set of data could take up a lot of time and may not be necessary for the goals that you want to get in the end with your model.

In this step, it is the responsibility of the Data Science to obtain a reduced representation of their set of data. We want this set to be smaller in size than some of the others, but inclusive enough that it will provide us with some of the same analysis outcomes that we want. This can be hard when we have a very large set of data, but there are a few reduction strategies for the data that we can apply. Some of these are going to include the numerosity reduction, aggregation, data cube, and dimensionality reduction, and more, based on the requirements that you have.

And finally, the fifth step of this is going to be known as data discretization. The set of data that you are working with will contain three types of attributes. These three attributes are going to include continuous, nominal, and ordinal. Some of the algorithms that you will choose to work with only handle the attributes that are categorical.

This step of data discretization can help someone in Data Science divide continuous attributes into intervals, and can also help reduce the size of the data. This helps us to prepare it for analysis. Take your time with this one to make sure that it all matches up and does some of the things that you are expecting.

Many of the methods and the techniques that you are able to use with this part of the process are going to be strong and can get a lot of the work with you. But even with all of these tools, it is still considered an area of research, one that many scientists are going to explore more and hopefully come up with some new strategies and techniques that you can use to get it done.

Handling the Missing Data

It is common for data to become missing in many applications of data analysis. One of the goals of working with the Pandas Library here is that we want to make working with some of this missing data as easy and as painless as possible. For example, all of the descriptive statistics that happen on the objects of Pandas exclude the missing data by default.

The way that this data is going to be represented in Pandas is going to have some problems, but it can be really useful for many of the users who decide to go with this kind of library. For some of the numeric data that we may have to work with, the Pandas library is going to work with a floating-point value that is known as NaN, or not a number, to represent the data that is missing inside of our set of data.

In the Pandas Library, we have adopted a convention that is used in the programming language of R in order to refer to the missing data. This missing data is going to show up as NA, which means not available right now. In the applications of statistics, NA data can either be data that doesn't exist at all, or that exists, but we are not going to be able to observe through problems with collecting the data. When cleaning up the data to be analyzed, it is often important to do some of the analysis on the missing data itself to help identify the collection of the data and any problems or potential biases in the data that has been caused by the missing data.

There are also times when the data is going to have duplicates. When you get information online or from other sets of data, it is possible that some of the results will be duplicated. If this happens often, then there is going to be a mess with the insights and predictions that you get. The data is going to lean towards the duplicates, and it will not work the way that you would like. There are ways that you can work with the Pandas library in order to really improve this and make sure that the duplicates are eliminated or are at least limited at least a little bit.

There is so much that we are able to do when it comes to working with data preparation in order to complete the process of data mining and getting the results that we want in no time with our analysis. Make sure to take some time on this part, as it can really make or break the system that we are trying to create. If you do spend enough time on it, and ensure that the data is as organized and clean as possible, you are going to be happy with the results and ready to take on the rest of the process.

CHAPTER 7:

What is Data Wrangling?

The next topic that we need to spend some time on is known as data wrangling. This is basically the process where we are able to clean, and then unify, the mess and complex sets of data that we have, in order to make them easier to access and analyze when we would like. This may seem like part of the boring stuff when it comes to our Data Science proves, but it is going to be so important to the final results, so we need to spend some time on seeing how this works.

With all of the vast amounts of data that are present in the world right now, and with all of the sources of that data growing at a rapid rate and always expanding, it is getting more and more essential for these large amounts of available data to get organized and ready to go before you try to accomplish any analysis. If you just leave the data in the messy form from before, then it is not going to provide you with an accurate analysis in the end, and you will be disappointed by the results. Now, the process of data wrangling is typically going to include a few steps. We may find that we need to manuallyconvert or map out data from one raw form into another format. The reason that this is done in the first place is that it allows us to have a more convenient consumption for the company who wants to use that data.

What Is Data Wrangling?

When you work with your own project in Data Science, there are going to be times when you gather a lot of data and it is incomplete or messy. This is pretty normal considering all of the types of data you have to collect from a variety of sources overall. The raw data that we are going to gather from allof those different sources is often going to be hard to use in the beginning. And this is why we need to spend some time cleaning it. Without the data being cleaned properly, it will not work with the analytical algorithm that we want to create.

Our algorithm is going to be an important part of this process as well. It is able to take all of the data you collect over time and will turn it into some good insights and predictions that can then help to propel your business into the future with success. But if you are feeding the analytical data, a lot of information that is unorganized or doesn't make sense for your goals, then you are going to end up with a mess. To ensure that the algorithm works the way that you want, you need to make sure that you clean it first, and this isthe process that we can call data wrangling. If you, as the programmer would like to create your efficient ETL pipeline, which is going to include extract, transform and load, or if you would like to create some great looking data visualizations of your work when you are done, then just get prepared now for the data wrangling. Like most data scientists, data analysts, and statisticians will admit, most of the time that they spend implementing an analysis is going to be devoted to cleaning or wrangling up the data on its own, rather than in actually coding or running the model or algorithm that they want to use with the data. According to the O'Reilly 2016 Data Science Salary Survey, almost 70 percent of data scientists will spend a big portion oftheir time dealing with a basic analysis of exploratory data, and then 53 percent will spend their time on the process of cleaning their data beforeusing in an algorithm. Data wrangling, as we can see here, is going to be an essential part of the Data Science process. And if you are able to gain some skills in data wrangling, and become more proficient with it, you will soon find that you are one of those people who can be trusted and relied on when itcomes to some of the cutting-edge Data Science work.

Data Wrangling with Pandas

Another topic that we can discuss in this chapter is the idea of data wrangling with Pandas. Pandas is seen as one of the most popular libraries in Python for Data Science, and specifically to help with data wrangling. Pandas is able to help us to learn a variety of techniques that work well with data wrangling, and when these come together to help us deal with some of the data formats that are the most common out there, along with some of their transformations. We have already spent a good deal of time talking about what the Pandas library is all about. And when it comes to Data Science, Pandas can definitely step in and help get a ton of the work done. With that said, it is especially good at helping us to get a lot of the data wrangling process that we want doing as well. There may be a few other libraries out there that can do the job, but none are going to be as efficient or as great to work with as the Pandas library. Pandas will have all of the functions and the tools that you need to really make your project stand out, and to ensure that we are going to see some great results in the process of data wrangling as well. So, when you are ready to work with data wrangling, make sure to download the Pandas library, and any of the other extensions that it needs.

Our Goals with Data Wrangling

When it comes to data wrangling, most data scientists are going to have a few goals that they would like to meet in order to get the best results. Some of the main goals that can come up with data wrangling, and should be high on the list of priorities, include:

6. Reveal a deep intelligence inside of the data that you are working with. This is often going to be accomplished by gathering data from multiple sources.

7. Provides us with accurate and actionable data and then puts it in the hands of n analyst for the business, in a timely manner so they can see what is there.

8. Reduce the time that is spent collecting, and even organizing some of the really unruly data, before it can be analyzed and utilized by that business.

9. Enables the data scientists, and any other analyst to focus on the analysis of the data, rather than just the process of wrangling.

10. Drives better skills for making decisions by senior leaders in that company.

The Key Steps with Data Wrangling

Just like with some of the other processes that we have discussed in this guidebook, there are a few key steps that need to come into play when it comes to data wrangling. There are three main steps that we can focus on for now, but depending on the goals you have and the data that you are trying to handle, there could be a few more that get added in as well. The three key steps that we are going to focus on here, though, will include data acquisition, joining data, and data cleansing. First on the list is Data Acquisition. How are you meant to organize and get the data ready for your model if you don't even have the data in the first place? In this part of the process, our goal is to first identify and then obtain access to the data that is in your preferred sources so that you can use it as you need in the model.

The second step is going to be where we join together the data. You have already been able to gather in the data that you want to use from a variety of sources and even did a bit of editing in the process. Now it is time for us to combine together the edited data for further use and more analysis in the process.

And then we can end up with the process that is known as data cleansing. Remember that we talked about this a bit in the last chapter, but it is still important as we work with the process of data wrangling. In the data cleansing process, we need to redesign the data into a format that is functional and usable, and then remove or correct any of the data that we consider as something bad.

What to Expect with Data Wrangling?

The process of data wrangling can be pretty complex, and we need to take some time to get through all of it and make sure that we have things in the right order. When people first get into the process of data wrangling, they are often surprised that there are a number of steps, but each of these is going to be important to ensure that we can see the results that we want.

To keep things simple for now, we are going to recognize that the data wrangling process is going to contain six iterative steps. These are going to include the following:

- The process of Discovering. Before you are able to dive into the data and the analysis that you want to do too deeply, we first need to gain a better understanding of what might be found in the data. This information is going to give you more guidance on how you would like to analyze the data. How you wrangle your customer data, as an example, maybe informed by where they are located, what the customer decided to buy, and what promotions they were sent and then used.

- The second iterative step that comes with the data wrangling process is going to be Structuring. This means that we need to organize the data. This is a necessary process because the raw data that we have collected may be useful, but it does come to us in a variety of shapes and sizes. A single column may actually turn into a few rows to make the analysis a bit easier to work within the end. One column can sometimes become two. No matter how we change up some of the work, remember that the movement of our data is necessary in order to allow our analysis and computation to become so much easier than before.

- Then we can go on to the process of Cleaning. We are not able to take that data and then just throw it at the model or the algorithm that we want to work with. We do not want to allow all of those outliers and errors into the data because they are likely to skew some of our data and ruin the results that we are going to get. This is why we want to clean off the data.

There are a number of things that are going to spend our time cleaning when it comes to the data in this step. We can get rid of some of the noise and the outliers we can take some of the null values and change this around to make them worth something. Sometimes it is as simple as adding in the standard format, changing the missing values, or handling some of the duplicates that show up in the data. The point of doing this, though, is to increase the quality of the data that you have, no matter what source you were able to find it from.

- Next on the list is the process of Enriching the Data. Here we are going to take stock of the data that we are working with, and then we can strategize about how some other additional data might be able to augment it out. This is going to be a stage of questions to make sure that it works, so get ready to put on your thinking cap.

Some of the questions that you may want to ask during this step could include things like: What new types of data can I derive from what I already have? What other information would better inform my decision making about this current data? This is the part where we will fill in some of the holes that may have found their way into the data, and then find the supplementation that is needed to make that data pop out.

From here, we can move on to the step of validation. The validation rules that we are going to work with this step in the Data Science process are going to be repetitive programming sequences. The point of working with these is that we want to check out and verify the consistency, quality, and security of our data to make sure that it is going to do the work that we want.

There are a lot of examples that come with the validation stage. But this can include something like ensuring the uniform distribution of attributes that should be distributed in a normal way, such as birth dates. It can also be used as a way to confirm the accuracy of fields through a check across the data.

- And the last stage is going to be Publishing. Analysts are going to be able to prepare the wrangled data to use downstream, whether by a software or a particular user. This one also needs us to go through and document any of the special steps that were taken or the logic that we used to wrangle this data. Those who have spent some time wrangling data understand that implementation of the insights is going to rely upon the ease with which we are able toget others the information, and how easy it is for these others to access and utilize the data at hand.

Data wrangling is an important part of our process and ensures that we are able to get the best results with any process that we undertake. We need to remember that this is going to help us to get ahead with many of the aspects of our Data Science project, and without the proper steps being taken, we are going to be disappointed in what we see as the result in the end. Make sure to understand what data wrangling is all about, and why it is so important so that it can be used to help with your Data Science project.

#### CHAPTER 8:

Taking Our Results and
Plotting Them to Visualize What We Learned

T he next topic that we need to take some time to learn about is known as Data Visualization. The point of this one is to take all of that data we have been collecting, and then learn how to plot it or turn it into some other form of graphical representation. This can then be presented, along with the other information you have on the findings to key decision-makers. Graphs and charts are much easier to read through and understand compared to large blocks of text, so this is another addition to your work that can ensure the key decision-makers actually understand what you did and what predictions and insights were found inside.

Data visualization is simply going to be the presentation of data in a graphical or pictorial format. It is helpful because it will enable key decision-makers to see analytics presented in a visual form. This makes it easier to grasp some difficult concepts quickly or even identify some brand-new patterns. With an interactive form of visualization, it is easier to take this concept even further by using a variety of technologies to drill down into charts and graphs for more detail, interactively changing what data you are going to see, and how this data can be processed.

The History of Data Visualization

The ideas that come with data visualization are going to be important to ensure that we can get the most out of what we see with our project. The concept of using any kind of picture or visual to help understand largeamounts of data is something that has been around for centuries. Look backto some of the early maps and graphs and even to the invention of the pie chart in the early 1800s. Several decades later, one of the most cited examples of one of these graphs occurred when Charles Minard was able to map the invasion of Russia by Napoleon.

This graph was truly amazing and helped to show us a lot of complex information in one picture. For example, this map was able to depict the size of the army throughout the invasion, as well as the path that Napoleon took in retreat from Moscow. And this information was also tied back to the temperature and time scales as well to make it even easier to understand the event and what was happening at the different stages.

It is technology however that is the thing that really added some fire to the process of data visualization. Computers have made it easier than ever to process a large amount of data at speeds that are faster than ever. Because of this, data visualization today has become a rapidly evolving blend of science, and it is going to be even bigger changes in the landscape of many businesses over the next few years.

Why Is This Data Visualization So Important?

The next question that we need to take a look at here is why this data visualization is so important. Due to the way that the human brain is able to process information, using graphs and charts and other options to visualize a large amount of data that is more complex, proves to be easier than pouring over reports and spreadsheets. We can learn a lot more from a chart than we are from ten pages of data and at a much faster rate.

Data visualization is helpful because it is quick and it is one of the easiest ways to convey concepts in an universal manner. And you can also move some of the information around and do some experimenting to make slight adjustments and see how that influences the data that you have. In addition, data visualization is also able to help with:

5. Identifying areas that need more attention or some improvement within them.

6. Clarify out which factors are the most likely to influence the behavior of the customer.

7. It can help us to understand which products we can place in different locations.

8. It is a great way to predict sales volumes.

How is Data Visualization Being Used?

The next thing that we need to take a look at here is how data visualization is actually being used. No matter the size of the industry, all types of businesses have found the value in using data visualization, and some of the tools that come with this, to help them make some more sense out of all that data they collected. There are a number of benefits to using this kind of tool in your Data Science project, and the way that you can use it will depend on what your overall goals are. Some of the ways that we can use data visualization to help make sense of our data will include:

It can help us to comprehend data and information faster. By using representations of our information in a graphic form, businesses have a better way to see large amounts of data in a clear and cohesive manner. They are then able to draw some conclusions based on that information. And since using this is going to be faster when it comes to analyzing the information, especially when compared to reading the information of a spreadsheet or another format, businesses are better able to address any problems or answer the needed questions in a timelier manner.

Another reason that a company would want to go with data visualization as part of their Data Science project is that it can help them to pinpoint some emerging trends. Using this tool to help discover new trends, both in the market and in the business itself, can give any business the edge that they need over their competition. And when we can beat out the competition, this helps to positively influence our bottom line.

A data visualization makes it so much easier to make this happen. With the data visualization, companies can find that it is much easier to spot any of the noise in the data, or the outliers that could affect the quality of the product or even the customer churn. Then they can address any of the issues that could affect them, long before these issues become bigger problems.

We can also see that this data visualization is going to help a business to identify relationships and patterns in their data. Even extensive amounts of complicated data can start making sense to us when we take it out of the words and turn it into a graph or a chart. Businesses that uses this method will start to recognize what parameters are there and how they can be highly correlated to one another at the same time.

Some of the correlations that show up in your data are going to be more obvious, and you will know why they are set up that way in the first place. But then there are some correlations that won't be as obvious. Being able to identify these relationships is a key to ensuring that organizations focus on the areas that are able to have some control over their most important goals, rather than wasting time and money in the process.

And finally, another way that we are able to see Data Science at work is when it communicates a story to others once a business has been able to uncover some of the new insights that are there through the process of data analytics, they then need to go through and communicate these insights to others, usually the key decision-makers or the stakeholders of that company.

With the help of graphs, charts, and other representations that can be seen as visually impactful, we are able to engage the other person, make the complex data easier to understand and ensure that the messages get across as quickly as possible. Those who have to use this information to make key business decisions are going to enjoy that they can just look through a graph and see the information that they want in one form.

Laying the Groundwork for Data Visualization

The next thing that we need to take a look at is some of the groundwork that needs to come into play before we are able to work with our Data Visualizations. Before we can implement any kind of new technology, there are a few steps that need to be taken. Not only do we need to have a good grasp on the data that we are using, but we also need to understand our own goals, the needs that our business has, and the audience overall. Having all of these in place and understanding how we want the data to help us can be important to see the results that we would like.

There are a number of steps that we need to do before we can work with data visualization and get it to work the way that we want. Preparing the business for the technology that helps with data visualization requires that we first do the following:

f)   We need to understand the data that we want to visualize. It is impossible to pick out the type of visualization that we want to work with if we know nothing about the data that will make up that visualization. We need to know the size of the data, and the cardinality, which includes how unique the data values are in a column.

g) We need to determine what we would like to visualize, and what kind of information is the most important to communicate in this process.

h) We need to know our audience well and understand how this audience is going to be able to visualize that information.

i) We need to use a visual to convey the information in the best, and often the simplest form, to the audience.

Once we have been able to answer the first four questions that we have above, including about the type of data we have and the audience who is most likely to consume this information, it is time to do some preparation. This needs to be done on the amount of data that you plan to work on for this visualization. As many businesses are finding out, big data can bring on some new challenges when we work with visualization.

When we factor in all of the large volumes, the different varieties, and some of the varying velocities of the big data, it is going to change the way that the visualization is able to work overall. Add to this that data can be generated at a much faster rate than ever before, and it is sometimes hard to manage or analyze it without a good method in place.

There are a lot of factors that we need to consider when it is time to create our visualization for our data. One of these includes the cardinality that shows up in the columns that we want to visualize. High cardinality means that there is going to be a large percentage of unique values. This could include something like bank account numbers since we want to have each of the items unique from the others.

Then it is possible that the cardinality is going to be lower. Low cardinality just means that the data in the column will contain a large percentage of values that are able to repeat again and again. This might be in the column that includes the gender of the customer.

Which Visual is the Right One for My Project?

One of the biggest challenges that we are going to face in this part of Data Science is figuring out which of the visuals are the best to represent all of that data and information we have been working on. There are a lot of choices when it comes to a good visual that will get your point across to the users, but we want to make sure that we are going with the one that will represent our data in the proper manner without any worries about errors or misrepresenting our work. When you first start to explore a new set of data, auto-charts are sometimes a useful tool to work with simply because they can give you a quick view of large amounts of data. This capability of data exploration is helpful, even to statisticians who are more experienced because it helps them to speed up the lifecycle process of their analysis. This happens because the auto-chart is able to eliminate the need for repeated sampling to determine what kind of data is going to be the best for each model that you create. There are also a lot of other types of visualizations that we are able to rely on based on what kind of data we explore and how we would like to view it. Some of the best types of data visualizations that we can do with the Python language will include:

4. **The scatterplot:** This is the visualization that is used to help us find any relationship that is present in bivariate data. It is going to be used in many cases to help us take two continuous variables and find the correlation between them.

5. **Histogram:** The histogram is going to help us to see the distribution that is there between a variable that is continuous. It is good for discovering the frequency distribution for a single variable when we arecompleting an analysis that is univariate.

6. **Bar chart:** This is the type of visualization that can be used to represent categorical data with either horizontal or vertical bars. It is a general type of plate that makes it easier to aggregate some of our categorical data based on a function. The default of this is going to be the mean, butyou can choose to have the function as something else.

7. **Pie chart:** This graph is going to be an example of a plot that is used to represent the portion of each category when we have categorical data. The whole pie is going to get divided up into slices, which are going to be the same as the number of categories.

Working with data visualization is going to be very important to the results that we are looking for with our Data Science project. Without the right visualization in process, it is really hard to see the data act the way that we want, and we may spend hours poring over spreadsheets and more, trying to guess what information is hidden inside. With the visualization, no matter what kind you use as long as it works for your data, this is no longer a big issue. We are able to focus on what is in the chart or graph, and see exactly

what trends, insights, and predictions, are found in our data right away.

CHAPTER 9:

Data Aggregation and Group Operations

T aking the time to categorize our set of data, and giving a function to each of the different groups that we have, whether it is transformation or aggregation, is often going to be a critical part of the workflow for data analysis. After we take the time to load, merge, and prepare a set of data, it is then time to compute some more information, such as the group statistics or the pivot tables. This is done to help with reporting or with visualizations of that data.

There are a few options that we are able to work with here to get this process done. But Pandas is one of the best because it provides us with an interface that is flexible. We can use this interface to slice, dice, and then summarize some of the sets of data we have in a more natural manner.

One reason that we see a lot of popularity for SQL and relational databases of all kinds, is because we can use them to ease up the process which joins, filters, transforms, and aggregates the data that we have. However, some of the query languages, including SQL, that we want to use are going to be moreconstrained in the kinds of group operations that we are able to perform right with them. As we are going to see with some of the expressiveness that happens with the Pandas library, and with Python, in general, we can performa lot of operations that are more complex. This is done by simply utilizingany function that is able to accept an array from NumPy or an object from Pandas. Each of the grouping keys that you want to work with can end up taking a variety of forms. And we can see that the keys don't have to all comein as the same type. Some of the forms that these grouping keys can come in for us to work on includes:

5. An array or a list that is the same length as the axis that we want to group.

6.   A value that is going to indicate the name of the column in a DataFrame.

7. A Dict or a Series that is going to give the correspondence between the

values of the axis that is being grouped here, and the group names you have.

8. A function that can then be invoked on the axis index, or on some of the individual labels in the index.

Note that the last three methods of this are going to be a type of shortcut that helps us to produce an array of values to be used when splitting up the object. This can seem a bit abstract right now, but don't let this bother you. It will all make more sense as we go through the steps and learn more about how all of this is meant to work. With this in mind, it is time to talk more about data aggregation and how we are able to make this work for our needs.

What Is Data Aggregation?

Data Aggregation is going to be any kind of process in which information can be gathered and then expressed in the form of a summary, usually for the purpose of analysis. One of the common purposes that come with aggregation is to help us get some more information about a particular topic or a group, based on a lot of variables like profession, income, and age.

The information about these groups is often going to be used in order to personalize a website, allowing them to choose what content and advertising that is likely to appeal to an individual who belongs to one or more groups where the data was originally collected from. Let's take a look at how this works.

We can work with a site that is responsible for selling music CDs. They could use the ideas of data aggregation in order to advertise specific types of CD's based on the age of the user, and the data aggregate that is collected for others in that age group. The OLAP, or Online Analytic Processing, is a simple option with data aggregation in which the market is going to use mechanisms for online reporting to help the business process through all of this information.

Data Aggregation can be a lot of different things as well. For example, it could be more user-based than some of the other programs that we may have seen in the past. Personal Data Aggregation Services are popular, and they will offer any user a single point for collection of their personal information from a host of other websites that we want to work with.

In these systems, the customer is going to work with a single master PIN, or personal identification number, which allows them the access they need to various accounts. This could include things like music clubs, book clubs, airlines, financial institutions, and so on. Performing this type of Data Aggregation can take some time and will be a more complex system to put in, but we will see that it comes under the title of screen scraping.

This is just one example of how we are able to work through the process of data aggregation. It is one of the best methods to help companies really gain the knowledge and the power that they need based on the users they have at the time. It often works well with Pandas, Python, and even databases because it can collect a lot of the information that is found in those, and then recommends options to our customers or our users, based on where they fit in with the rest of the information.

Yes, there are always going to be some outliers to the information, and times when the information is not going to apply to a person, no matter where they fit in the database or how good the data aggregation algorithms are. But it will be able to increase the likelihood that you will reach the customers and the users you want, providing them with the information and the content that they need, based on their own features and how they will react compared to other similar customers.

CHAPTER 10:

What Is the Time Series?

Another topic that we need to spend some time discussing in this guidebook that can help us learn more about the process of Data Science and what it all entails is the idea of a Time Series. This is a bit different than some of the other topics that we have had some time to explore so far, but it is still an important part of the process that we need to be able to look through. The first question here is what a Time Series is all about. A Time Series is going to be a sequence of numerical points that happen in successive order. When we talk about investing, for example, a time series is able to track the movement of any points of data that you choose, such as the price of a security over a specified time period with the points of data recorded at intervals that are regular, such as once a day. When it comes to Data Science, we are able to work with this in a slightly different way. But it is still the same idea. We will find the object that we want to track, such as customer satisfaction, and then follow these at regular intervals to see what is happening with the satisfaction of our customers and whether the new improvements we are working with are going to really help provide us with a higher amount of customer satisfaction overall.

There isn't going to be a minimum or even a maximum amount of time that we need to include with our Time Series. This allows the business to gather and collect their data in a manner that will provide the information they need.If they find that they can gather the information in a shorter amount of time, then the business can stop doing some of the analysis a bit earlier. If they feelthat this is something that they should monitor and watch for a longer period of time to get accurate results, then this is what they can do.

This is one of the nice things that come with the Time Series. We are able to make some customizations to it, especially when it comes to how long we want the intervals for testing to be, and how long we wish to keep the time series going for. This customization is going to ensure that we can get it to work the right way that we need for our project.

Understanding the Time Series

Let's dive a bit more into what the time series is all about. A Time Series can be taken on any kind of variable that we want, as long as this variable changes over time. When we see this in investing, for example, it is common to work with the time series in order to track the price of a security over time. With your business, you may use it to track the level of customer satisfaction that you have, or how well the market is accepting your new product.

We are able to track the time series over the short term, such as the price of something over the hour, or even the full course of a business day. And then there is the possibility that we want to track the variable over the long term, such as looking at the price of the security when you get to the close on the last day of each month over two or three years.

We can also perform what is known as a time series analysis. This can be a useful tool to use because it helps us to really track and look through how a given economic variable, security, or asset is going to change over time. We can also use this when it is time to examine how the changes associated with the point of data we chose compare to shifts in other variables over a similar period of time.

For example, let's say that we want to go back to the idea of investing for a bit and analyze the Time Series of a closing stock daily with the prices, looking at the stock for a year. You would first need to obtain a list of the prices for that stock at closing for each day in the past year, and then getthese listed out in chronological order. This would be the time series for the closing price of one year for the stock. We can use this to figure out what the peaks and troughs are with that stock, so we can make some better predictions of how it will behave in the future.

You can also use this to figure out your profits and how they vary from one part of the year to another. You could do this same idea, monitoring the monthly gross profit each month for three years and write these out. With this information in place, we are able to see that the price goes up at some points of the year, and down at other points of the year. This makes it easier to figure out when to extend hours, how many employees to have on hand at different parts of the year, and more.

Another neat thing that we are able to do here when it comes to working with the time series is to use it in some of our forecasting endeavors. Time Series

Forecasting is helpful because it is going to use information regarding historical values and associated patterns to make it easier to predict the future activity of the variable you are monitoring.

This could include a lot of different parts, but may relate to trending analysis, issues with seasonality (is one season of the year naturally a slower period for you?), and a cyclical fluctuation analysis. As with all of the forecasting methods, success is not going to be guaranteed, but it can help with planning and ensuring that you can best serve your customers, create high-quality products, and get the most profits possible.

Working with the Time Series is a great way to enhance the knowledge you have about a particular topic and can help you determine whether it is something that you need to pursue or not. It can even make it easier to plan out some of the work that you need to do with your business, adding so muchmore to your business that other competitors are not able to beat out.

CHAPTER 11:

What Is Machine learning and How It Fits with Data Science

The next topic that we need to take a look at here is Machine learning and how it can come into play when we work with Data Science and all of the neat things that we are able to do with this topic. Machine Learning can definitely be an important part of the Data Science process, as long as we use it in the proper manner.

Remember, as we go through this process, that part of Data Science is working on data analysis. This helps us to take a lot of the data we have collected along the way, and then actually see the insights and the predictions that are inside of it. To make this happen, we need to be able to create our own models, models that are able to sort through all of the data, find the hidden patterns, and provide us with our insights.

To help us make these models, and to make sure that they actually work the way that we want, we need to have a variety of good algorithms in place, and this is where Machine Learning is going to come into play quite a bit. You will find that with the help of Machine Learning, and the variety of algorithms that are present in Machine Learning, we can create models that are able to go through any kind of data we have, whether it is big or small, and provide us with the answers that we need here.

Machine Learning is basically a process that we can use in order to make the system or the machine we are working with think in a manner that humans do. This allows the algorithm to really go through and find hidden patterns in the same manner that a human would be able to do, but it can do it much faster and more efficiently than any human could do manually.

Think about how hard this would be to do manually for any human, or even for a group of people who are trying to get through all of that data. It could take them years to get through all of that data and find the insights that they need. And with how fast data is being generated and collected, those predictions and insights would be worthless by the time we got to that point anyway.

Machine Learning can make this process so much easier. It allows us to have a way to think through the data and find the hidden patterns and insights that are inside for our needs. With the right Machine Learning algorithm, we are able to really learn how the process works, and all of the steps that are necessary to make this happen for us. With this in mind, it is time to take a closer look at Machine Learning, and all of the parts that we need to know to make this work for our needs.

What is Machine learning?

The first thing that we need to take a look at here is the basics of Machine Learning. Machine Learning is going to be one of the applications of artificial intelligence that can provide a system with the ability to learn, all on its own, without the help of a programmer telling the system what to do. The system can even take this a bit further and can work to improve based on its own experience, and none of this is done with the system being explicitly programmed in the process. The idea of Machine Learning is going to be done with a focus on the development of programs on the computer that is able to access any data you have, and can then use that presented data to learn something new, and how you would like it to behave.

There are going to be a few different applications that we can look at when it comes to using Machine Learning. As we start to explore more about what Machine learning is able to do, you may notice that over the years, it has been able to change and develop into something that programmers are going to enjoy working with more than ever. When you want to make your machine orsystem do a lot of the work on its own, without you having to step in and program every step, then Machine Learning is the right option for you.

When it comes to the world of technology, we will find that Machine Learning is pretty unique and can add to a level of fun to the coding that we do. There are already a lot of companies, in a variety of industries (which we will talk about in a bit), that will use Machine learning and are already receiving a ton of benefits from it.

There are a lot of different applications when it comes to using Machine Learning, and it is amazing what all we can do with this kind of artificial intelligence. Some of the best methods that we are able to follow and focus our time on when it comes to Machine Learning include:

9. **Research on statistics:** Machine Learning is already making some headway when it comes to the world of IT. You will find that Machine Learning is able to help you go through a ton of complex data, looking for the large and important patterns that are in the data. Some of the different applications of Machine Learning underthis category will include things like spam filtering, credit cards, and search engines.

10. **An analysis of Big Data:** There are a lot of companies who have spent time collecting what is known as Big Data, and now they have to find a way to sort through and learn from that data in a short amount of time. These companies are able to use this data to learn more about how money is spent by the customers, and even to help them make important decisions about the future. If we had someone go through and manually do the work, it would take much too long. But with Machine Learning, weare able to get it all done. Options like the medical field, election campaigns, and even retail stores have started to turn to Machine Learning to gain some of these benefits.

11. **The financial world:** There are many financial companies that have been able to rely on Machine Learning. Stock trading online, for example, will rely on this kind of work, and we will find that Machine Learning can help with fraud detection, loan approvals, and more.

To help us get going with this one, and to understand how we are able to receive the value that we want out of Machine Learning, we have to make sure that we pair the best algorithms with the right processes and tools. If youare using the wrong kind of algorithm to sort through this data, you are basically going to get a lot of inaccurate information, and the results will not give you the help that you need. Working with the right algorithm the whole time will make a big difference.

The really cool thing that we will see with this one is that there are a lot of Machine learning algorithms that we can choose from at this point to work on your model. Each of these works in a different manner than the others, but this ensures that you are able to handle any kind of problem that comes along with your own project. With this in mind though, you will notice that some of the different algorithms that are available, and really great at doing your job, and finding the insights that you want, include random forests, neural networks, clustering, support vector machines, and more. As we are working on some of the models that we want to produce, we will also notice that there are a ton of tools and other processes that are available for us to work with. We need to make sure that we pick the right one to ensure that the algorithm, and the model that you are working with, will perform the way that youwould like. The different tools that are available with Machine learning will include:

4. Comprehensive management and data quality.

5. Automated ensemble evaluation of the model to help see where the best performers will show up.

6. GUIs for helping to build up the models that you want along with the process flows being built up as well.

7. Easy deployment of this so that you can get results that are reliable and repeatable in a quick manner.

8. Interactive exploration of the data and even some visualizations that help us to view the information easier.

9. A platform that is integrated and end to end to help with the automation of some of the data to decision process that you would like to follow.

10. A tool to compare the different models of Machine learning to help us identify the best one to use in a quick and efficient manner.

The Benefits of Machine learning

We also need to take some time to look at a few of the benefits that come with Machine learning. There are a lot of reasons why we would want to choose to go with Machine Learning to help our Data Science Project. It is impossible to create some good algorithms or models that can accurately make predictions out of the data you send through it. And there are a lot of other benefits that can come with this as well. Some of the best benefits that we can see when we decide to work with Machine learning include:

3. **Marketing products are easier:** When you are able to reach your customers right where they are looking for you, online and on social media, it can increase the sales. You can use Machine Learning to figure out what your target audience is going to respond to, and you can make sure that the products you are releasing work for what the customer wants as well.

4. **Machine Learning can help with accurate medical predictions:** The medical field is always busy, and it is believed that a lot of the current job openings are going to be left unfilled. Even a regular doctor, with no specialties, will need to go through and deal with lots of patients throughout the day. Keeping up with all of this can be a hassle. But with the help of Machine learning, we can create a model that is able to look at images, and recognize when something is wrong or not. This can save doctors a lot of time and hassle and can make them more efficient at their jobs.

This is just one area where Machine learning will be able to help out with the medical field. It can assist with surgeries, helps with taking notes for adoctor, looking for things in x-rays and other imaging, and even helping with front desk operations.

5. **Can make data entry easier:** There are times when we need to make sure that all the information is entered into a database in an efficient and quick manner. If there is a ton of data to sort through, and we are short on time, this can seem like a task that is impossible. But with Machine Learning and the tools that come with it, we are able to get it all done in no time.

6. **Helps with spam detection:** Thanks to some of the learning processes that come with Machine Learning, we find that this can be used to prevent spam. Most of the major email servers right nowwill use some form of Machine learning in order to handle spam and keep it away from your regular inbox.

7. **Can improve the financial world:** Machine Learning is able to come in and work with a lot of the different tasks of the financial world. It helps with detecting fraud, offering new products to customers, approving loans, and so much more.

8. **Can make manufacturing more efficient:** Those in the manufacturing world are able to use Machine Learning to help them be more efficient and better at their job. It can figure outwhen things are going to be slowing the process down and needs tobe fixed, it will look at when a piece of a machine is likely to die out, and so much more.

9. **It provides us with a better understanding of the customer:** All companies want to know as much about their customers as possible, ensuring that they can really learn how to market to these individuals, what products to offer, and which methods they can take to make the customer as happy as possible.

Supervised Machine learning

The first type of Machine learning algorithm that we will take a look at is known as supervised Machine learning. This Machine learning type is the kind where someone is going to train the system, and the way that they dothis is by making sure to provide input, with the corresponding output, to the system so it knows the right answers. You also have to take the time tofurnish the feedback into the system, based on whether the system or the machine was accurate in the predictions that it made.

This is a process that takes time, and you need to have a good deal of data present in order to make it happen. The trainer has to show a bunch of different and diverse examples to that system, and then also show the system the output, or the corresponding answers, so that it can learn how it issupposed to behave in the process as well.

After the completion of the training, the algorithm will need to apply what it learned from the data earlier on to make the best predictions. The concept that comes with supervised learning can be seen to be similar to learning under the supervision of a teacher to their students. The teacher is going to give a lesson to the students with some examples, and then the student is going to derive the new rules and knowledge from these examples. They can then take the knowledge and apply it to different situations, even if they don't match up directly to the examples that the teacher gives.

In supervised Machine learning, we are going to spend our time looking at how to train, and then test the method we are working with. We need to have lots of data to present to the model, and it needs to be labeled or structured in format. This can take some time to accomplish, and often we need to go through quite a few iterations of the training and testing before we are able to find the results that we need. When the model is properly trained, we will be able to handle the data that you present to it later, and then we can receive the predictions and more that we need.

Unsupervised Machine learning

Now we can move on to the idea of Unsupervised Machine learning and see how this one is going to work compared to supervised learning. With unsupervised Machine learning, we will find that there are going to be a big difference when it is compared to the other methods but can train the system how to behave, without all of the examples and labeled data along the way.

We will find that with unsupervised learning, the model is not going to be provided with the output for it to be taught how to behave. This is because the goal of this kind of learning is that we want the machine to learn what is there, based on the unknown input. The machine is able to learn how to do this all on its own, rather than having the programmer come in and do all of the work on it.

This process, or this approach, is something that is known as deep learning. Deep learning is a form of Machine learning that basically lets the computer learn on its own, rather than having to be trained the whole time. This kind of deep learning is going to be an iterative approach because it is able to review all of the data it is holding onto, and then figure out the conclusions that it wants to make from there.

What this does is make an unsupervised learning approach more suitable for use in a variety of processing tasks, which can be more complex than what you would do with supervised learning algorithms. This means that the learning algorithms that are unsupervised are going to learn just from examples, without getting any responses to it. The algorithm will strive tofind the patterns that come from those examples all on its own, rather than being told the answers.

Many of the recommender types of systems that you encounter, such as when you are purchasing something online, are going to work with the help of an unsupervised learning algorithm. In this kind of case, the algorithm is going to derive what to suggest to you to purchase based on what you went through and purchased before. The algorithm then has to estimate the customers you resemble the most based on your purchases and then will provide you with some good recommendations from there.

Reinforcement Machine learning

The third type of Machine learning method that we need to take a look at here is going to be known as reinforcement Machine learning. This algorithm type is newer than the other two, and it is going to be the one that we work with any time that the presented algorithm has examples, but these examples are not going to have any labels on them at all.

This is often the algorithm that is going to happen in a way that looks similar to unsupervised Machine learning. And sometimes, if we are not familiar with this type of learning, it may seem like the two categories are going to be the same thing. But there are some differences, mainly that it works with trial and error compared to the other option. The reinforcement Machine learning method is going to rely more on positive feedback, and sometimes negative feedback. This is going to be based on the solution that is proposed by our algorithm, and whether it all ends up matching up to what the programmer is looking for.

With reinforcement Machine learning, we will find that it is used with any kind of application that has the algorithm to make some decisions. These decisions will face some kind of consequence, either positive or negative, based on what the decision was and how it relates to your conditions.

Errors are fine in this because they are going to become useful in the learning process when they are associated with a penalty, such as loss of time, cost, and pain. In the process of reinforced learning, some actions are going to be more likely to succeed while others are less likely to succeed.

Machine Learning processes are going to be similar to what we see with predictive modeling and data mining. In both cases, patterns are then going to be adjusted inside the program accordingly. A good example of Machine learning is the recommender system. If you purchase an item online, you will then see an ad that is going to be related to that item.

There are some people who see reinforcement learning as the same thing as unsupervised learning because they are so similar, but it is important to understand that they are different. First, the input that is given to these algorithms will need to have some mechanisms for feedback. You can set these up to be either negative or positive based on the algorithm that you decide to write out.

So, if you decide to work with this method of Machine learning, you are going to work with a Machine learning Technique that is similar to trial and error. Think about when you are doing something with a younger child. When they go through and perform an action that you don't want them to repeat, you will stop by letting them know the action is not something they are allowed to do. You explain that they need to stop, or they will end up in a time out or another action that you want here.

There is so much that we will be able to do when it comes to working with Machine learning. There are a lot of benefits that we can look for when it is time to explore Machine learning, and we can look at the three different types of Machine learning. Each of these three types, including supervised, unsupervised, and reinforcement Machine learning, can help us to get the results that we want as we work with Data Science and to really see the insights and the predictions that are needed out of our data.

Machine Learning is a buzzword that is creating a stir in many businesses, no matter what industry they fall in. Understanding how this process works, and how you are able to use it with your own Data Science project, can help us to get the insights and predictions that we are looking for.

CHAPTER 12:

Other Libraries That Can Help with Python

We have already spent a good deal of time in this guidebook exploring the different types of coding that we can do, and even a few of the options with Python Libraries that help out with Data Science. This can make it easier than ever to take some of the ease of use and the power of Python, and put it all to good use for those Data Science models. The libraries that we have already spent some time discussing in this chapter are going to be useful because they can handle a lot of the various tasks and more that you want to do with Python.

With that said, we also need to take some time to look at a few of the other libraries that we can add to the mix, and that will help us to get things done. There are a lot of Machine learning, Deep Learning, and Data Science libraries out there that can help us with each step of the process of our data analysis. Some of the additional libraries that a programmer can consider using along with the Python Language in Data Science includes:

IPython

The first library that we are going to take a look at is known as IPython. This is going to be an interactive shell that works with the Python programming language and is able to offer an enhanced introspection, lab completion, and additional syntax for the shell that we are not able to get with some of the other options.

This brings up the idea of why you would want to work with IPython in the first place. There is already a basic shell that comes with the traditional Python library and will help us to get a lot of the coding and work did that we need. But in some cases, the shell that you are able to get with Python is going to seem a little bit basic, and many programmers find that they want something a little bit more. And IPython is able to provide that to us.

If you find that the default shell that comes with the Python Language is a bit too basic to help you out, then the alternative of using IPython is a great one to work with. You will get all of the same features and functions that are available with the Basic interpreter, but it also provides us with a lot of extras that make some of our coding a bit easier. You may find that it comes with things like a help function, editing that is more advanced, line numbers, and more.

When it is time to do some of the models and algorithms that you want to accomplish in Data Science, you may find that working with the basic shell of Python is just not going to be enough to get it all done. With the help of IPython and all of the neat things that it is able to provide, we will be able to take some of our codings to the next level and really see some results in no time.

Jupyter

Jupyter is the next library that is on our list that we can explore a little bit here. The Jupyter Notebook is a unique addition to Python and Data Science and it is able to combine live code, visualizations, graphics, and text into some notebooks that are shareable and run well in the web browser of your choice.

The idea with this one is that at some point, we all need to be able to show off our work. Most of the programming work that is done out there will either be shared as the code that is raw still or as a compiled executable that others can try out. The source of the code is going to provide us with the complete information that we need, but it is going to be done in a manner that "tells" the other person things, rather than "shows" anything. Then we have the executable code that will show us exactly what that kind of software does. But even when it is shipped out with some of the source code, it is still difficult to figure out exactly how all of this is supposed to work.

Imagine how frustrating this could be? And imagine how it would feel if you were able to view the code and then still execute it in the same user interface. This could allow you to make the changes that you need to the code, and then still see the results of any changes you made, instantly in real-time? If this is something that interests you at all, then the Jupyter Notebook is the right option for you.

This Notebook was created with the idea that it needed to be easier for a coder to show their programming work, and to let others join in and make suggestions or even changes. This Notebook is going to allow us to take one interactive document, which is known as a notebook, and combine together the code, multimedia, comments, and visualizations in one place. In addition to this, we can take that interactive document and share it with others, re-useit as needed, and even re-work some of the parts that are needed.

And hosting this kind of Notebook is pretty easy as well. Since the Jupyter Notebook is going to run via a web browser, the notebook on its own can be hosted on either a remote server or even on the local machine that you are using. You can choose to put this where it is the most convenient for your needs.

There are a lot of benefits that come with the Jupyter Notebook, which is why it is one of the most popular interfaces out there for programmers to work with. This was originally developed for various applications of Data Science that were written in Julia, R, and Python. In addition, it can make its way intoa lot of other projects as well.

To start, this Notebook is going to be great when you want to focus on data visualization. Most of those who gain exposure to Jupyter will do so while working on their data visualization. Jupyter Notebook is a great option that lets the author create their own visualizations, while also sharing these and allowing for some interactive changes to the shared code and the set of data.

Another benefit is that this allows for some code sharing. There are several cloud services, including Pastebin and GitHub, that will provide us with ways to share the code. But while these do offer that service, we have to remember that these are not going to be interactive. When we add in this Notebook, we are able to view the code, execute it, and then display the results directly to the web browser that we are using.

It is also possible to work with some live interaction in your code. The Notebook that we are taking a look at here is not going to be static. It is designed to be edited and re-run incrementally in real-time. With the feedback that is provided directly in the browser, we know that this can allget done in no time. Notebooks are able to embed some of the controls from the user, which can then be used as the sources of input in the code.

And finally, another benefit that a programmer may like about the Jupyter Notebook is that it can help document code samples. If you have a piece of code and your goal is to explain how it works going one line at a time, with some feedback that is live along the way, you may want to use this Notebook. The best thing with this one is that while you do this process, the code will maintain its functionality. You can just add along in an interactive manner with the explanation, basically being able to show and tell all at the same time.

It is also important to take a look at some of the components that come with the Jupyter Notebook. This notebook is going to require a few different ingredients in order to make sure that it can behave in the manner that we want. Each of these ingredients also has to be organized out, so they are in their own discrete blocks. Some of the components that have to be in placefor the Jupyter Notebook to work include:

4. **The HTML and Text**: Plain text, or text annotated in the Markdown syntax to help us generate some HTML, can be inserted inside of your document, no matter which point you would like it to be at. CSS styling is also something that we can include inline, or we can add it to the template that is used to help generate the notebook.

5. **The code and the output**: The code that we will see with this kind of notebook is often going to be Python, but it does work with a few other languages if you would choose. The results of the code that you choose to execute are going to show up right after the blocks of code. And these blocks of code can be executed, as well as re-executed, in any order that you want, and as often as you would like.

6. **Visuals**: Things like charts and graphs can be generated from code by way of modules, including Bokeh, Plotly, or Matplotlib. Like the output, these are going to appear inline, right next to whatever code generates them. However, the code can be changed up inorder to write these out as external files any time it is needed.

7. **Multimedia**: Because this Notebook is going to be built on web technology, it is able to display all types of multimedia that you want, and will support them in the web page. You can include them in a notebook as the elements of HTML, or you can decide to

generate them programmatically using IPython.A display module.

8. **Data:** The data that you have for this notebook is going to be provided in a separate file alongside the .ipynb file. This is going to constitute a Jupyter Notebook, or it can be imported by doing the process programmatically. For example, it can do this by including some code into the notebook and telling it to download the data from an internet repository that is free or access it by a connection to another database.

Scikit-Learn

Another library that we can focus on when it is time to do some work with Python and Data Science is known as Scikit-Learn. This is a key library with the programming language of Python that is used to help out with a variety of Machine learning projects. For the most part, this library is going to be focused on a lot of tools that work on Machine learning projects, including statistical, mathematical, and general-purpose algorithms. These algorithms can all work together to help us form the basis of many Machine learning Technologies that we want to do.

Because this is a free tool that has a tremendous amount of power behind it, it makes sense that this is one of the libraries that we need to focus on in Machine learning and Data Science for that matter. Scikit-Learn can behelpful with the development of many algorithms that work with Machine learning, and many of the other technologies that you may want to create.

Some of the key parts and elements that come with Scikit-Learn make it particularly helpful when we work in Machine learning. Some of the algorithms that it is able to work with, including clustering, regression, and classification, can help with almost any kind of model we want to create for data analysis. For example, this library is able to support work with random forests, where the individual tree nodes hold onto information that can combine with the architecture of other trees, achieving a look like a forest.

But the random forest is not the only thing that we are able to do with this kind of library. In addition to this algorithm, Scikit-Learn can be a great option to help out with things like gradient boosting, vector machines, and some of the other elements of Machine learning that can be seen as key to achieving the results that you want. As a resource that is able to gather up a lot of algorithms and make them easier to use, this is definitely one of the libraries that we want to spend our time on.

TensorFlow

The final library that we are going to take some time to explore in this guidebook is known as the TensorFlow library. This library is currently one of the best-known deep learning libraries in the world. It was developed by Google to help with one of their projects and is designed to be used in Machine learning for things like recommendation systems, image captioning, translation, and search engine results. The architecture that comes with TensorFlow is going to come in with three parts that you can use, and these will include:

3. The ability to take the data you have and preprocess it.

4. It helps you to build up the model that you want to use, adding in the right algorithms to make this happen.

5. It can help you to train and estimate the model.

The reason that we call this library TensorFlow is that it is going to take input in as an array that is multi-dimensional, which is also called a tensor. You are able to construct a type of flowchart of the operations that you use, which is called a graph, that all comes together to perform on your input. With this one, the input is going to head in one end, and then will flow through the system, with many operations in the process, until it comes out on the other side as the output that you will rely on. TensorFlow is also able to meet some hardware and software requirements. These are going to include a few classifications that help the program run smoothly. First, there is the development phase. This is going to be part of the program where you workto train the model. Training is going to be done on a laptop or a desktop in most cases. Then we can move on to the phase that is known as the runphase, r the inference phase. When all of the training is done, the TensorFlowprogram is going to be available to run on any operating system or platform that you would like to use. This means that the programmer will be able to take their model and run it on some of the following:

4. A desktop that is able to use the Linux, macOS, or Windows operating systems.

5. The cloud as a web service.

6. A mobile device including Android and iOS.

You can also train the model that you are doing on more than one machine. This allows it to run on a different machine as well, as soon as the model is completely trained.

To add to some of this, we are able to train the TensorFlow model to work with CPUs and GPUs. GPUs, until late 2010, was only used for video games.But since it was discovered that the GPU is also a good one to work with when handling algebra and matrix operations, and can handle these kinds of calculations in a quick manner, it is becoming more prevalent to see these shows up in the various models that are designed.

All of these libraries can be great additions to help us get some of the work that we want to be done in a short amount of time. It is not always as easy asit may seem in the beginning, but working with some of the right codings,and deciding what kind of library we want to work with when handling aData Science or deep learning project, can be the number one key to ensuringthat we will actually get this set up and ready to go and see results with our work.

CHAPTER 13:

Practical Examples of Python Data Science

Now that we have spent some time looking at Data Science and how Python data can be used with it, it is time for us to work on the next part that comes with this. We are going to look closer at some of the practical examples that we can do when it comes to writing out codes to create the models you need in Data Science. There are a lot of different options that we are able to work with here, and you can choose the one that is the best for your needs and will help you to create the model that helps us sort through the data we want. Some of the best examples of how you can complete your own Python Data Science model will include:

K-Means Clustering

The first example that we are going to take a look at when it comes to Python Data Science is the K-means clustering. Clustering is a simple but common process that helps with a lot of data analytics projects with Machine learning, and it can help us to take all of the data points that we want to work with and then divides them up into groups. The points that are in the same cluster are going to share a lot of similarities to one another, and the ones that are in other clusters are going to not be as similar to the others.

For example, you may decide to go through the data points that we want to look at, and then separate out the customers into females and males. With this one, we are going to end up with two clusters, and when the algorithm is able to sort through all of the data it has, they will get all of the points in your data to fit into one out of the two clusters.

That was a pretty simple option to work with, but we can go through and sort through the data in a different manner. You could create a model where you want to learn more about your customers and see who is the most likely to purchase a certain product, and which group they are likely to fall into. This is going to help us with some of the marketing and the sales that you would like to work with. In this case, maybe you would need five clusters so that you can get the best idea of the customers you are working with, and even some of the outliers to see if there is a new customer base you can reach through.

The idea that we will see here is that any of the objects or the data points that are in the same cluster are going to be the ones that are related to one another closely. And if something shows up in a different cluster, they won't really share similarities with one another. The amount of similarity that comes with this is going to be important because it is going to help us learn the main metric that we are able to use to help us see how strong the relationship becomes between two or more objects that we want to look over.

If you want to work with k-means clustering, it may sound complicated and you are worried that it is going to not work for the project that you want. But this code is not meant to be too difficult, and when it is done with the Python language, it can really make a strong model that works well with DataScience. An example of the kind of code that you will want to write out whenit comes to the k-means clustering algorithm will include:

- *import numpy as np*
- *import matplotlib.pyplot as plt*

```
def d(u, v):
    diff = u - v
    return diff.dot(diff)


def cost(X, R, M):
    cost = 0
    for k in xrange(len(M)):
        for n in xrange(len(X)):
            cost += R[n,k]*d(M[k], X[n])
```

return cost

def plot_k_means(X, K, max_iter=20, beta=1.0):

    N, D = X.shape

    M = np.zeros((K, D))

    R = np.ones((N, K)) / K

    # initialize M to random

    for k in xrange(K):

        M[k] = X[np.random.choice(N)]

    grid_width = 5

    grid_height = max_iter / grid_width

    random_colors = np.random.random((K, 3))

    plt.figure()

    costs = np.zeros(max_iter)

    for i in xrange(max_iter):

        # moved the plot inside the for loop

        colors = R.dot(random_colors)

        plt.subplot(grid_width, grid_height, i+1)

        plt.scatter(X[:,0], X[:,1], c=colors)

        # step 1: determine assignments / resposibilities

        # is this inefficient?

        for k in xrange(K):

            for n in xrange(N):

                *R[n,k] = np.exp(-beta*d(M[k], X[n])) / np.sum(np.exp(-*

beta*d(M[j], X[n])) for j in xrange(K))

 # step 2: recalculate means

      for k in xrange(K):

         M[k] = R[:,k].dot(X) / R[:,k].sum()

      costs[i] = cost(X, R, M)

      if i > 0:

         if np.abs(costs[i] - costs[i-1]) < 10e-5:

            break

  plt.show()

def main():

  # assume 3 means

  D = 2 # so we can visualize it more easily

  s = 4 # separation so we can control how far apart the means are

  mu1 = np.array([0, 0])

  mu2 = np.array([s, s])

  mu3 = np.array([0, s])

  N = 900 # number of samples

  X = np.zeros((N, D))

  X[:300, :] = np.random.randn(300, D) + mu1

  X[300:600, :] = np.random.randn(300, D) + mu2

  X[600:, :] = np.random.randn(300, D) + mu3

  # what does it look like without clustering?

  plt.scatter(X[:,0], X[:,1])

```
plt.show()

K = 3 # luckily, we already know this

plot_k_means(X, K)

# K = 5 # what happens if we choose a "bad" K?

# plot_k_means(X, K, max_iter=30)


# K = 5 # what happens if we change beta?

# plot_k_means(X, K, max_iter=30, beta=0.3)


if __name__ == '__main__':

    main()
```

As you take a look through some of that code, it may seem like a lot to handle, and you may be worried that you won't be able to make this work for your needs at all. But remember that in the beginning, we are just pulling alot of libraries out, and then we simply ask them to take the various points of data that we are working with and turn them into a form that is easier to understand after reading through.

Being able to create these clusters, and then reading through the data to determine where each of the points of data should fall, and which cluster they fit into, is a challenge, but this is where the K-Means clustering algorithm is going to come into play. With the code above and a little bit of practice, you will be able to make all of this come together for you.

Neural Networks

Now that we have had some time to discuss what the K-Means clustering algorithm is all about, it is time for us to move on to the second example that we are going to work with is known as a neural network. When it comes to working with neural networks, we will see that they are really powerful codes, and it can take us some time to learn the best way to handle them.

Once you learn how to handle the neural networks, we will find that they will help us to handle the codes, and this shows us why so many programmers like to add these into their data analysis. But let's explore it a bit more to learn how it can work with artificial intelligence, why it fits in with Machine learning, and how we can use this to create the best models for our Data Science project.

These neural networks are going to be set up in a manner that they can teach our system how to think similar to the human mind. Through learning and remembering some of the things it has learned and done in the past, the neural network is able to become 'smarter" and can make better decisions in the future. The more work that it does, the faster and more efficient it will get at doing these tasks. You will quickly find that when you create a model that relies on neural networks, it will be really good at its job.

Neural networks are useful simply because they are able to work in a manner that is similar to what we see with the human brain. It is done through our chosen system or machine; however, to get it to work in this manner, we will need to make sure that we rely on the right procedure to get it done. If we end up picking out bad information or information that is low-quality, then it is going to train the algorithm in the wrong way, and it won't give you the results that you want.

Always remember with the neural networks, the higher the quality of data that you can feed into the machine, the better. This helps us to make sure that the model is going to work the way that we want. With this higher quality information, we will ensure that the neural network will give the right predictions and insights. And in the process, we will have the system learn what it needs to do in an accurate and faster method than before.

Keep in mind with this one that when creating our Neural Network, there are going to be many parts that have to come together. But for now, we are going to take a detour and focus on the code that is needed to get the neural network started and ready to go. While the neural network may seem difficult to work with, but there is a simple code that we can work with to get the basic neural network ready to go. The code that we need to work with, using the Python coding language along the way, to go through our data and make sure that the model learns along the way includes:

- *import torch*

- *import torch.nn as nn*

- *import torch.nn.functional as F*

class Net(nn.Module):

```python
def __init__(self):
    super(Net, self).__init__()
    # 1 input image channel, 6 output channels, 3x3 square convolution
    # kernel
    self.conv1 = nn.Conv2d(1, 6, 3)
    self.conv2 = nn.Conv2d(6, 16, 3)
    # an affine operation: y = Wx + b
    self.fc1 = nn.Linear(16 * 6 * 6, 120)  # 6*6 from image dimension
    self.fc2 = nn.Linear(120, 84)
    self.fc3 = nn.Linear(84, 10)

def forward(self, x):
    # Max pooling over a (2, 2) window
    x = F.max_pool2d(F.relu(self.conv1(x)), (2, 2))
    # If the size is a square you can only specify a single number
    x = F.max_pool2d(F.relu(self.conv2(x)), 2)
    x = x.view(-1, self.num_flat_features(x))
    x = F.relu(self.fc1(x))
    x = F.relu(self.fc2(x))
    x = self.fc3(x)
    return x


def num_flat_features(self, x):
    size = x.size()[1:]  # all dimensions except the batch dimension
    num_features = 1
    for s in size:
        num_features *= s
    return num_features
```

```
net = Net()

print(net)
```

Many programmers worry that they will not be able to work with neural networks because they feel that these networks are going to be too difficult for them to handle. These are more advanced than what we will see with some of the other forms of coding, and some of the other Machine learning algorithms that you want to work with. But with some of the work that we did with the coding above, neural networks are not going to be so bad, but the tasks that they can take on, and the way they work, can improve the model that you are writing, and what you can do when you bring Python into your Data Science project.

Conclusion

Thank you for making it through to the end of *Data Science Python*, let's hope it was informative and able to provide you with all of the tools you need to achieve your goals whatever they may be. The next step is to start putting the information and examples that we talked about in this guidebook to good use. There is a lot of information inside all that data that we have been collecting for some time now. But all of that data is worthless if we are not able to analyze it and find out what predictions and insights are in there. This is part of what the process of Data Science is all about, and when it is combined together with the Python language, we are going to see some amazing results in the process as well.

This guidebook took some time to explore more about Data Science and what it all entails. This is an in-depth and complex process, one that often includes more steps than what data scientists were aware of when they first get started. But if a business wants to be able to actually learn the insights that are in their data, and they want to gain that competitive edge in so many ways, they need to be willing to take on these steps of Data Science, and make it workfor their needs.

This guidebook went through all of the steps that you need to know in order to get started with Data Science and some of the basic parts of the Python code. We can then put all of this together to create the right analyticalalgorithm that, once it is trained properly and tested with the right kinds of data, will work to make predictions, provide information, and even show us insights that were never possible before. And all that you need to do to getthis information is to use the steps that we outline and discuss in this guidebook.

There are so many great ways that you can use the data you have been collecting for some time now, and being able to complete the process of data visualization will ensure that you get it all done. When you are ready to get started with Python Data Science, make sure to check out this guidebook to learn how.

Finally, if you found this book useful in any way, a review on Amazon is always appreciated!